Berlitz

RHODES
POCKET GUIDE

Discover the world's best destinations with the Insight Guides Walking Eye app, available to download for free in the App Store and Google Play.

The container app provides easy access to fantastic free content on events and activities taking place in your current location or chosen destination, with the possibility of booking, as well as the regularly-updated Insight Guides travel blog: Inspire Me. In addition, you can purchase curated, premium destination guides through the app, which feature local highlights, hotel, bar, restaurant and shopping listings, an A to Z of practical information and more. Or purchase and download Insight Guides eBooks straight to your device.

TOP 10 ATTRACTIONS

RHODES NEW TOWN
The main surprise here is whimsical Italian architecture in a variety of 1920s and 1930s styles. See page 46.

PETALOÚDES
The Valley of the Butterflies offers an idyllic escape from summer heat, and sightings of rare Jersey tiger moths. See page 68.

LÍNDOS
A collection of old sea captains' mansions sit beneath the towering Acropolis with its ancient Temple of Athena. See page 59.

SÝMI ISLAND
Deservedly the most popular day-trip destination from Rhodes, the port presents a stunning tableau of preserved neoclassical mansions. See page 79.

PALACE OF THE GRAND MASTERS
The imposing centrepiece of Rhodes Old Town houses two excellent museums with some fascinating ancient and medieval exhibits. See page 37.

KAMEIROS
The most scenic and untouched of the island's ancient sites. See page 70.

THÁRRI MONASTERY
The 14th- and 15th-century frescoes in its church are the most noteworthy on Rhodes. See page 63.

TSAMBÍKA BAY
Soft golden sand meets sparkling aquamarine water at this lovely beach. See page 57.

KRITINÍA CASTLE
Though a ruined shell, this fort offers great views of the western islets. See page 72.

STREET OF THE KNIGHTS
This 14th-century street in Rhodes Old Town is so atmospheric that it is frequently used as a film location. See page 35.

A PERFECT TOUR

Day 1

Rhodes Town

Head to the Grand Masters' Palace before the crowds, then follow Odón Ippotón to the Archaeological Museum. Have lunch at Hatzikelis in the old Jewish quarter, then visit nearby Kal Kadosh Shalom synagogue-museum. Swim at Élli beach, then stop at the late-opening Aquarium at the cape. Dine at Marco Polo Café, or Steno.

Day 3

Rhodes East Coast

Return to Rhodes by midday, meet pre-booked hire car at your arrival dock. Reach Pigés Kallithéas Art Deco monument before it closes, then lunch and a dip at Oasis lido. Continue south towards the accommodation of your choice, near or at Líndos, then treat yourself to dinner at Mavrikos in Líndos after another sunset swim.

Day 4

Líndos and around

Get onto ancient Líndos acropolis before temperatures soar, and while morning light flatters the sweeping coastal views. Point your car north towards Tsambíka beach, with lunch at Stegná, and then visit the Eptá Pigés oasis. Return to Líndos for a second overnight.

Day 2

Sými Break

Take a morning catamaran or conventional craft to Sými, check into accommodation there, then view Horió's museum before it closes. Bus service is limited, so rent a scooter or car to explore the island, or use taxi-boats to beaches. Marathoúnda and Nanoú bays both have suitable lunch tavernas. Explore Gialós in the evening; dine at a taverna (see page 108).

OF **RHODES**

Day 6

Around the West Coast

With an early start, visit Prassonísi to try your hand at wind- or kite-surfing. Lunch is best taken up the coast at Palios Monolithos in that village, prior to visiting Monólithos castle, and swimming at Foúrni. En route back to Rhodes Town, pause at Kritinía castle and, in summer when it opens late, ancient Kameiros. Return to Rhodes Town accommodation, keeping your hire car.

Day 5

The Far South

Head west to Thárri monastery, then swing by the frescoed church at Asklipió. Swim at Kiotári or Gennádi, scheduling lunch at idyllic Plátanos in lower Lahaniá. Overnight at the Paraktio Apartments, with dinner inland at Váti or Profýlia.

Day 7 pm

Northwest Highlights

Go to ancient Ialysos and Filérimos monastery, and time permitting Petaloúdes. Return to town for sunset on Monte Smith's Apollo Temple. Final dinner at Petaladika in Old Town, then drive yourself to the airport that evening or next morning.

Day 7 am

Round-up

Catch whatever you've missed in town. Obvious choices include the Museum of Modern Greek Art at '100 Palms Square', with perhaps a temporary exhibition at one of its annexes. Try to get into Mandráki's Evangelismós Cathedral for Photis Kontoglou's neo-Byzantine frescoes. Lunch at Meltemi at Élli.

CONTENTS

INTRODUCTION

It is impossible not to feel the weight of history when you arrive in Rhodes. The granite of Dorian settlements, marble of Classical sites and sandstone of medieval churches and castles are all tangible legacies of a long historical timeline. However, to think that Rhodes is only of interest to archaeology buffs would be a mistake. With long, hot summer days, a balmy sea lapping numerous beaches, and lots to do, the island is a holidaymakers' paradise.

Rhodes is the largest island in the Dodecanese, an archipelago lying in the southeastern Aegean Sea between Greece and Turkey. Originally made up of 12 major islands (*dódeka nisiá* means '12 islands' in Greek) that coordinated action against Ottoman and Italian repression early in the 20th century, the group is now an administrative region of Greece comprising several dozen islands and islets, though only 21 have a permanent population.

A TURBULENT HISTORY

The ebb and flow of history has washed over Rhodes, with periods of influence and great wealth alternating with centuries as a backwater. Lying only 10 nautical miles from the Asia Minor coastline, Rhodes was an important stepping-stone on the trade routes between east and west throughout Classical, Hellenistic and Roman times. The Rhodians were adept at commerce and cultivated trading partners around the Mediterranean, bringing sustained prosperity to the island. Traces of this flourishing culture can be seen at the ruins of their three main city-states – Líndos, Kameiros and Ialysos.

After the Roman Empire disintegrated, this strategically important territory became a lightly defended outpost of Byzantium, left to the mercy of raiding pirates and barbarian tribes. Its population

lived in fear until the early
14th century, when it
became home to the Order
of the Knights Hospitaller
of St John, recently ousted
from the Holy Land by
Muslim forces. The Knights
changed the island's landscape irrevocably, under-
taking a huge building
programme that created
some of the strongest fortifications in Europe. Rhodes
Old Town still stands as a
monument to their wealth,
steadfastness and faith.

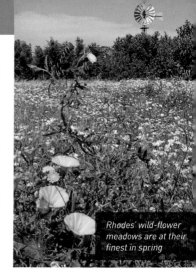

Rhodes' wild-flower
meadows are at their
finest in spring

The influence of the island's subsequent rulers can also be
seen. When Ottoman Turkish forces drove the Knights out and
took up residence in 1523, they created a comfortable Islamic outpost, complete with carved marble fountains, delicate wooden-
balconied windows, elegant minarets and majestic mosque
domes. The Italians, who supplanted the Turks just before World
War I, invested vast sums of money, creating a new administrative centre in Rhodes New Town, restoring many historic buildings
and directing their archaeologists' attention to the ancient sites.

TRADITIONAL ISLAND LIFE

Despite these various overlords, the basic way of life for the ordinary Rhodian people, governed by seasons of planting, tending
and harvesting, changed little over 5,000 years. Since the Bronze
Age the seas have provided abundant food, the long summers
have brought forth crops of grain, and well-established olive

trees and vines have borne fruit. The island's hillsides have always provided good grazing for livestock, and donkeys and mules furnished a reliable means of transport.

From the early Christian era onwards the fabric of life was sustained by religion. The Orthodox Church became a cornerstone of Greek identity long before the modern state emerged in 1832. In times of natural disaster, war, disease and occupation, the church served as a place of refuge and solace – physically and spiritually.

Yet island life has seen more change in the last 70 years than in the previous thousand. Rhodes is now 'invaded' by almost 2 million people annually, creating both fantastic opportunities and great pressures for the island and its people. Over half of the island population now lives in Rhodes Town, taking advantage of the many amenities in this university centre and provincial capital. But despite the growth of the main city and tourist resorts, rural lifestyles still exist in the far south and interior of the island.

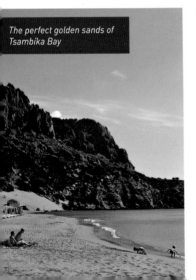

The perfect golden sands of Tsambíka Bay

Although Rhodes has given up many of its traditional ways, some things haven't changed. Life still revolves around the family, and each new addition is proudly shown off at the evening stroll (vólta). Children play happily and safely in the streets, watched over by doting grandparents. A Greek gathering of family and

friends would not be com-
plete without ardent debate.
After all, this was the country that invented democratic
decision-making through
discussion. In both rounds of
the inconclusive 2012 elections, extreme right and left
parties did less well here
than the national average,

Women at worship

Women have traditionally
formed the majority of the
congregation, praying on
behalf of fathers, husbands
and sons off studying
abroad or away at sea in
merchant fleets.

with Rhodians staying loyal to the traditional parties PASOK and
ND. In both 2015 elections, however, more Rhodians voted for the
victorious left-wing SYRIZA party, only to be bitterly disappointed
when they abolished the preferential VAT rate, which east Aegean
islands had enjoyed until then. The next election, due to take
place by autumn 2019, is expected to result in a hung parliament.

RHODES OF THE RESORTS

The major resorts are international territory, with foreign-lan-
guage restaurant signs and menus along with daily English-
language newspapers, imported beers and bars with televised
sports matches. Since most hotel and tourism workers speak
English, it can be easy to forget that you are in Greece if you
choose not to venture out of your resort. Those who do explore
the island will discover that Rhodian hospitality is both genuine and refreshing. A smattering of Greek phrases used at the
taverna will earn you honest appreciation.

Tourism has brought wealth and security, and the current
generation expects more than the precarious existence expe-
rienced by their parents and grandparents. Since EU subsidies
began in the 1980s, farmers have replaced their trusty donkeys
with trucks; many have given up their trade altogether to open

Rhodes Old Town in the summer months

a bar or car-rental office. Some fishermen now use their boats to ferry tourists to nearby beaches rather than to catch fish.

Today, mobile phones are heard more frequently than the bells of grazing live-stock, and only old-timers have leisure to linger over a game of backgammon at the *kafenío* while the younger men try to impress the girls with new motor-bikes. There is a veneer of sophistication here not found in most other Aegean towns – a casino, a top national art museum, trendy boutiques, and teenage girls out on the town until 1am – something unthinkable only a generation ago.

Rhodes has grasped with both hands the opportunity of catering for the modern worshippers of the sun god Helios, and it provides an excellent product for its visitors. Good transport connections, a plethora of eateries, bars and nightclubs and a relaxed lifestyle all contribute to a great holiday experience. Spring or autumn are ideal times for clambering up ancient ruins, castles or the odd hiking trail, while in summer you can simply take in some rays or enjoy a range of watersports, golf or jeep safaris into the remote interior. No matter what time of year, the world-class architectural showcases of Rhodes Old Town and Líndos are worth a visit. Whatever your interests, there is bound to be something on Rhodes to suit you. Perhaps that's why so many people keep coming back for more.

A BRIEF HISTORY

Few traces remain of Rhodes' first inhabitants, rugged immigrants from Anatolia who could fashion simple tools and pottery. During the Middle Bronze Age (2500–1500 BC), Carians from Asia Minor and Phoenicians from Lebanon settled on the island before moving west to Crete. Traffic was two-way – Minoan merchants from Crete set up shop in Rhodes, which at the time was part of a lucrative trading network that included Egypt and the Levant. In around 1625 BC a major natural disaster caused by the eruption and collapse of a volcano on ancient Thera (now Santoríni) brought about the destruction of Minoan society by 1400BC.

Mycenaeans from the Greek mainland soon occupied both Crete and Rhodes. These seafaring warriors are still famous for the legendary war they waged against the Trojans around 1220 BC, as recounted in Homer's *Iliad*. According to Homer, 'nine ships of the arrogant Rhodians' sailed in Agamemnon's 1,000-strong fleet. The 10-year siege ended with the destruction of Troy, but it also left the exhausted conquerors vulnerable to attack. The so-called 'Sea Peoples' from beyond the Black Sea appeared in about 1150 BC, devastating all cultures in their path. Many Greeks emigrated from the mainland to Rhodes. Over time, fusion of the 'Sea Peoples' with the area's previous inhabitants resulted in the Classical Greek civilisation.

Heavenly gift

According to legend the sun god Helios gave the island as a gift to his favourite nymph, Rodon, who in turn gave her name to the place. Others claim that the word is a corruption of *rodi*, 'pomegranate' in Greek.

THE RHODIAN CITY-STATES

The first major settlements on Rhodes were the city-states of Líndos, Kameiros and Ialysos (named after the mythical grandsons of the sun god Helios), which reached their zenith during the 1st millennium BC. By 700 BC, the three city-states, together with the Asia Minor ports of Halikarnasos (now Bodrum) and Knidos, plus the island of Kos, had set up a six-city trading and religious league, the Dorian Hexapolis. Each city minted its own coins (money had just been invented in Asia Minor), and Lindian ships sailed as far as the western Mediterranean.

In the 5th century BC, a large force dispatched by the king of Persia, Darius I the Great, reached the Aegean. The city-states of mainland Greece – Athens and Sparta – stood in the way of this invasion. Anticipating a Greek defeat, Rhodes and many neighbouring islands joined forces with the Persians, but the tide turned at the land battle of Marathon in 490 BC. When the Greeks sank the fleet of Darius' son, Xerxes, at the epic naval battle of Salamis 10 years later, there were around 40 Rhodian ships among the victims. The Greeks exacted swift retribution on those islands allied with the defeated enemy.

The Delian League was founded soon afterwards, under the leadership of

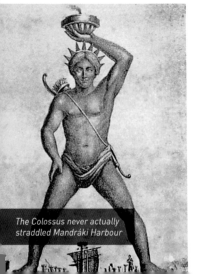

The Colossus never actually straddled Mandráki Harbour

Athens, as an attempt to bring unity and security to the Greek city- and island-states, and Rhodes became a taxpaying member. This league did much to ensure economic and political strength for the region over the coming centuries.

THE FOUNDING OF RHODES TOWN

Due to its strategic position on vital trade routes in the eastern Mediterranean, Rhodes grew in importance as a maritime power and financial centre. By 408 BC, the volume of trade and shipping had become too much for the island's three existing ports to handle. By the mutual consent of the three existing city-states, the town of Rhodes was founded at a spot on the northern tip of the island with three natural harbours. The new city's gridiron street plan was laid out by the famous architect Hippodamos of Miletos, and many of today's thoroughfares still follow their predecessors. The new city prospered, while Ialysos and Kameiros declined to become little more than religious cult centres – though Líndos remained important thanks to its two well-protected harbours.

When Alexander the Great rose to power, Rhodes allied itself with the Macedonian and prospered as part of his empire, in particular benefiting from trade concessions with Egypt. After the great leader's death in 323 BC, Rhodes refused to join an expedition by his successor, Antigonos, against Ptolemy I, the Macedonian general who had become the king of Egypt.

As a result Antigonos' son Demetrios Polyorketes, 'Besieger of Many Cities', led one of the most celebrated campaigns of ancient times against Rhodes in 305 BC. Demetrios had an army of 40,000 troops and a fleet of over 200 ships with which to blockade the city. Against this the Rhodians could only muster about 25,000 soldiers, most of them foreign mercenaries or local slaves promised their freedom in the event of victory. After unsuccessful attacks on the harbour walls, Demetrios deployed the Helepolis, an ingenious, 125-tonne siege machine nine storeys high and 27m (89ft) wide at the base. Sheathed in leather and heavy-gauge bronze, it was propelled on oaken wheels by a crew of 3,400 people up against the landward ramparts of the city, firing missiles and landing commandos. In response, Rhodian engineers tunnelled under the walls and undermined the path of the machine, causing it to founder.

After nearly a year's siege, the hostilities ended in a truce that confirmed Rhodes' independence, but required the island to assist any Macedonian military efforts not directed against

⊙ A WORLD WONDER

Contrary to popular belief, the Colossus of Rhodes did not straddle the entrance to Mandráki Harbour – its 20 tonnes of bronze would have sunk immediately into the soft seabed. More credible theories place this statue of the sun god Helios near today's Palace of the Grand Masters.

It took sculptor Khares of Líndos 12 years to cast the 35m (115ft) Colossus – each finger was supposedly the size of a man. Khares committed suicide after discovering an apparently critical design flaw, and the work was finished by his disciple Lakhes. During an earthquake less than 70 years after its completion, the Colossus cracked at the knees and crashed to the ground – perhaps vindicating Khares' remorse.

The Rhodians consulted the Delphic Oracle, which warned them not to restore the statue. The crumpled image lay where it had fallen for nearly 900 years until AD 653, when Arab pirates sacked Rhodes and sold off the bronze as scrap to a Jewish merchant from Syria who, legend says, needed 900 camels to carry it off.

Ptolemy. Demetrios handed over the remains of his siege engine to the Rhodians, on condition that they sell it and build a commemorative monument from the proceeds. Thus was born the famous Kolossós (Colossus), one of the Seven Wonders of the Ancient World.

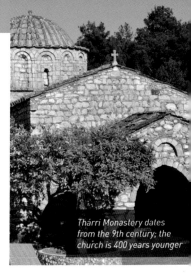

Thárri Monastery dates from the 9th century; the church is 400 years younger

HELLENISTIC HEYDAY, ROMAN DOMINANCE

At the peak of its power, and with a population slightly more than today's 110,000, Rhodes enjoyed a golden age during the 3rd century BC. The island won fame as a cultural and intellectual centre, with a renowned school of rhetoric founded in 342 BC by the Athenian Aeskhines. Rhodian artists and craftsmen enjoyed a privileged social standing and were highly regarded throughout the area. When the Colossus was toppled by an earthquake in 227BC, the rest of the city was destroyed too, but such was its prestige in the Hellenistic world that ample financial and technical help was sent to rebuild it.

Early in the 2nd century BC, Rhodes became an important ally of the Romans, but between 171 and 168 BC angered them by siding with King Perseus of Macedonia. As punishment, Rome declared the island of Delos a free port, thus depriving Rhodes of a substantial income from port duties. The Rhodians hastily renewed their alliance with Rome, but soon became embroiled in the Roman civil wars. Rhodes supported Pompey against Julius Caesar, but after his victory Caesar forgave them. Then Cassius and Brutus, Caesar's assassins, demanded Rhodian help in their war against the Senate. When this was refused, Cassius conquered and sacked Rhodes. He dispatched 3,000 statues to Rome, leaving only *The Sun* – a famous sculpture of Helios' chariot by Lysippos, too heavy to remove. Most of this precious art was destroyed when Rome burned in AD 64.

CRUSADERS AND KNIGHTS

Christianity took root during the 1st century AD, aided by St Paul, who visited the island in 58 AD. However, the new religion did not bring divine protection – Rhodes city was shattered by earthquakes in 155, 178 and 515. Much weakened, it was plundered by Goths in 263, and overrun by the Persians and Arabs during the 7th century and by the Seljuks in the 9th century. Although nominally part of the Byzantine Empire, Rhodes was a poorly defended backwater, unceasingly harassed by pirates.

By the 11th century, followers of Muhammad had conquered Jerusalem, Islamised Persia and North Africa, converted the Turks and occupied much of Spain's territory. They represented a serious challenge to Christianity and the security of Europe. During this period Rhodes'

Ottoman forces gather outside the walls of Rhodes in 1480

ties with Western Europe were strengthened by trade and the passage of the first crusaders on their way east to Jerusalem in 1097. In 1191, Richard the Lionheart and Philippe II Auguste of France landed in Rhodes to recruit crusaders. However, despite gaining significant territory in the interim, by 1291 the crusaders had relinquished their foothold in the Holy Land.

Among the retreating Christians were the Knights Hospitaller of the Order of St John, founded in Jerusalem around 1100 to offer assistance to ailing pilgrims. During the Crusades, these Knights Hospitaller became increasingly militaristic, learning the value of both pitched battles and fortifications. They initially settled on Cyprus, but moved to Rhodes in 1306, having found Cyprus uncongenial. Over the next three years they wrested control of the island from Genoese adventurers acting for the Byzantine Empire. By 1309 the Knights were well entrenched, and over the next 213 years they overhauled the flimsy Byzantine defences of the city in successive phases.

Beyond the city, the Knights relied on a network of nearly 30 fortresses scattered across Rhodes, on smaller nearby islands, and at Bodrum on the Anatolian mainland. The Knights were formidable warriors, and aided by Rhodian supporters they repelled attacks by the Sultan of Egypt in 1440 and 1444. In 1480 they also brilliantly outmanoeuvred the massed forces of Ottoman Sultan Mehmet II.

THE OTTOMAN CONQUEST

Nonetheless, Ottoman naval power was growing in the eastern Mediterranean, and Rhodes was a perennial concern. On 26 June 1522 Süleyman the Magnificent's fleet appeared off the island's north tip. Shuttling back and forth from the Anatolian mainland, 400 ships carried 100,000 soldiers, sappers, sailors, equipment, food and supplies, and by 9 July the city was besieged.

Over the next few months, the Ottomans lost almost 50,000 men in their attempt to take the fortified city. They were on the verge of giving up in late September when a traitor, Grand Chancellor Andrea d'Amaral, revealed that the Christians were also at the limits of their resolve. The Ottomans renewed their attacks all through October and November, breaching the walls at several spots and penetrating the town. On 10 December the Knights, urged on in part by the civilians who hoped to emerge alive, ran up the white flag, and 12 days later a formal surrender was signed between the Knights' Grand Master and Süleyman. Its terms were generous: on 1 January 1523 the 180 surviving Knights were allowed to sail away with honour and their arms, taking with them 5,000 Christians, plus whatever treasure and religious relics the Ottomans had not already plundered. Within seven years they established a new base on Malta.

For nearly four centuries, until 1912, Rhodes remained a sleepy Ottoman provincial possession. Several large mosques and some baths were built, but as often Christian churches were converted to Islamic use. The Palace of the Grand Masters became a barn, and the inns of the Knights served as barracks or the dwellings of governors. Only Muslims and Jews were allowed to live within the walled city; at sunset, any Greeks working there had to leave for their homes in the *marásia*, or surrounding suburbs, which had been established outside the city walls. This segregation ensured that Greek culture survived and that religious apostasy was kept to a minimum.

ITALIAN RULE AND UNION WITH GREECE

The Ottomans brutally suppressed Rhodian attempts to join the 1821 Greek revolution on the mainland, and when an independent Greek state was established in 1832 the island was not part of it. By the end of the 19th century the Ottoman

Empire was in decline, but hopes of union with Greece were dashed in 1912 when Rhodes and the other Dodecanese fell to the Italians during a war with the Ottomans over Libya. Although a 1915 conference committed Italy to handing over the Dodecanese (except Rhodes) to Greece, the 1920 Treaty of Sèvres confirmed Italian sovereignty.

The Italians left their mark in Rhodes New Town

After the Fascists came to power in late 1922, they began a programme to make Rhodes more Italian. The entire townscape was replanned and many Mediterranean Art Deco and Rationalist structures erected. Although many Rhodians suffered considerable hardship under the occupation, the Italians made the island far more accessible, with regular sea-plane services, and built the first tourist hotels. They also excavated and restored ancient and medieval sites, and constructed roads and rural colonies for Italian colonists.

Despite the Treaty of Sèvres being nullified by the 1923 Treaty of Lausanne, it became increasingly clear that Italy had no intention of ceding the Dodecanese – or rather, the *Isole Italiane del'Egeo* – to Greece. In 1936, Italian became the official language, with both the Greek language and the Greek Orthodox Church suppressed.

Following Mussolini's capitulation in September 1943, German troops took over all Italian military bases in the

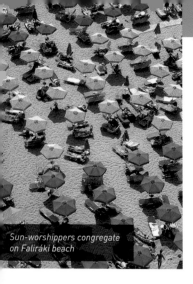

Sun-worshippers congregate on Faliráki beach

Dodecanese. The islands were liberated one at a time by British forces between September 1944 and May 1945, and, after a 22-month occupation while the Italo-Greek peace treaty was finalised, they were handed over to the Greek military authorities on 31 March 1947. On 9 January 1948, the Dodecanese were officially annexed by Greece. Rhodes gained duty-free status, but mass tourism didn't really take off until the end of the 1960s. For most of that decade, Rhodes – especially Líndos – was largely a bohemian hangout. The first charters and package tours arrived in the early 1970s, which saw the construction of many hotels and apartments.

More recently, Faliráki resort achieved notoriety as a venue for youthful excess, an era which ended abruptly with the 2003 fatal stabbing of a British youth and an official crackdown that wiped out the Faliráki club scene. Local tourism has since entered a brave new world, especially given a global economic turndown – and the appearance of Rhodes as a destination for many no-frills airlines. All-inclusive packages, particularly aimed at customers from the former communist economies, are becoming dominant, today you are as likely to hear Russian, Turkish, Spanish, Serbian or Hebrew spoken in the cobbled old town streets as you are English or Finnish.

HISTORICAL LANDMARKS

1450–1200 BC Rhodes settled by Minoan Cretans, then Mycenaeans.

1150 BC Invasion of the so-called 'Sea Peoples'.

c. 700 BC Rhodian city-states found the Dorian Hexapolis.

408 BC Ialysos, Líndos and Kameiros unite to establish Rhodes Town at the north tip of the island.

305 BC Unsuccessful siege of Rhodes by the Macedonian Demetrios Polyorketes; the Colossus is built afterwards.

227 BC Colossus collapses in an earthquake which wrecks Rhodes.

42 BC Cassius sacks the city and carries off many treasures to Rome.

AD 58 St Paul visits Rhodes.

2nd–12th centuries AD The island is a Byzantine backwater, assailed by earthquakes, pirates and various invaders.

1309 Knights Hospitaller of St John assume control of Rhodes.

1440–80 The Knights repel several attacks by the Egyptians and Ottomans.

1523 The Knights surrender the island to Sultan Süleyman after a six-month siege, and retire to Malta.

16th–17th century Ottoman monuments built in the walled city; Orthodox marásia appear outside.

1912 Italians oust Ottomans from Rhodes and the rest of the Dodecanese.

1923–39 First archaeological excavations; Italian urban planning.

1940 Italy attacks Greece; Rhodes an important Italian base.

1943 Italy capitulates, Germany occupies Rhodes.

1944 Rhodian Jews deported; Rhodes Old Town heavily bombed.

1945 Germany surrenders Rhodes to the British.

1947 British hand over Dodecanese to Greek military governor.

1960s Beginning of mass tourism in Rhodes.

2010–12 Greek economy in freefall, country dependent on EU/IMF bailouts; 2012 elections produce centre-right, pro-bailout coalition government.

2015 Left-wing SYRIZA party wins both 2015 elections, forming a coalition with the anti-EU ANEL; Alexis Tsipras (SYRIZA) is prime minister.

2016–18 Rhodes seldom has even 200 refugees resident, compared to nearby, overwhelmed islands. Air BnB causes many Old Town inns to close.

Columns at the partially reconstructed
Hellenistic stoa on the acropolis at Lindos

WHERE TO GO

Rhodes is an easy island to explore, with a good road network and public transport for independent sightseeing. The old quarters of Rhodes Town and Líndos are mostly car-free, and make ideal places to wander through on foot. There are also numerous tour companies for those who want an organised itinerary.

This guide is divided into several sections, exploring Rhodes Old and New Town first. Then there's a tour of the eastern coast, with a separate section for the ancient settlement of Líndos and the area south of it, followed by another section covering the western side of the island. Finally, day excursions are suggested.

RHODES OLD TOWN

Nothing quite prepares you for the spectacle of **Rhodes Old Town (Ródos) ❶**, especially seen from an approaching boat. An immense citadel with high sandstone walls 4km (2.5 miles) around, facing the town's three natural harbours, it has survived various sieges and bombardments, plus the visibly corrosive effects of damp sea air.

Built on the site of ancient Rhodes, itself founded some four centuries prior to the birth of Christ, the Old Town served from 1309 onwards as the headquarters of the Knights Hospitaller of St John, one of the most powerful of the Christian military orders. Originally established to provide medical care for pilgrims on their journeys to the Holy Land, they soon became one of the leading military opponents of Islam, harrying both Arab and Kurdish armies and later the Ottoman Empire.

In December 1522, after a long siege, Ottoman forces wrested Rhodes from the grasp of the crusader-knights and inaugurated nearly four centuries of Muslim Turkish rule. Vestiges of their influence are still obvious within the walls. The turn of the 20th century saw accelerated Ottoman decline and, in 1912, following the Italian-Turkish War, the Dodecanese islands (including Rhodes) were occupied by Italy. In contrast to Ottoman neglect, the Italians invested considerable effort and money into the Isole Italiane d'Egeo (Italian Islands of the Aegean), as they styled this cherished Mediterranean colony.

In the northernmost sector of the Old Town is the Knights' Quarter or **Collachium** (*kollákio* in Greek), where each of eight *langues* (nationalities) within the order had its inn and the Grand Master had his palace. Beyond this is the Boúrgos or civilian area, where you will find a fascinating maze of streets, comprising the former Turkish and Jewish sectors of the town.

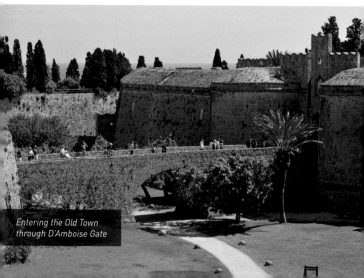

Entering the Old Town through D'Amboise Gate

THE WALLS AND GATES

The first impressive feature of the town is the walls themselves. Dating mostly from preparations for the 1480 siege, they sit strong and proud, especially beautiful at dawn, rosy-hued in the sun's first rays, or at night, lit by the soft glow of wrought-iron lamps. The Knights did not begin the citadel from scratch; they elaborated a series of relatively modest

Conqueror's gate

Victorious Ottoman Sultan Süleyman entered town through the southwesterly Ágios Athanásios Gate in 1523 and ordered it sealed up thereafter; it was only reopened by the Italians. The gate is, however, now universally referred to as 'Ágios Frangískos' after the Italian-built Catholic church of that name just outside.

Byzantine defences, creating eight sections of curtain walls, each one the responsibility of a separate *langue* (see page 30).

At one time each curtain had a gate; today there are 12 gates in use, each uniquely designed. Many are only wide enough to accept pedestrians or scooters. The most interesting is the **D'Amboise Gate Ⓐ**: situated in the northwest corner near the Palace of the Grand Masters (see page 37), it was built in 1512, during the reign of Grand Master Emery d'Amboise. It curves in an S-shape to outwit attackers and is then followed by a second, much simpler gate, **Ágios Andónios** (St Anthony's), which lies between two curtain walls.

Beside this gate is one of four discreetly signed entry tunnel-stairways leading to the **dry moat Ⓑ**, attractively landscaped on the west and southeast sides. You can follow a path in the moat from here all the way around the landward walls to the Akandiá Gate on the east side of the city. The walk takes about 30 minutes. However, it is not possible to gain direct access to many of the gates on this route as they sit high in the walls above,

⊙ THE ORDER OF THE KNIGHTS HOSPITALLER OF ST JOHN

This religious military order had three classes of membership, each bound by vows of chastity, poverty and obedience. Fully fledged knights were recruited from Europe's noblest families and numbered around 650; commoners could serve as soldiers or nurses, while chaplains saw to their spiritual needs. There were eight *langues* or 'tongues': English, German, French, Provençal, Auvergnat, Aragonese (in fact Catalan), Castilian and Italian. Each *langue* lived in a compound called an inn, under an appointed prior. For security, they went about in pairs and left the walled domain only on horseback.

French influence outweighed the other tongues when it came to electing the lifelong post of Grand Master. Thus, 14 of the 19 Grand Masters were from one of the French *langues*, and French was the Order's spoken language (Latin was used for official documents). The Italians' maritime talents made them the obvious choice to command the fleet, while other tongues each defended a section, or 'curtain', of the city walls.

After being expelled from Rhodes, the knights were without a base for seven years, until the island of Malta was offered to them by Holy Roman Emperor Charles V. They changed their name to the Knights of Malta and successfully repelled a four-month Ottoman siege in 1565. Despite this, the order was fast becoming obsolete; nations could now outfit their own fleets more efficiently, and the new trade routes to the Americas and the Far East dwarfed the significance of the Mediterranean.

Nowadays the order has been revived in many countries (including England's St John Ambulance Brigade) and engages in various medical and charitable activities. You can learn more at www.orderofmalta.int.

with bridges over the moat linking the Old Town to the outside world.

On the eastern side of the fortifications, facing Kolóna Harbour, is the impressive Marine Gate (see page 50), plus in the northeast, linking Kolóna and Mandráki harbours, the smaller Ágios Pávlos (St Paul's) Gate (see page 50). In 1924 the Italians decided that traffic would need access along the waterfront. They altered the walls, creating widened entrances for automobiles on the shore between Mandráki and Kolóna ports. The most important of these, **Freedom Gate** (Pýli Eleftherías) is located just west of St Paul's Gate, isolating it and the now-vestigial Naillac Tower from the rest of the citadel. Today many visitors enter the Old Town through this gate as it is the nearest to the taxi stand and main Mandráki bus stations.

Platía Argyrokástrou

THE KNIGHTS' QUARTER

All the living and administrative quarters of the Knights are at the northern end of the Old Town. Just inside the Freedom Gate lies **Platía Sýmis** (Sými Square), focused on the remnants of a 3rd-century BC **Temple of Aphrodite**. Only a few columns and a section of entablature are on view, though other remains were found in the ancient shipyards behind the two buildings to the west. One of these houses a spacious, well-lit **annexe** (Mon–Fri 8am–3pm; www.

mgamuseum.gr/en/info.php) of the **Modern Greek Art Museum ⓒ** (see page 49), hosting worthwhile temporary exhibitions.

Platía Argyrokástrou

Beyond the temple is **Platía Argyrokástrou**, decorated by a fountain with a dolphin spout. The base of the fountain is in fact a Byzantine baptismal font discovered by Italian archaeologists in southern Rhodes. The square is flanked on the east by the splendid **Inn of Auvergne**, built in the 16th century for the *langue* of Auvergne – one of three French-speaking *langues* within the Knights' Order (see page 30).

Behind the fountain is a building of 14th-century origin thought to have been the original hospital for the Order, although it was later used as an arsenal – Oplothíki in Greek, its modern official name. It now houses the archives of the Dodecanesian Institute of Archaeology and, in its southern wing, the **Decorative Arts Museum ⓓ**, which re-opened in 2018 after a long restoration (summer Tue–Sun 8am–7.40pm; winter earlier closure). The museum is home to an interesting collection of Rhodian painted pottery and carved wooden furniture.

Museum Square

Further south, through an archway, is **Platía Mousíou** (Museum Square), flanked by several important buildings. On the eastern side is the church of **Panagía tou Kástrou ⓔ** (Our Lady of the Castle), built by the Byzantines and completed by the Knights of St John, who made it into their cathedral. Its austere stone walls retain faint 14th-century fresco fragments from its time as a church, though it became a mosque during the Ottoman period. It formerly housed a collection of powerful icons, mostly from the 14th and 15th centuries, and post-Byzantine frescoes rescued from neglected chapels on Rhodes and the surrounding islands. However, these items have been moved to the Palace of the Grand Masters and the monument itself refurbished for an uncertain future role.

At the southeastern corner of the square, by the **Arnáldou Gate**, stands the **Inn of England** (1483), rebuilt by the Italians after it was destroyed in 1856.

Portrait bust of Helios

Archaeological Museum

The western side of Museum Square is dominated by one of the most important buildings in the Old Town – the Knights' New Hospital, which now houses the **Archaeological Museum of Rhodes** (Apr–Oct daily 8am–7.40pm; Nov–Mar Tue–Sun 8am–2.40pm). As well as displaying finds from all the ancient sites on the island, the building itself pays testament to the wealth of the order and the considerable engineering prowess of its medieval builders.

Construction began in 1440 under Grand Master Jean Bonpar de Lastic, after the previous Grand Master, Anton Flavian de Ripa, bequeathed a 10,000-gold-florin building fund, but the building was not fully completed until 1489 under Grand Master Pierre d'Aubusson. The hospital was state-of-the-art for its time, and its doctors treated Christians from all over Europe. Restoration began during the Italian era, with more needed following bomb damage in World War II.

The beautiful Aphrodite Bathing

Inside the building is a large **courtyard** flanked by arched porticoes, one of them graced by a lion statue of Hellenistic origin. There are also piles of cannonballs used in various sieges against the town, including that of Süleyman the Magnificent.

To the left of the courtyard, a stone staircase leads up to the **infirmary hall**. A vast open space, with a roof supported by several stone columns, it gives the impression of a medieval courtroom. This was the main ward of the hospital, with a capacity for over 100 beds and several small recessed rooms for the very sick. It had a fireplace at one end but very few other luxuries. Today, the room houses relics from the era of the Knights. The gravestones of illustrious members are on display here, with coats-of-arms depicting several lineages.

The rooms on the rest of the floor, including the large refectory, have been divided into smaller spaces to display mostly painted pottery, pithoi (urns) and grave artefacts found at ancient Ialysos and Kameiros, as well as other sites on the island. Rooms 6 to 8 display finds from Ialysos, which range from the 9th to the 4th century BC, while rooms 9 to 15 exhibit finds from Kameiros. Both sites were initially excavated during the Italian period.

The **atrium** area to the north, which was once the hospital kitchen, contains some splendid Classical statuary and grave steles, in particular one donated by Krito for her mother

Timarista. It was carved around 410 BC by a local artist, in the Athenian style prevalent at the time, and was found at Kameiros. Nearby is an Archaic-era kouros and a small head of Zeus found near his temple on Mount Atávyros.

Other rooms display very fine Hellenistic and Roman statuary, including two marble versions of Aphrodite: Thalassia or Aidoumene, celebrated by Lawrence Durrell as the 'Marine Venus' but lent a rather eerie aspect by her sea-dissolved face, and the more accessible *Aphrodite Bathing*, with the goddess crouched and fanning out her hair. This was carved in the 1st century BC but is considered to be a copy of a lost 3rd-century BC work. On the same level is a sculpture garden with a curious collection of stylised beasts real and mythical – a dolphin head, a lion and a sea serpent – posed among potted plants.

Via the ground-floor rear garden area, one may visit the sumptuous Villaragut Mansion, first built by a 15th-century Aragonese knight but much adapted by the Ottomans.

Street of the Knights

North of the museum is **Odós Ippotón Ⓖ** (Street of the Knights), where many of the Inns of the crusading order were based. One of the most complete medieval streets in the world, its buildings of finely chiselled sandstone form one uninterrupted facade that rises to a double archway spanning the road at its peak. Small square windows and fine arched doorways pierce the masonry – doors wide enough for horse and carriage or a single rider atop his steed. There are many other small details to be seen here, including carved ornamentation and commemorative plaques.

During the day Odós Ippotón is crowded with strolling visitors and large tour groups striding to the next location on their itinerary. This can make it difficult to imagine Knights arriving on horseback or walking between inns for strategy meetings,

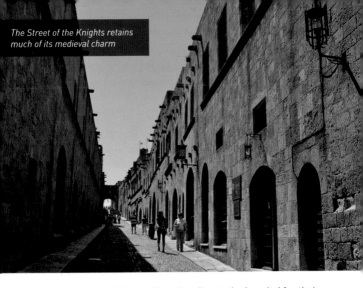

The Street of the Knights retains much of its medieval charm

or the lower-ranking brothers heading to the hospital for their medical duties. It is easier to imagine yourself back in the 14th century at night, when the street takes on a more magical atmosphere with the waxy glow of the streetlights reminiscent of medieval oil-lamps, and the only sound is the gurgle of the fountain in the Villaragut Mansion garden.

The first building on the right (north) is the **Inn of Italy**, with a plaque honouring Grand Master Fabrizio del Carretto (1513–21) above its entranceway. Across the street, further uphill you will see a small garden with a trickling Ottoman fountain; this is the courtyard of the 15th-century **Villaragut Mansion**, restored in 2002 but only accessible via the archaeological museum. Immediately opposite stands the highly decorated **Inn of France**, where a splendid life-sized carving of a knight in repose is set in stone – perhaps once a tombstone – just inside the courtyard, which also has a chapel dating from the era of

Grand Master Raymond Berenger (1365–74), though the street frontage dates from over a century later.

Near the top of Ippotón are two final **inns**, those of **Provence** (1418), on the right (north), and **Spain**, on the left (south), which housed two separate *langues*, those of Aragón and Castile. Around 1462, Grand Master Pedro Ramón Zacosta contrived to divide the Spanish *langue* into that of Aragón (actually Catalan-speaking) and Castile, in a move to counter the overwhelming influence of the French inns.

At the very top of the street, to the left, are the scant remains of the **Church of St John of the Collachium**, named after the order's patron, where the Grand Masters were buried. The Ottomans used its basement as a gunpowder magazine, and in 1856 lightning set off a powerful explosion that not only vaporised the church, but destroyed much of the town and killed over 800 people.

Palace of the Grand Masters

At the top of the Street of the Knights is the **Palace of the Grand Masters** ❶ (May–Oct daily 8am–7.40pm; Nov–Apr

---

⊙ RESTORING THE STREET OF THE KNIGHTS

Grand Tourists and Belle Époque travellers noted the picturesque dilapidation of the Street of the Knights, where Muslim families had adapted the grand inns for their needs by adding projected wooden structures with latticed gratings to upper-floor windows. These served to protect the virtue of the womenfolk from prying eyes, while allowing them in turn to survey the street. When the Italians took control of the island, these additions were summarily swept away and restoration carried out according to notions of a vanished medieval ideal.

Tue–Sun 8am–2.40pm). This was the administrative heart of the Order of the Knights of St John and the most important building in the Knights' Quarter. Left to fall into a state of disrepair by the Ottomans – they used it as a prison before the 1856 explosion nearly levelled it – it was renovated by the Italians with results that remain controversial for various reasons. The original ground-plan of the palace was not adhered to, with many modernising features added to the interior – including statuary and mosaics brought from other Dodecanese islands.

Greek archaeologists would have preferred to demolish the ruins of the palace to excavate the site in search of a Classical temple thought to lie directly beneath. Instead, the Italians saw an opportunity to create an impressive summer retreat for their royal family (none of whom ever used it), and so the palace was rebuilt.

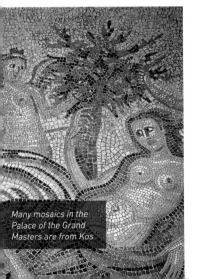

Many mosaics in the Palace of the Grand Masters are from Kos

However, the Italians employed poor-quality materials and workmanship, even by the standards of the 1930s, which has resulted in frequent, costly repairs since the 1990s as iron struts in the concrete core of the building corrode and expand.

Despite these issues, the building rarely fails to impress, retaining a majesty that befits its old role. Columns and capitals from ancient sites have been used throughout the interior, and the exterior stone cladding shows how the whole of the Knights' Quarter would have appeared in its prime. Look for the magnificent wooden ceilings, and the translucent panes of onyx in the windows that let in a soft light. Many of the main rooms have spectacular Hellenistic and Roman mosaics taken from sites across nearby Kos, and while it is ethically questionable whether they should be here, they have at least been carefully preserved.

Palace battlements

The palace's entrance lies between two imposing semi-circular towers; a grand marble staircase leads to the airy upper-storey rooms, sparsely furnished to allow a better appreciation of the structure and mosaics. The latter include depictions of the Nine Muses, another with a Nereid riding a sea-monster, and another showing the head of Medusa; fish and dolphins are also popular themes.

The ground-floor rooms, which originally acted as stables or grain and munitions stores during the great sieges, flank a courtyard sporting a series of Classical statues. These rooms house a permanent **exhibition** of finds from the first 2,400 years of Rhodes' history, as well as a medieval gallery covering the period up to the Ottoman conquest, and there are also temporary exhibitions. The **collections** are excellent – better organised and labelled than the Archaeological Museum's – though they close at 4.45pm, unlike the rest of the Palace.

Odós Sokrátous is lined with shops and a few cafés

THE BOÚRGOS

At the time of the Knights, the town's civilian population, though not permitted to live within the Collachium, still resided within the city walls. After the Ottoman conquest, only Muslims and Jews were allowed to live in the citadel, and the town acquired a new profile as mosques were built and minarets pierced the skyline. Although some Ottoman buildings were destroyed after their departure, most survive (if often in poor condition – part of the Recep Pasha Mosque collapsed in 2012), and two mosques are still in use.

Odós Sokrátous and Platía Ippokrátous

Throughout the old town, a maze of pebble-paved alleyways – some busy with people, others deserted – leads to hidden corners where you never know what's around the next bend. Yet no matter where you wander, you won't get hopelessly lost

– everything eventually leads back to a main thoroughfare, **Odós Sokrátous** (Socrates Street), abounding in shops interspersed with a few cafés. This has been the main commercial street since ancient times, though the Ottomans, with their flair for bazaar culture, accentuated its role.

Early in the morning before the shopfronts have opened, Sokrátous appears superficially much as it did a century or so ago. Later in the day, however, cruise-ship patrons crowd the pavements, and the windows of the numerous shops along the main drag and in the little alleyways either side display everything from gold jewellery and designer watches to knock-off handbags, fridge magnets, bangles and cheap footwear.

At the western end of the street, where it meets Odós Orféos and Odós Ippodámou, are several important buildings. The most impressive is the **Süleymaniye Mosque ❶**, with its magenta-tinted walls and distinctive minaret. This mosque, built in 1523 to mark the Ottoman takeover of the island, has emerged from a long renovation process (including a new minaret), but is still not yet open to the public and so can only be viewed from the outside. A small flight of steps on Odós Orféos affords the best views of the large dome that tops the building.

Odós Orféos also leads to the **Rolóï** (open all day and evening), a clock tower erected in 1851 on the site of a Byzantine-era tower. The tower gives impressive views over the Old Town's rooftops; you can clearly see what a labyrinth it is and yet how small an area it covers.

Opposite the mosque at the intersection of Sokrátous and Odós Ippodámou is a **Muslim library ❷**, founded in 1794; among its priceless collection of Persian and Arabic manuscripts are a number of rare handwritten Korans dating from the 15th and 16th centuries. The elegant Arabic script around the doorway will tell you that you are in the right place.

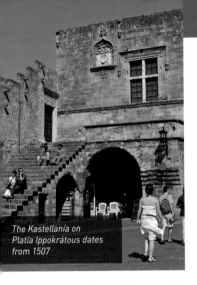

The Kastellanía on Platía Ippokrátous dates from 1507

The other building, right at the corner, is the **Imaret** 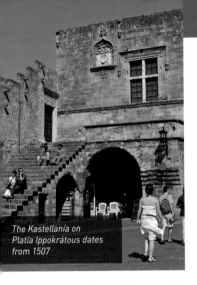 (the Paleó Syssítio in Greek), once an alms house for theological students; the lovely vaulted café inside is not currently operating, nor is the small gallery, an annexe of the Modern Greek Art Museum, across the pebble-paved courtyard. Theoretically it is home to a collection of rare engravings donated by the heirs of Noël Rees, 1940s British Vice-Consul in Izmir and a coordinator of Greek resistance to the Axis.

The east end of Sokrátous opens out onto **Platía Ippokrátous** (Hippocrates Square), one of the main meeting places in the Old Town, a few steps south of the Marine Gate with its massive towers. In the centre of the square is the **Syndriváni**, a fountain topped by an Italian ornament and normally bedecked by pigeons. In the southeastern corner of the square, the **Kastellanía** ⓛ was the medieval courthouse and commercial tribunal of the Knights, completed in 1507 and restored by the Italians between 1925 and 1935. The building now houses the public library and town archives.

The Turkish Quarter

South of Sokrátous and west of Pythagóra lies the heart of the former **Turkish Quarter**, perhaps the most intriguing area in the Old Town. Streets such as **Agíou Fanouríou**, **Pythagóra** and **Sofokléous** make good starting points for exploration, as does focal Platía Aríonos with its hamam (shut indefinitely) and the adjacent, minaret-less Sultan Mustafa Mosque, now used for wedding and circumcision ceremonies. Narrow, twisting lanes lead to empty, sun-baked squares, disused, semi-derelict mosques, medieval chapels with minarets tacked onto them, neoclassical mansion facades, Ottoman wooden

⊘ THE TURKS OF RHODES

The Turkish community of Rhodes was established in 1523, when an Ottoman garrison and civil servants settled principally in and around the main town. Their numbers were boosted between 1897 and 1912 by Greek-speaking Muslims fleeing unsettled conditions on Crete. These refugees founded the seaside suburb of Kritiká, about 3km (2 miles) southwest.

Some Old Town Turks claim to trace their ancestry to the original conquest, and feel that they have every right to be considered native Rhodians. However, the Greek authorities rarely agree, and their bureaucratic treatment of the Rhodian Turks often reflects the current state of relations between Greece and Turkey. The years after 1948 saw a sharp decline in the Muslim population, from about 6,500 to under 2,000. Around 1974, when the war in Cyprus made the position of Rhodian Turks very precarious, many wealthier Muslims sold their property in Rhodes Old Town and Líndos at knockdown prices.

However, since a European Court of Human Rights decision in 1997, Rhodian Turks cannot be stripped of Greek nationality no matter how long they have been resident in Turkey, Australia or elsewhere, and can return freely. As a result the local population has stabilised at around 2,500.

A quiet back street

balconies and ochre or powder-blue stucco-rendered ancient walls. Worth a special mention is the elaborate Hadji Khalil mansion of 1880, straddling Pythagóra. Beautiful stone buttresses arching overhead are designed to provide structural support in the event of an earthquake. In the evenings, as taverna street-tables begin to fill, this area awakens from its mid-afternoon sleep.

The Jewish Quarter

From Platía Ippokrátous at the eastern end of Odós Sokrátous, Odós Aristotélous extends east towards **Platía Evréon Martýron** (Square of the Jewish Martyrs), named in honour of the inhabitants of the adjacent Jewish Quarter who were sent to Auschwitz by the Nazis in the summer of 1944. At the centre of the square is a black granite, multilingual memorial to the victims. Flanking the *platía* on its north is the 15th-century **Navarhío** or Admiralty of the Knights; this later became the seat of the local Orthodox archbishop.

The **Kal Kadosh Shalom Synagogue** Ⓜ (Apr–Oct Sun–Fri 10am–3pm; donation; www.rhodesjewishmuseum.org), on Odós Simíou, just off the square, was first built in the 16th century and has been carefully renovated with funds sent by emigrated Jewish Rhodians; to one side is an excellent three-room

museum which thematically covers the community's history both in Rhodes Town and overseas.

Heading east out of the square towards the Pýli Panagías (Gate of the All-Holy) opening onto Kolóna Harbour, you'll pass the ruined **Panagía tou Boúrgou** church Ⓝ, which was

⊙ THE JEWS OF RHODES

Jews have lived on Rhodes since the 2nd century BC. In return for their support during the 1522 siege, the Ottomans assigned the Jews their own quarter in the east of the walled city. Under the Italians, who favoured them as a counter to Greek nationalism, the Jewish population grew to around 4,000 by the 1920s. A highly regarded rabbinical school at Kritiká attracted students from across the Sephardic world.

Thereafter, the *Rodesli* (as Rhodian Jews call themselves) began to emigrate in large numbers to the Belgian Congo, Rhodesia, Egypt, South America and the US. By the time anti-Semitic laws were promulgated and enforced in 1938–39, and war broke out between Italy and the Allies shortly after, some 2,000 *Rodesli* were safely overseas, avoiding the fate of the 1,973 *Rodesli* and 120 Jews from Kos deported to Auschwitz by the Nazis in July 1944.

Of these, just 161 (plus 53 with Turkish nationality, who were saved by Turkey's consul in Rhodes) survived. Today there are only about 25 in Rhodes Town, mostly elderly Jews from the Greek mainland, who resettled here early in the 1960s on the orders of Greece's head rabbi to ensure a continued Jewish presence on the island. The last community-supported rabbi left Rhodes in 1936, so one comes annually from Israel to conduct Rosh Hashanah and Yom Kippur services.

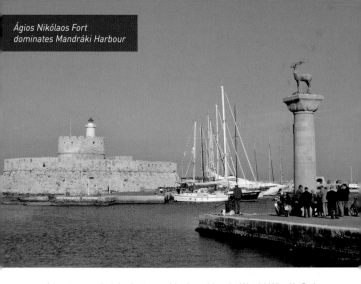

Ágios Nikólaos Fort dominates Mandráki Harbour

almost completely destroyed by bombing in World War II. Only the Gothic triple apse remains standing; a little stage within sometimes hosts special events.

A block further east stands the **Xenónas Agías Ekaterínis** 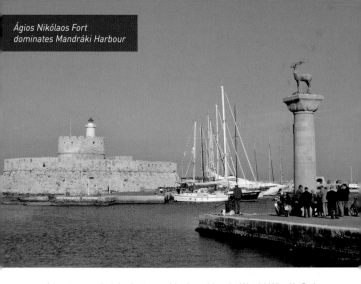 (St Catherine's Inn; unreliable opening hours; free), originally built in 1391–92 and meant to host distinguished guests of the Knights. Mostly restored in 1988–95, with the eastern, war-demolished wing now being rebuilt, it is well worth a peek inside (if open) for its fine votsalotó floors and antique furniture.

RHODES NEW TOWN

During the Ottoman occupation, the Greek population and others who were not allowed to live in the Old Town inhabited the area immediately outside the city walls, in the marásia or suburbs. Once distinct villages with their own parish churches, over time these settlements have merged to form **Rhodes New Town**.

MANDRÁKI HARBOUR

Just north of Freedom Gate, **Mandráki Harbour** , once the ancient city's main port, has anchorage for numerous private sailboats along its long easterly quay with its three **windmills**. At the far end of this jetty sits **Ágios Nikólaos Fort** Ⓠ, originally built by the Knights and last used militarily during World War II. Today its lighthouse assists the modern vessels that negotiate the port's north entrance. Despite wishful thinking and its portrayal on tea-towels, T-shirts and posters, the ancient Colossus never actually stood here. Today, two columns frame the narrow opening, topped by two bronze **statues** of Rhodian deer, a doe and stag.

During summer, the southwest quays are home to numerous colourful excursion boats, which head down the coast to Líndos, or over to nearby islands. Immediately across the busy boulevard from this quay stands the orientalised Art Deco **Néa Agorá** Ⓡ (New Market), built by the Italians on the site of a much older bazaar. This serves as a focus of transport activity, with a main taxi rank and two bus stations just outside. The interior is largely disappointing in terms of shops and tavernas, but at the centre is a wonderful raised open rotunda from 1925–26, originally used to auction fish.

Further along the west quay is the Italian-built (1924–25) cathedral of St John, today the Orthodox **Cathedral of Evangelismós** Ⓢ (Annunciation). It is worth trying to gain admission (easiest on Sunday) to see the frescoes painted between 1951 and 1961 by Photis Kontoglou, the great neo-Byzantine artist from Asia Minor – especially the *Annunciation* on the north wall, the *Virgin Platytéra* in the conch of the apse, and the *Psalmody* on the south wall, with figures holding period instruments.

The three famous windmills

Around the church is the **Foro Italico** , the main Italian administrative complex. When the Italians took control of the island, they set about redeveloping the northern part of the New Town, now known as **Neohóri**, giving it a new street plan and building the whimsical Governor's Palace, Town Hall, Courthouse, Port Authority (once the Fascist HQ), Post Office and the Municipal Theatre (originally the Puccini Opera House). These buildings were erected in two phases (1924–7 and 1932–9) by distinguished architects working first in orientalised Art Deco, and later the more severe Rationalist (essentially updated neoclassical) styles, impelled by the social imperatives of Fascism. Since the millennium these buildings have received some long-overdue recognition and conservation work. Just north of the theatre looms the bulbous-topped minaret of the **Murad Reis Mosque** , renovated in 2008. Peer through the wrought-iron railings at the exquisitely carved if neglected headstones in the old cemetery, one of the few that the Italians left alone during their remodelling. Murad Reis, one of Süleyman's admirals, met his end during the 1522 siege, and is entombed inside the circular mausoleum beside the mosque.

ÉLLI AND AROUND

Beyond the mosque sprawls **Élli** Ⓥ, the main town beach, backed at the east end by the domed, Italian-built Ronda bathing establishment and at the centre by the enormous casino, the largest in Greece, originally the Italian Albergo delle Rose. At the western end of the beach and on the very northern tip of the island stands the Italian-built **Aquarium** Ⓦ (Enydrío; Apr–Oct daily 9am–8.30pm, Nov–Mar daily 9am–4.30pm; http://rhodes-aquarium.hcmr.gr), with subterranean tanks full of creatures that live in the seas around Rhodes, plus interesting displays about the building itself.

Immediately south of here, on the oval plaza popularly known as Ekatón Hourmadiés (100 Date Palms), is the **Modern Greek Art Museum** Ⓧ (Tue–Sat 8am–2pm, Fri also 5–8pm; www.mgamuseum.gr), the richest collection of 20th-century Greek painting outside of Athens. All the big names – semi-abstract Níkos Hatzikyriákos-Ghíkas, Spýros Vassilíou, Yiánnis Tsaroúhis with his trademark portraits of young men, surrealist Níkos Engonópoulos, naïve artist Theóphilos, neo-Byzantinist Phótis Kóntoglou

Writer's residence

A plaque on the Italian Villa Kleoboulos (Cleobulus) at the edge of the Murad Reis cemetery commemorates Lawrence Durrell's residence in this tiny cottage between 1945 and 1947. The writer was working as a British civil servant at the time.

– are well represented. An annexe around the corner hosts temporary exhibits.

A short way south of Ekatón Hourmadiés, between Íonos Dragoúmi and Kathopoúli, stands the engaging neo-Gothic Catholic church of **Santa Maria della Vittoria Y**, originally dating from 1742 and not Italian-built despite appearances. Today it is used by a variety of foreign denominations, and usually left open so that you can enter at either the front or the back, to enjoy the calm, quirky interior.

KOLÓNA HARBOUR

Southeast of Mandráki Harbour you can walk along the waterside and through **St Paul's Gate**, an outer defensive bastion of the Old Town, emerging at the northwest end of **Kolóna 2**,

Élli beach, with the Aquarium in the background

the middle one of Rhodes' three ports, busy with colourful fishing boats, ferries from Turkey, cruise ships and large catamarans. A favourite vantage point is the foundations of the otherwise vanished **Naillac Tower** just east of St Paul's Gate, with unrivalled views towards Mandráki, particularly at dawn and dusk. Just south of Kolóna's fishing port stands one of the most dramatic entrances to the walled town, the **Marine Gate**, flanked by two large round towers and retaining

remnants of the mecha-
nisms that once operated
the gate.

SOUTHERN AND WESTERN NEW TOWN

Most of the modern town
extends south and west
of the Old Town. Just 2km
(just over 1 mile, less than
half an hour's walk) west
of the citadel is the high
ground of **Monte Smith**
(Ágios Stéfanos). Signposts
often read 'Akrópoli', as
the Italian renaming of the

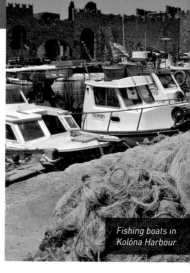

Fishing boats in Kolóna Harbour

heights after Sir Sydney Smith, a 19th-century British admiral
who established a lookout point here during the Napoleonic
Wars, is now falling into disfavour. At 110m (365ft) high, the
summit offers an excellent view of the whole town, the surrounding islands and the Turkish coast, particularly at sunset.
The hill is also home to the ruined Doric **Temple of Apollo**
(always open), of which three columns and an architrave were
re-erected by the Italians. The distance from here to Kolóna
gives you a good idea of the ancient city's size – nearly as extensive as modern Rhodes Town. Below the temple are the scant
remains of an ancient *odeion* (small theatre) and a stadium.

Rodíni Park (daily dawn to dusk; free), 3km (2 miles) south
of the Ágios Athanásios Gate, is the place to go to cool off on
a hot day. Fragrant conifers shade this parkland where the
knights used to cultivate medicinal herbs, while shrieking
peacocks patrol either side of an Ottoman aqueduct. Walking

The Mikrí Rotónda overlooks the coast at Pigés Kallithéas

trails loop around and across a spring-fed stream, interrupted by little dams to the delight of the resident ducks. Scholars say that this was the location of a famous ancient school of oratory; nowadays every August there's a nocturnal festival with grilled *souvláki* and all the Rhodian wine you can drink for a set price. At other times a bar-restaurant operates near the main entrance.

THE NORTHEAST COAST

Rhodes' eastern coast is sheltered from the prevailing summer winds blowing down from the Aegean. The shoreline presents a mix of wide sandy bays and small pebbly coves, with evocatively sculpted limestone bluffs interrupting the flow of the main coastal road. In addition to several seaside resorts, there are numerous interesting excursions into the hills.

KALLITHÉA AND FALIRÁKI

Travelling south from Rhodes, the first resort is **Kallithéa**, which is soon followed by the mock-Moorish, Art Deco spa of **Pigés Kallithéas** ❷ (Apr–Oct daily 8am–8pm, Nov–May daily 8am–4pm), 7km (4.5 miles) from Rhodes. Healing springs have flowed here since ancient times, and the Ottomans maintained a bathing establishment here from the 1880s onwards. The current Italian-built spa dates from 1929 and emerged from a lengthy restoration in 2007. The iconic image of the place is the **Mikrí Rotónda** dome in its clump of palms, just inland from a swimming lido used by beginners' scuba classes and a fancy bar serving from inside the original artificial grottoes.

⊙ OH DEER

Prompted by the Delphic Oracle, small fallow deer (*Dama dama*) – a bit bigger than a mastiff– were introduced to Rhodes during ancient times to combat the island's snakes. These were said to be repelled by the odour of deer urine, or dispatched using their sharp antlers (accounts vary). The knights introduced more as game, but during Ottoman times they were hunted to local extinction, and the Italians had to restock them.

For decades after the union of Rhodes with Greece, many semi-tame deer lived in the Old Town's moat, but after eight were killed by feral dogs in 1994, action was taken to save the survivors. Some deer have been released into the wild interior and south of the island – you may see them in the forests near Láerma – some were sent to live in the castle of Límnos island, while dozens of others reside in a large reserve on the clifftop flanking the canyon in Rodíni Park.

The sprawling **Megáli Rotónda** higher up hosts changing modern art exhibitions and a permanent collection of still photos showing the spa in its post-war heyday and as it was when it featured in 1961's The Guns of Navarone. Though the waters no longer flow, the bigger rotonda is regularly hired out as a venue for banquets, weddings and fashion shoots.

From Pigés Kallithéas, the coast road continues towards the first, multi-star hotels on **Faliráki Bay**, one of the best beaches on the island and unsurprisingly exploited for tourism. Towards the south end of the sand is central **Faliráki ❸** resort, long notorious among the Mediterranean's top nightlife meccas. However, following a drink-fuelled crime spree in 2003 (including one murder), local police clamped down hard and the party moved on to Zákynthos Island and Mália on Crete.

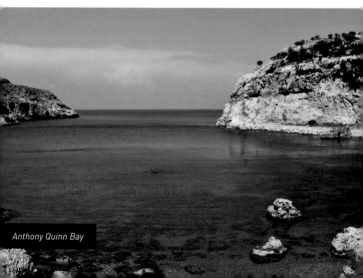

Anthony Quinn Bay

Faliráki is now struggling to reinvent itself as a resort for families and young couples. Just a handful of bars and mega-clubs survive from the dozens here at the resort's zenith. By day the beach remains busy, as it is the parasailing hotspot of the Dodecanese. There are also ringos and banana rides on offer, as well as hundreds of umbrellas for the more sedentary to lie under. Near the south end of the strip is the original village's fishing anchorage and chapel, with a couple of tavernas nearby that serve an approximation of traditional Greek fare.

Perfect Koskinoú

Inland from Kallithéa, the village of Koskinoú is noted for its clusters of traditional 18th-century Rhodian houses, which are kept in pristine condition. Every door and window frame receives a regular dose of bright paint, and the whole effect is enhanced with plants in ceramic pots.

AFÁNDOU AND EPTÁ PIGÉS

Afándou ❹, 5km (3 miles) south of Faliráki, is the next major settlement, situated inland from the centre of a long, eponymous bay. Just as you enter the coastal plain, there are signposts to the only 18-hole golf course (www.afandougolfcourse.com) on Rhodes. The island's climate means that greens here often have a decidedly brown appearance, and the fairways are extra firm. Afándou means 'invisible', referring to the fact that the village cannot be seen from the sea, which protected it from medieval pirate raids. The village's inhabitants have cultivated apricot orchards for many generations, and the local carpet-weaving tradition only recently died out. The main access road to the beach is flanked by atmospheric 16th-century Panagía Katholikí church (always open), with recently cleaned frescoes, including

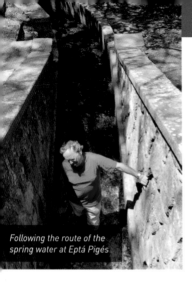
Following the route of the spring water at Eptá Pigés

an almond-eyed Panagía Enthroned. The beach itself, minimally developed other than for sun loungers and showers, is one of Rhodes' best. The most scenic portion is **Traganoú** ⑤ at the north end, where there are rock formations and caves to explore.

From Afándou it is possible to travel via the village of Psínthos to Petaloúdes (Valley of the Butterflies; see page 68).

From the crossroads at Kolýmbia further south, a road leads inland to **Eptá Pigés** ⑥ (Seven Springs), the perfect antidote to hot summer days in town or on the beach. This oasis has been exploited by farmers since Ottoman times; later, the Italians planted a pine forest to shelter numerous species of wild orchids, and their engineers channelled the springs to form a small artificial lake in the forest.

Many visitors enjoy following the route of the springs from their origin, paddling through above-ground channels into a large tunnel that passes under a nearby hillside to the reservoir. You can traverse the tunnel, nearly 200m (650ft) long, with the aid of a torch, but watch out for people coming back in the other direction – it's not really made for two-way traffic. For the claustrophobic, there is also an overground path to the artificial lake. Alternatively, visitors can sit in the shady café and watch the ducks, geese and peacocks strut about.

TSAMBÍKA

Panagía Tsambíka Monastery ❼ sits on the peak of a rocky promontory overlooking the coast just a little south of Eptá Pigés. Although a narrow, steep but drivable concrete lane leads most of the way there, female pilgrims usually walk (or crawl on hands and knees) from the main road to pray for fertility and the chance of a child, especially during the festival on 8 September. While modern fertility treatments have lowered their numbers, you will still meet many people called Tsambíka or Tsambíkos – a sure sign that the Virgin answered their mother's prayer. Even from the parking lot and taverna there are still 298 steps up to the pinnacle, a breathtaking walk in all senses of the word. The original, vaulted, 17th-century church retains fresco fragments; the wonder-working icon resides in a separate recess, emblazoned with *támmata* (votive offerings). The views from the 2009-remodelled grounds along the coast are second to none.

Some 326m (1,070ft) directly below is sandy **Tsambíka Bay ❽**, which has many watersports franchises but only one permanent building. Gently shelving, it is the first beach on Rhodes that becomes comfortably swimmable, in April. Beyond this, several bays are visible as far as Líndos, and other rugged limestone promontories fill the panorama.

ARHÁNGELOS TO LÍNDOS

Further south, **Arhángelos ❾**, guarded by its crumbled Knights' castle, is one of the

Anthony Quinn Bay

Tucked into the headland of Ladikó closing off Faliráki Bay to the south is scenic, rock-girt 'Anthony Quinn Bay', named in honour of the actor, who fell in love with Rhodes while here filming *The Guns of Navarone*. He thought that he had purchased land just inland, but never obtained proper title to it.

The village of Arhángelos retains a traditional feel

largest villages on the island. It has remained outside the tourist mainstream, making a living largely from farming. There are still a few ceramic kilns and showrooms, especially on the main bypass road, but only one traditional boot-maker remains to supply the high-cut, supple footwear designed to guard against both snakes and thornbushes. From Arhángelos a twisty, steep road leads down to the small beach resort at **Stegná ❿**, which has some excellent tavernas and is not overdeveloped.

Further along the main road, a left turn leads to **Haráki ⓫**, where several tavernas line the seafront. Above the village looms **Faraklós Castle**, once one of the largest fortifications on the island. Unfortunately, little remains of the castle today, but once it must have been impressive – it was the first position established by the Knights in 1306, and the last to surrender to Ottoman forces in the 1520s, well after Rhodes Town itself had fallen. The road that leads to the castle continues on to the gently shelving **Agía Agathí beach** just north. With some of the finest sand on Rhodes, it is a popular destination for excursion boats, with watersports available and some beach bars.

The main east-coast highway crosses the wide **Mássari Plain** on its way south. Hidden among the area's main citrus orchards is an old airstrip used by both the Italian and German forces during World War II. Eventually, after passing the turnoff for superb, unspoilt **Kálathos beach** ⑫, the road climbs to a bend revealing a photogenic view of the citadel and village of Líndos.

LÍNDOS AND THE SOUTHEAST

In ancient times **Líndos** ⑬ was the most cosmopolitan and commercial of Rhodes' three original city-states. Its 'golden age' occurred during the 6th century BC under the tyrant Kleoboulos, considered one of the 'seven sages' of antiquity – in ancient times the title 'tyrant' did not have the pejorative associations of today. It was he who established the Temple of Athena on the Acropolis, which allowed ancient Líndos to remain the island's most important religious sanctuary even after Rhodes Town was founded in 408 BC.

Perched upon a sheer-sided coastal precipice, this was always an excellent stronghold, and the Byzantines and Knights both

Kleoboulos' tomb

Such pithy maxims as 'Nothing in Excess', inscribed at the sanctuary at Delphi on the mainland, are ascribed to the Lindian ruler Kleoboulos. A round Hellenistic structure on the headland of Ágios Emilianós – now a chapel – is purported to be the great sage's tomb, but since it was built five centuries too late it seems unlikely to be his actual resting place.

fortified the site before it fell into decline during Ottoman rule. The village of Líndos remained a historical backwater, aside from a brief period of prosperity in late medieval times, when its sea captains plied the entire Mediterranean and built themselves sumptuous houses. During the 1960s bohemian types favoured the village as an idyllic hangout and the fashionable set soon followed; money rolled in to renovate the captains' mansions and create a whitewashed 'postcard-perfect' settlement.

LÍNDOS VILLAGE

Today Líndos has a permanent population of just a few hundred people – most Lindians now live in nearby villages and commute here to work in the all-dominating tourist trade. As one of the most photographed locations in the Aegean, the village can get

Líndos village sits beneath
the ancient Acropolis

unbearably crowded in high season. If you wish to wander in peace and sense some of the atmosphere of the place it is advisable to come early in the day or outside peak season. Most vehicles are banned from the village itself, with parking (fees usually charged) allowed only on the outskirts. Buses and taxis drop visitors in the Indian-fig-shaded square with its gurgling fountain of excellent water. From here a maze of narrow streets criss-cross the lower hill, the main ones lined with souvenir shops, noisy bars and restaurants with roof gardens looking to the Acropolis.

Líndos is one place on Rhodes where you can still find the traditional monóhoro or one-room house – given by a girl's family as a dowry on her marriage. Surrounded by high walls with ornate gateways, these dwellings, usually divided inside by a soaring arch, had outer courtyards whose floors were laid with votsalotó (pebble mosaic), and flanked the kitchen and other extra rooms that were built subsequently. Today, many are holiday studios managed by package tour operators. The grander captains' mansions are usually expatriate properties, or have been converted into restaurants or bars. One that isn't, the **Papakonstandís Mansion**, functions as a museum (notional hours 11am–2pm).

The route to the Acropolis, indicated by small hand-painted signs, passes **Kímisis Theotókou** church (Dormition of the Mother of God; daily 7am–7pm). It contains exquisite post-Byzantine frescoes by Gregory of Sými, mostly Christ's miracles but also a dog-headed Saint Christopher, plus a fine votsalotó floor.

THE ACROPOLIS

The climb to the **Acropolis** (Apr–Oct Tue–Sun 8am–7.40pm, Mon 8am–2.40pm; Nov–Mar Tue–Sun 8.15am–2.40pm) is steep, made more arduous in summer by the hot air that hangs heavily in the often windless village. An alternative is

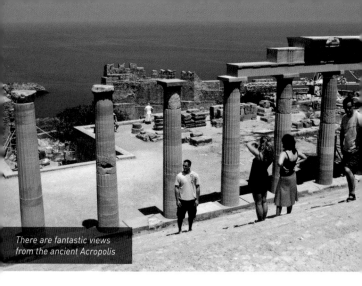

There are fantastic views from the ancient Acropolis

to ride a donkey to the top – the station is by the main square – for about €5 (but minimum hire two donkeys). The route towards the looming walls passes women peddling lace and cotton fabric and affords spectacular views over the invitingly azure sea with excursion caiques and expensive speedboats moored offshore.

A ticket booth sits inside the citadel's lower gate, just before a monumental staircase to the summit. At the bottom of the steps on the rocks to the left there is a **relief of a Hellenistic trireme** (warship). At the top is the **Residence of the Knights' Commander**, which adjoins the remains of originally Byzantine **Ágios Ioánnis** (St John) church.

Beyond the church is the base of the main ancient monument, the **Sanctuary of Athena Lindia**. The sanctuary is entered via a large **Hellenistic stoa** (covered walkway), 87m (285ft) long and constructed around 200 BC, which would have contained shops selling offerings to take into the sanctuary. Beyond the stoa, a wide staircase leads to the **propylaia** – the sanctuary entrance. This consisted of a series of colonnades surrounding the inner **Temple of Athena Lindia** at the highest seaward point on the rock. The remains seen today – columns of the propylaia and inner bemas (raised platforms) – date from 342 BC; the original sanctuary built by Kleoboulos was destroyed by fire in 392 BC, although post-millennium restoration works have re-erected much of the temple itself.

The Knights' 14th-century fortifications offer superb views of **Líndos Bay** to the north, the town to the west, and perfectly sheltered **St Paul's Bay** to the south. This was where St Paul supposedly landed when thrown off course by a fierce storm in AD 58. The gap in the rocks here is said to have been miraculously opened by lightning, allowing his boat to land safely. A small, whitewashed church, popular for baptisms, marks the spot.

INLAND TO THÁRRI

Beyond Líndos, the coast road passes through **Péfki ⓮** resort, with its secluded coves at the base of low cliffs, and **Lárdos** village slightly inland, also well geared to tourism. From Lárdos it's 12km (7 miles) to **Láerma** village, which, like many in this part of the island, has lost its younger generation to the coastal resorts and Rhodes Town.

Begun in the 9th century, **Thárri Monastery ⓯**, 5km (3 miles) south of Láerma in fire-scarred pine forest, is the oldest on Rhodes. Now home to a small community of monks, its church of the Archangel Michael (open during daylight hours) shelters stunning, well-cleaned frescoes dating from 1300 to 1450, mostly showing the acts of Christ.

SOUTH TO PRASSONÍSI

South of Péfki, the next major coastal resort is **Kiotári ⑯**, which sprung up in the mid-1990s with several, mostly all-inclusive, hotels along the main highway above the quiet beach road with its tavernas and summer cottages.

From Kiotári a road runs inland to the village of **Asklipió ⑰**, nestled in the lee of yet another Knights' castle. Also on the hill above the town is an ancient Greek shrine to Asklepios, the god of healing, which functioned as a therapeutic centre and was staffed by healer-priests. Today Asklipió remains one of the most traditional villages on Rhodes, with the odd loaded donkey or working wood-fired oven in the backstreets. The exquisite, dead-central 11th-century church of **Kímisis Theotókou** (daily 9am–5pm) is a beautiful example of Byzantine design. Every nook and cranny of the interior is decorated with rich 15th-century frescoes depicting Old and New Testament scenes in a vividly coloured 'cartoon strip' scheme.

Beyond Kiotári, **Gennádi ⑱** is the last major holiday resort on this coast, with limited accommodation but an endless, clean beach. The centre of the village is picturesque and inhabited nowadays by more immigrant Albanians than native islanders. **Lahaniá ⑲**, located 7km (4 miles) south of Gennádi, is an old village partly hidden in a ravine, whose lovely lower square has two Ottoman fountains. From both Lahaniá and Gennádi roads lead to **Plimýri ⑳**, a popular if windy sandy cove with

Remote lighthouse

The 1890-vintage lighthouse situated at the far southern tip of the Prassonísi islet used to be staffed, but has been automated (and solar-powered) since the 1980s, though a keeper still commutes out from Kattaviá to perform maintenance.

a medieval chapel and friendly tavern adjacent.

Prassonísi 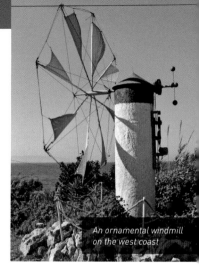, the southernmost point of Rhodes beyond Kattaviá village, has been really opened up to tourism by the paving of the road in; travel time from Líndos is now around 30 minutes non-stop. This is where the Aegean Sea to the northwest meets the Mediterranean Sea to the southeast, so it's almost always windy here, with either the dominant northerlies or rarer southeast wind delighting the windsurfing set, who have three schools (and two sides of the spit) to choose from. Prassonísi is a cape linked to the main island. During 1996 severe storms breached the sandbank, creating a channel between the Aegean and Mediterranean sides and making the cape an islet. However, two decades-plus later, the sand spit has returned.

An ornamental windmill on the west coast

THE WEST COAST

As a rule, Rhodes' western coast is not as stimulating or picturesque as the eastern one. The beaches are not as wide or as sandy, and the prevailing winds and tides carry debris down the Aegean and deposit it directly on the shoreline. However, there are several interesting attractions, and resort facilities in the northwest – close to Rhodes Town – are among the best on the island.

IALYSOS AND THE NORTHWEST

Diagóras Airport ㉒ lies on the coast 16km (10 miles) south of Rhodes Town, and there are several villages en route. However, as hotels have multiplied since the 1960s, these separate settlements appear to have blended into one resort 'strip'. The first resort, **Ixiá** ㉓, has the most established tourist area, with several large and luxurious hotels, but was never a village per se. Further south, **Triánda**, **Kremastí** and **Paradísi** (by the airport) villages have grown due to tourism but still support some Greek domestic activities.

From Triánda or Kremastí it's easy to travel inland to visit the remains of one of ancient Rhodes' most important settlements, **Ialysos** ㉔. Unfortunately little remains of the city-state that was one of a powerful triumvirate with Kameiros and Líndos during the 1st millennium BC – though it was once so extensive that it stretched down the hillside to the coast. The site, on high ground overlooking Rhodes Town, made it a prime strategic position throughout the island's history. It was from here that the Knights consolidated their hold on the island in 1308–9, and also here that Sultan Süleyman had his headquarters during the 1522 siege.

The ruins later became a quarry for stone to build newer towns and structures, including the main attraction at the site, **Filérimos Monastery**, which has had a chequered life. Revered by Orthodox Christians, it was used as stables by the Ottomans, renovated by the Italians and bombarded by German forces in September 1943 to dislodge its Italian garrison, before being restored again after World War II. Today, its tranquil dignity shines through, and it's well worth spending a few moments in quiet reflection among the pines. The monastery's most impressive building is the 14th-century **Church of Our Lady of Filérimos**, with its rib-vaulted chambers (one built by the Grand Master Pierre d'Aubusson) and small cloister. The mosaic floor in the innermost chapel dates from the 6th century AD, as does a cruciform baptismal font outside, though the stone used was originally part of a Classical temple – illustrating the numerous rebirths of the place.

A mosaic icon at Filérimos Monastery

At the threshold of the church are the remaining foundations of the Classical temples to **Athena Polias** and **Zeus Polieus**. Below these, near the car park, is the entrance to the subterranean Byzantine chapel of **Aï-Giórgis Hostós**, decorated with often faint 14th- and 15th-century frescoes.

Outside the site entrance lies a 4th-century BC **Doric fountain**, which came to light after a landslide in 1926, but is now off-limits again owing to more earth movement. Even if you can't visit the fountain, take a stroll down the pine-shaded avenue with a series of bronze reliefs depicting the **Stations of the Cross**, laid out by the Italians. At the end of the lane sprouts a huge, nocturnally illuminated **cross** perched atop the 265m (875ft) hillside. The Italians destroyed the original in 1941 to deprive Allied airmen of a navigational aid, but it was re-erected in 1995. You can climb the cross and enjoy panoramic views south over the Italians' hidden airstrip (now a Greek air force base) and north to Sými and Turkey.

THE VALLEY OF THE BUTTERFLIES

South of the airport developments peter out, though there are occasional beaches signposted to seaward from the main road through grassland or fields. These are quieter than the main resort beaches except at weekends, when local families take a break from town life.

From the main road a left turn leads up into the hills to **Petaloúdes** ❷⑤. This literally translates as 'butterflies', and the area is usually known in English as the **Valley of the Butterflies** (Apr–Oct daily 8am–5pm; charge varies by season),

⊙ THE BUTTERFLIES (OR MOTHS) OF RHODES

Petaloúdes is actually a seasonal home not to butterflies but Jersey tiger moths *(Panaxia quadripunctaria)*, which are attracted by the oriental sweetgum *(Liquidamber orientalis)* trees which grow densely in this valley. Hundreds of thousands of these creatures settle on the tree trunks here between May and September, with peak arrival time during July and August. The moths cannot eat during this final phase of their life cycle, so rest to conserve energy for mating, then die of starvation soon afterwards.

When at rest, the moths are a well-camouflaged black and yellow, but careful examination reveals hundreds resting inconspicuously on the tree trunks. Their Latin name derives from four spots visible when their wings are open, which is augmented by a flash of their cherry-red overwings when in flight. Though it is tempting to startle the moths into taking to the air by making a sudden loud sound or vibration, this stresses the moths and interferes with their reproduction, so the reserve has strict rules against deliberately disturbing them.

The Valley of the Butterflies

one of the island's beauty spots. The whole valley has been set aside as a well-laid-out reserve for visitors, who can walk through the trees, over streams and around ponds and waterfalls, looking out for the winged creatures. The climb to the relatively uninteresting 18th-century chapel of **Kalópetra** at the top of the valley takes about one hour; on the way down there is a snack bar to stop at.

Some 2km (1 mile) downhill from Petaloúdes is the **Microwinery of Anastasia Triantafyllou** (daily 8.30am–7pm; tel: 22410 82041), where you can sample up to 10 varieties annually of their red, white and rosé bottlings.

THE PROFÍTIS ILÍAS RANGE

The coastal road continues southwest, with the Profítis Ilías range, the island's third-highest, rising inland; a paved side road at Soroní leads towards it. First stop on the north slope of the mountain is strange-looking **Eleoússa** ㉖, built in 1935–6 as the Italian agricultural colony of Campochiaro. On its western outskirts spreads an enormous Art Deco **fountain-pool**, now home to captive specimens of the rare local *gizáni* fish, about the size and colour of a guppy. Some 2km (1 mile) west of this stands the tiny Byzantine chapel of **Ágios Nikólaos Foundouklí** ㉗. Once part of a larger monastery complex, the four-apsed structure has very damp-blurred 13th- to 15th-century frescoes.

The same road from Eleoússa then passes wooded **Profítis Ilías** peak ㉘ (798m/2,618ft). Although the summit itself is off-limits owing to military and telecoms facilities, a network of prepared paths through the fragrant mixed conifer forest allows you to explore the lower slopes. From the small **Monastery of Profítis Ilías**, another path descends to Sálakos village just to the north. Beside the monastery is an Italian-built chalet-style hotel which has been restored and returned to service (see page 139).

KAMEIROS

Beyond Soroní the coast highway threads through seasonally changing farmland until it reaches the turning to the site of ancient Kameiros, just inland. Despite being the smallest of Rhodes' three Dorian cities, **Kameiros** ㉙ (daily May–Oct 8am–7.40pm; Nov–Apr Tue–Sun 8am–2.40pm) is the best preserved, and it brings to life the daily routine of ordinary people from the Archaic era onwards. Although founded around 1450 BC, when Cretans fled their devastated homeland and settled here, the ruins visible today date mainly from after 226 BC, when most earlier buildings were destroyed by a powerful earthquake.

The ruins cover the hillside in distinct urban zones typical of the era. Near the site entrance is the lower **agora**, the main public meeting place, flanked by two temples. Climb the steps ahead of you and turn right to follow the main street trodden by so many ancient sandals, passing numerous small, square rooms to either side; each was a Hellenistic dwelling. Above this residential area, buttressed by a massive retaining wall, lie the remains of a massive **stoa** 200m (660ft) in length, built in the 3rd century BC. In its time, the shops would have been at the rear, while an open front supported by a series of double Doric columns allowed the townspeople – and today's visitors – to survey the whole city below them. Beyond the retaining wall's north end yawns a huge **cistern** dating from the 6th century BC, which supplied water to the lower town via a sophisticated system of pipes.

At the town's highest point are the remains of a **Temple of Athena**. There is no Acropolis per se, nor any fortifications, and it seems the peaceable, Minoan-influenced culture and a population largely made up of farmers and craftsmen ensured an unwarlike profile. The rise of Rhodes Town after 408 BC resulted in the gradual abandonment of Kameiros. Luckily for modern archaeologists the city was never plundered or overbuilt, only being rediscovered in 1859, and first excavated in 1929.

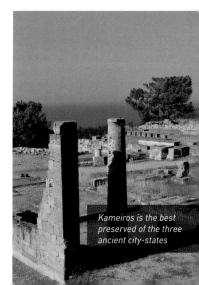

Kameiros is the best preserved of the three ancient city-states

To Hálki from Skála Kámiros

There are currently three small craft competing on this route: *Fedon* (tel 6942 799487), *Nissos Halki* (tel 6946 519817) and Nikos Express (tel 6946 826095). Most days there are departures at 9.15am and 5–5.30pm, with odd morning services on Weds and Fri at 11.30am and a 2.30–2.40pm service on Mon, Tue, Fri and Sat, plus at 3.30pm on Weds. Journey time in calm seas is 75min.

There are several fish tavernas at **Ágios Minás beach ㉚**, downhill from ancient Kameiros, though some cater to tour-bus clients and can be busy at lunchtime. An alternate lunch spot is **Kámiros Skála ㉛** (Kámiros Harbour), 15km (9 miles) further southwest, with its fishing fleet and nets spread on the quay. After lunch you can watch the comings and goings of the daily caiques to the island of Hálki just off the coast.

KRITINÍA AND AROUND

As the road climbs away from Kámiros Skála, ruined **Kritinía Castle ㉜** (sometimes called Kastéllo) comes impressively into view on your right. Since the access road is too steep and twisty to allow tour-coach passage, you will likely share the premises with only a few other people. The castle was built by the Knights of St John during the 14th century as one of a series of strongholds to protect Rhodes' western coast, in visual contact with their castles on Alimniá islet and Hálki to the west. Its keep is built around the rocky summit, with the curtain walls swooping steeply down; a population of 'Rhodes dragons' – agama lizards – scurry along these and disappear between cracks in the masonry. There is at present no charge or opening schedule, despite the vaulted chapel being restored in 2008 and a ticket booth installed at the entrance.

Kritinía village perches a little way inland from the castle, with its amphitheatrically tiered houses looking out to sea and an atmospheric kafenío on the square. The name supposedly derives from the Cretan origins of the inhabitants.

Beyond here the road heads inland to the slopes of Mount Atávyros, at 1,215m (3,949ft) the highest peak on the island, and to **Émbona** ❸ village on its north flank, the centre of Rhodian winemaking. During the late summer grape harvest the air here takes on a sweet, heavy perfume as the grapes are crushed to produce the must for fermentation. The mega-wineries of CAIR and Emery are the most publicised, but it's far preferable to seek out family-run micro-wineries like Alexandris (www.facebook.com/alexandriswinery), which makes the excellent Citizen of the World red and Apiro rosé, or Kounakis, known for its soúma (see box p.75). In the next village 14km/8.5 miles east, Apóllona, the Piperis winery (www.piperiswinery.com) produces a range of good labels.

Nearby, sleepy **Ágios Isídoros** is the best starting point for hikes to the summit of **Mount Atávyros** ❹, with the trailhead signposted at the north edge of the village. This barren hump, with just a few giant oaks, could not be more different from Profítis Ilías, just a little way north.

Émbona village

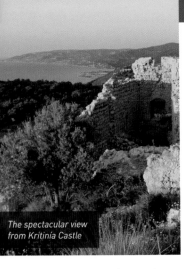

The spectacular view from Kritinía Castle

The round trip takes about five hours, but you will be rewarded with magnificent views as far as Crete on a clear day. There are also remains of a Bronze Age **Temple to Zeus**, next to a modern radar 'golf ball'.

THE SOUTHWEST

Continuing south from Kritinía, the main road veers inland through partly forested mountain scenery. The first village is **Siánna ㉟**, famous for producing the honey and *soúma* (see box) sold at the roadside.

Soon after the road enters **Monólithos** village ㊱, whose older flat-roofed houses around the main church have sweeping views south. But there are even better ones 2km (1 mile) west from yet another Knights' castle sitting atop an impressive rocky pinnacle 250m (820ft) above sea level – hence the name Monólithos, meaning 'single rock'. There are great photographic opportunities from the access road and, despite appearances, an easy stair-path leads to the summit. Inside the walls, there is little left of the other castle structures, but a tiny whitewashed chapel adds a typical Greek touch. The paved road continues about 5km (3 miles) to various secluded beaches at **Foúrni ㊲**, some of the best on the west coast, though there's only one tiny snack-bar at one cove – the closest proper tavernas are in Monólithos.

South of Monólithos, the broad road passes through Apolakkiá to **Kattaviá**, the southernmost village the island, which gives access to Prassonísi (see page 65). Alternatively, another fast road cuts through the forest from Apolakkiá to Gennádi on the east coast (see page 64). Finally, in 2012–13 the rough road between Ágios Isídoros and Láerma (see page 63) was improved, providing another invaluable link while touring.

EXCURSIONS

As part of the larger Dodecanese archipelago, Rhodes offers opportunities to visit several neighbours, each on a separate day trip.

Village of Soúma

Siánna is one of three villages on Rhodes (along with Kritiniá and Émbona) allowed every autumn to make *soúma*, a distillation of grape pulp, skins and seeds left over after most of the fruit has been pressed for wine. The result, initially about 22 percent alcohol but then concentrated to double that strength, is identical to Italian *grappa*, and in fact the local distilling licence dates from Italian times. Unlabelled bottles of this clear liquid are on sale everywhere in Siánna and Kritiniá.

Sister catamarans *Dodecanese Express* and *Dodecanese Pride* make it possible to design your own itineraries, offering advantageous day-return tickets, without signing on to expensive organised excursions. You can also pop over to Marmaris in Turkey, which lies just north of Rhodes' northernmost point.

KOS

A two-and-a-half-to-four hour catamaran trip northwest of Rhodes (depending on stops), **Kos ⊛** ranks second among the Dodecanese in population and size, and has been settled since ancient times, thanks to wide fertile plains, and a good harbour opposite Asia Minor. Contemporary Kos is popular with

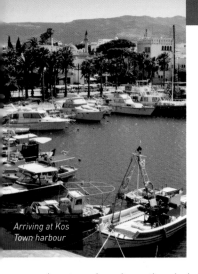

Arriving at Kos Town harbour

package-holidaymakers, thanks to its many fine beaches, castles and other attractions. It is also a uniquely bicycle-friendly island, with a network of bike lanes, and visitors can get the most out of Kos Town and environs by renting a push-bike for the day (or longer).

Kos Town, near the northeastern tip of the island, has been the main settlement since antiquity, and remains a fascinating place to explore. An earthquake in 1933 damaged much of the town centre, but allowed Italian archaeologists to expose and excavate a large section of the Roman city directly underneath. Today it is possible to explore the old **agora** (daylight hours; free), and to walk along Roman roads past exposed patches of mosaics west of the centre, all now a bit lower than the ground level of adjacent modern thoroughfares.

Like Rhodes, the town became a stronghold of the Knights Hospitaller of St John early in the 14th century, and between 1450 and 1514 they built the huge waterfront **Neratziás Castle** (June–Sept Tue–Sun 8am–6.40pm, Oct–May Tue–Sun 8am–2.40pm) to replace an earlier, flimsier Byzantine fort. The fortification walls make an excellent vantage point for photographs over **Mandráki Harbour** with its excursion boats, while the interior is filled with carved marble plaques, statuary and cannons.

The Knights departed in 1523 without firing a shot, as part of the treaty which surrendered Rhodes (and most of the Dodecanese) to the Ottomans. Nearly four centuries of Ottoman rule are attested to just inland from the castle, where the 18th-century **Loggia Mosque**, the largest on Kos, now stands silent and closed, its windows damaged during World War II (though shops occupy its ground floor). There are several smaller mosques scattered across town and in Platáni village, still used by the small local Muslim population of about 700.

The town's main square, **Platía Eleftherías**, is 150m/yds inland from the waterfront along pedestrianised Vassiléos Pávlou. The square is surrounded by various fanciful Italian buildings, including the 2015-renovated **Archaeological Museum** (Apr–Oct Tue–Sun 8am–7.40pm, Nov–Mar closes 2.40pm), which displays excellent Hellenistic and Roman mosaics and statuary, including two portrayals of Kos' favourite son, Hippocrates, who was born on the island around 460 BC (see box page 79).

At the southern outskirts of the town, on Grigoríou tou Pémptou, lies a Roman *odeion* or small theatre (open all day), used in summer for performances. Nearby the **Casa Romana** (Tue–Sun 10am–5.40pm) is a 3rd-century AD Roman villa whose mosaic floors show various land and sea creatures and whose exhibits illuminate daily life of the era.

The **Asklepion** (Apr–Oct daily 8am–7.40pm, Nov–Mar Tue–Sun 8am–2.40pm), situated 4km (2.5 miles) outside of Kos Town, can be reached by bicycle, local buses or a green-and-white, rubber-wheeled 'train' that departs from near the waterfront tourist office. The Asklepion was a religious shrine, spa and therapeutic centre founded shortly after the death of Hippocrates in 370 BC. The most conspicuous remains date from the Roman rather than the

Hellenistic era, and the site was plundered for masonry by the Knights of St John when they built their castle in Kos Town. The main Doric temple to Asklepios, god of healing, stood on the highest of the three terraces. The site itself was chosen for its mineral-rich spring water, which still flows – you can also still see sections of half-buried clay plumbing feeding the baths – and perhaps also for the fine views across to Anatolia.

Statue of Asklepios at the Asklepion

HÁLKI

The largest of a group of islands lying a few nautical miles off the west coast of Rhodes, barren, quiet **Hálki** ⑨ is the diametric opposite of its larger sibling. It relies on Rhodes for almost everything (except meat from the many sheep and goats), and both the local population and visitor numbers remain relatively low – ensuring a tranquil atmosphere.

The islanders made a decent living from sponge-diving until the Italians put restrictions on the trade in 1916. This spurred mass emigration to Florida, where natives of Hálki and other Dodecanese islands founded the town of Tarpon Springs and carried on their traditional livelihood. Hálki slumbered in neglect until the 1980s, when first Unesco and later conventional tourism companies discovered the island and began to restore many of the handsome houses as accommodation.

Boats dock at the main settlement of **Emborió**, where the lanes are lined by colourful restored mansions. The town is also home to **Ágios Nikólaos** church, with its elegant campanile and, just south, the tallest clock tower in the Dodecanese. On the pedestrianised waterfront, several eateries are perfect for a leisurely lunch.

West of Emborió, Tarpon Springs Boulevard, the island's first paved road – funded by Floridian émigrés – leads past the sandy bay of **Póndamos** to the abandoned hillside village of **Horió**, deserted except around 15 August when a festival is celebrated at its **Panagía** church. Otherwise Hálki is best explored on foot, or – in midsummer when temperatures climb – by taxi-boats serving remote beaches with poor overland access.

SÝMI

Despite being infertile and waterless, the small island of **Sými** ④ was one of the wealthiest in the Aegean from the 1880s until 1910, prospering from shipbuilding, maritime

---

⊘ BIG OLD TREE

Beside the Loggia Mosque in Kos Town –indeed almost overshadowing it – grows a huge plane tree. Its branches extend so far and its trunk has split into so many sections that for many years it has been supported by scaffolding. The islanders proudly proclaim this as the Tree of Hippocrates, under which the 'Father of Medicine', a native of the island whose bronze statue adorns the harbourfront, supposedly lectured his students some 2,400 years ago. However, although the tree is among the oldest in Europe, most experts reckon it to be well under 1,000 years old and therefore not of Hippocrates' era.

trading and sponge diving. The shipyard owners, captains and tradesmen built fine mansions and ornate churches. However, the island's fortunes changed when the arrival of steam-powered ships coincided with new Italian restrictions on sponge-gathering. Soon Sými's streets fell silent as most of the workforce emigrated to the US and Australia, leaving the island's grand buildings gradually to crumble away. However, beginning in the early 1980s, foreign connoisseurs and rich Athenians fell in love with this picturesque backwater and snapped up the decaying mansions for restoration as second homes. Like Rhodes Old Town, Sými is protected by the state archaeological service, which ensures that all renovations are done in accordance with traditional architecture and materials.

The small permanent population of just under 3,000 is more than doubled by expat homeowners and holidaymakers in high season. There are no huge resorts on the island, so accommodation is in small to medium-sized hotels, apartments or restored houses. Most people visit Sými as a day trip from Rhodes, 50 minutes away by the fastest craft. Visitors typically disembark from ships between 9.30 and 10.30am and depart at 4–5.30pm. Consequently, the island has two distinct moods – daytime bustle and relaxed languor in the late afternoon and evening.

Arrival at Sými's major port, **Gialós**, offers one of the most impressive vistas in Greece. Hundreds of neoclassical stone facades and iron balconies combined with thousands of pastel-hued shutters rise from the harbourside up the slopes. Gialós was always the commercial hub of the island, though now the trade is in T-shirts, packaged spices, small trinkets and imported carpets rather than sponges. There are still sponges of all sizes on display, but these are mostly imported from the Caribbean and Asia. Waterfront restaurants entice visitors to stop for a delicious seafood meal, but there is much more to see on the island.

High above Gialós and just out of sight lies **Horió**, the island's inland village, reached either by 357 broad stone steps, the **Kalí Stráta** (the 'Good Road'), or, less strenuously, by bus from the south quay. Horió is crowned by the inevitable Knights' castle, built amid the ruins of Sými's ancient citadel. At the far side of the village is the very

Sými's tribute

When the Knights surrendered the Dodecanese in 1523, the Greek civilian population of Sými, already noted as sponge-divers, sent Sultan Süleyman a placatory gift of the finest sponges for his harem. The sultan, duly impressed, granted Sými effective autonomy thereafter in exchange for a yearly tribute of sponges, an arrangement honoured until the Italian era.

Sými's major port, Gialós

worthwhile local **museum** (Apr–Oct Tue–Sun 8am–2.30pm), highlighting Byzantine and medieval Sými with its displays on some of the island's dozens of frescoed rural churches and an ethnographic collection.

Most day trips to the island from Rhodes call for about half an hour at **Panormítis Monastery** in the south of the island as part of their itinerary. Unfortunately this means that the monastery can be very crowded if several boats happen to arrive at the same time. In the middle of the compound's pebble-paved courtyard is the church of **Taxiárhis Mihaïl**, with its highly revered icons of the Archangel Michael, patron saint of Dodecanesian sailors.

MARMARIS (TURKEY)

Although the protracted conflict between Greece and Turkey carried on well into the 20th century, the two nations have mostly put the past behind them, despite the occasional belligerent statement from Turkey's long-serving President Erdoğan. Rhodes is very close to Turkey's western coast, so it is possible to enjoy a day (or longer) in this totally different, yet strangely similar, country. You'll need your passport and some small euro or sterling notes for entry formalities (including a tourist visa if you intend to stay overnight; UK passport-holders do not need one for a day trip).

Although Turkey officially uses the Turkish lira, almost all transactions can be conducted (at a slight mark-up) in euro or sterling.

The nearest Turkish port to Rhodes is **Marmaris** ❹, an hour away by catamaran. The town occupies the head of a wide bay backed by pine-clad hills that shelter it from north winds – consequently, it is much hotter and more humid in summer than Rhodes. The resort strip, one of the largest in Turkey, dominates the shore just west with a rash of high-rise hotels set behind a coarse-sand beach. East of the centre sprawls a marina with berths for hundreds of yachts.

On a hill in the old quarter is **Marmaris Castle** (signposted *Müze* or museum; Tue–Sun 8.30am–noon and 1–6.30pm), which offers wonderful views over the bay as well as a small archaeological and ethnographical collection. The climb to the little restored fort, built by Sultan Süleyman, passes the few remaining old houses of the **Kaleiçi** district.

The town's main attraction is its *çarşı*, or **bazaar** – a warren of lanes around a hall. Mass-produced trinkets predominate, though there are also spices, leather goods, jewellery, beads, İznik and Kütahya tiles, counterfeit designer apparel (often of shoddy quality) including fake pashminas, and discounted 'end of season' clothing. A sense of humour is useful, as sales tactics are more intense than in Greece, and prices are not necessarily any cheaper than on Rhodes.

After a spot of retail therapy, shun fast-food snacks in the bazaar and head down to the easterly waterside for lunch, while watching the distinctive wooden tour *gulets* as they come and go. Many menu items are the same as on Rhodes – only the name changes, and even then not always. This is because Greeks and Turks have lived together, though not always happily, for almost a millennium, and their cultures are more similar than some would like to admit.

Shopping in Rhodes Old Town,
near Platía Ippokrátous

WHAT TO DO

Rhodes is not only an excellent holiday destination in terms of ancient sites, museums and historic attractions – it also offers a fabulous range of sporting, shopping and entertainment opportunities. Tour companies also offer excursions, both from resorts to nearby attractions and to other nearby islands.

SPORTS AND OUTDOOR ACTIVITIES

WATERSPORTS

There is a huge range of watersports available on Rhodes. Operators at the more frequented beaches provide lots of activities for those in search of an adrenalin rush. **Jet-skis** are available almost everywhere to rent by the quarter- or half-hour, and there are plenty of **water rides** where a speedboat pulls along an inflatable ring or banana boat. **Waterskiing** is also on offer at many of the popular bays, including Vlýha. Those who wish to take it one step further and get airborne should head to Faliráki, which has become the **parasailing** capital of the Dodecanese.

With its strong breezes, Rhodes is also one of the best places in Greece to try **windsurfing**. The best locations are wide, fairly shallow sandy bays and where there are no cliffs to disrupt the prevailing winds. Perfect conditions exist at Prassonísi in the far south, a magnet for serious windsurfers. The friendliest places to learn here are Prasonísi Center (tel: 22440 91044, www.prasonisicenter.com), and adjacent Wind4Fun (tel:6944 337443 , www.wind4fun.pl/en/), which also offers kiteboarding. Wind conditions are also good at Ixiá, where Surfline (www.surflinerhodes.gr, tel: 22410 69507) – the northernmost school

The clear, warm water is ideal for swimming

– makes a point of offering individual instruction.

Many beaches also have **pedalos** or **kayaks** for hire if you want to try something more sedate.

Local **scuba diving** outfitters have finally succeeded in expanding the number of permitted areas around Rhodes – the Greek state has always tightly controlled diving owing to the potential for theft of submerged antiquities. The dull beginners' area at Pigés Kallithéas lido has now been joined by more exciting, deeper wall-dives at Ladikó and Líndos, beach diving at Kolýmbia and a wreck dive at Plimýri. The Aegean – or rather, the Mediterranean on the most-dived side of the island – is warm and clear, but don't expect a tropical profusion of fish.

By far the best beginner or intermediate diving experience around Rhodes, however, is to be had at or near privately run Blutopia Marine Park, around Makrís islet, some 3 nautical miles from Kámiros Skála on the western shore. Snorkellers or scuba-divers of all levels can swim with a wide variety of marine life, including tuna, giant rays, grouper swordfish, barracuda and dolphins, as well as smaller fish and colourful sedentary species. Snorkelling trips cost €20–35 per person (minimum group of 4). It's more affordable to dive outside the reserve boundaries, around Hálki, Alimniá islet or near Monólithos, where attractions include wrecks and caves. Scuba outings cost €55 for one introductory boat dive, €90 for two; within Blutopia boundaries, budget €100 for a single dive, €160 for a two-tank day out. Blutopia operates 15 April to 31 October (tel 22410 60170; www. blutopia.gr). At Mandráki quay, two dive operators Waterhoppers (www.waterhoppers.com) and Trident (www.tridentdivingschool. com) compete for business in front of their boats; offering days out to destinations along the east coast (depart 9.30am, return from site 5pm), including return boat transfer, equipment and two dives. Prices are marginally less than at Blutopia.

Reputable dive operators are affiliated with one or two of three certifying bodies: PADI (Professional Association of

⊙ BEST BEACHES

Rhodes' beaches come in all shapes and sizes, from tiny coves where you can spend the day alone, to wide sandy bays where you are guaranteed the company of hundreds. The beaches may consist of sand, pebbles or a mixture of the two.

Although many people prefer soft sand over pebbles, when the summer *meltémi* winds blow across the Aegean and cool the west coast (plus more exposed parts of the southeast-facing shore), coin-sized pebbles won't blow around and spoil your day. Pebbles predominate on the coastline around Ixiá, although partly sheltered Élli beach in Rhodes Town is mostly sand. The best sandy beaches line the more protected east coast – broad ones at Faliráki, Afándou, Kálathos and Gennádi, with wonderful small bays at Stegná, Agía Agathí, Glýstra and Líndos.

On almost all beaches topless sunbathing is accepted, except directly in front of a taverna or within sight of a church. Complete nudism is indulged in at one cove near Líndos, and at very remote bays without facilities between Plimýri and Prassonísi.

Diving Instructors), BSAC (British Sub-Aqua Club) or CMAS (Confédération Mondiale des Activités Subaquatiques). If you're not already a qualified diver, you can obtain the basic Open Water Diver qualification over five days of theoretical instruction and practice in a swimming pool, then the sea. 'Try Dive' days are also available if you're not ready to commit yourself. Just snorkelling allows you to explore the shallows, glimpsing sea anemones, shoals of fish and even small octopuses that make their homes in rocky crevices just offshore.

WALKING AND HIKING

Although there are few recognised, marked trails (as opposed to forestry jeep tracks) on the island, the Rhodian landscape offers a seasonally changing experience.

In early spring the hillsides are awash with wild flowers, while later on grain crops give the fields a golden hue. As summer progresses and the crops are harvested (mostly by early July), the terrain becomes drier and dustier. The distinctive trill of the cicada dominates the hottest daylight hours, when no sensible person is out walking. Autumn is perhaps the most pleasant season, even though the days are shorter. Spring or autumn offer the clearest air for views and photography; heat haze rises in summer, reducing long-distance visibility.

Inland, you can hike to the summit of Mount Atávyros from Ágios Isídoros, around the lower slopes of Profítis Ilías from Sálakos, and along the Akramýtis ridge between Siánna and Monólithos, with wonderful forested scenery. The coastal walk from Faliráki to the Ladikó headland coves is a favourite, and there are also hiking possibilities between Tsambíka beach and Haráki. Much the best local walking, however, is on Sými, with paths to remote coves and old chapels, though you must stay there at least two nights to enjoy them. Be sure to take enough water plus snack food, and wear sturdy footwear.

HORSE RIDING

There are a handful of horse-riding centres on Rhodes. The most established and reputable include Kadmos, between Ialysos and Asgoúrou (tel: 22410 96651, www.rhodesriding.com), and Fivos Riding Centre near Faliráki and Afándou (tel: 6946369918, www.fivos-horse-riding.com).

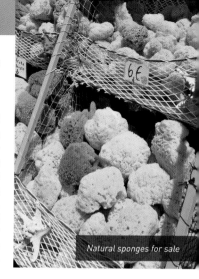
Natural sponges for sale

SHOPPING

The maze-like lanes of the old quarters in Rhodes Town and Líndos host a fascinating mixture of art and ceramics galleries, jewellers, clothing outlets, trinket stalls and out-and-out kitsch displays. Shopping is perhaps the easiest diversion in Rhodes, and the walled city still retains some of the atmosphere of an oriental bazaar. In sharp contrast are the numerous air-conditioned boutiques in the New Town selling brand-name watches, jewellery and designer clothing.

Antiques. For serious collectors there are very few genuine antiquities (officially classified as anything made before 1821) to be found. These are usually ceramics, jewellery or icons, and will often require authentication certificates and an export permit – the dealer should be able to advise you in this process. For those

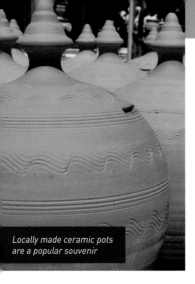

Locally made ceramic pots are a popular souvenir

whose budget or expertise does not stretch to the real thing, there are many reproductions of such items, of varying quality and price.

Ceramics and sculpture. Rhodes still supports a ceramics industry, evident in the numerous roadside workshops and retail stores. Plates, jugs and bowls are produced in a bewildering number of patterns and colours. Popular traditional themes include Minoan patterns from Crete, or scenes taken from ancient Greek frescoes or mosaics. Elegant painted house-number tiles make useful souvenirs.

Copies of Classical sculptures are also popular. Prices vary according to the quality of the materials and the skills of the artisan. You will soon discern the variation after visiting a few different stores and closely examining items. In particular, take note of the weight of a piece of pottery or sculpture and the detail in the decoration or carving.

Olive wood items. Olive wood can be laboriously carved into practical souvenirs, ranging from coasters or flat-candle holders to large salad bowls or cutting boards, the latter fairly expensive. Cutting boards should preferably be one piece, not glued sections. Protect your investment by oiling it occasionally with linseed oil, and never leaving it immersed in water. Sadly, much olive wood is improperly cured, being worked while still green; thus bowls may crack within a year as they continue drying after purchase.

Brass and copperware. Until the 1960s, every household used brass and copper utensils and tools, the copper ones tinned inside for use with food. Since the arrival of stainless steel ware, electric kitchen appliances and the like, these items – including tureens, ewers, trays, coffee grinders, bowls and bríkia (small pots for making coffee) – have found their way to dealers in the Old Town. One worthwhile specialist metal antiques shop is at Agíou Fanouríou 6, with an annexe adjacent – but the items are not cheap, especially if they are of Ottoman vintage. Light-gauge, lower-quality modern ornamental copper and brass objects are less expensive and easier to find.

Clothing. Both Rhodes Town and Líndos have plenty of shops whose wall racks are festooned with cool cotton or muslin trousers, tops and dresses ideal for summer. You will also find plenty of T-shirts, swimwear and footwear. Umbrellas, especially in Neohóri, are excellent value and come in a myriad of patterns.

Neohóri is also home to an improbable number of designer clothes shops, especially around Platía Kýprou. Storefronts range from British favourites like Marks & Spencer to more upscale brands like Benetton and the multistorey, multi-label emporium known as Scarabee. The well-attended August sales coincide with the end of the main tourist season, but you'll have to be quick to find something in your size. The EU is cracking down on cut-rate imitation designer apparel, which is generally sold by itinerant street peddlers, rather than the posh Neohóri boutiques.

Leather and fur. The Rhodian islanders have always worked the leather from their herds and now make handbags, purses, belts and footwear in a variety of styles and patterns. Specialist boutiques in Rhodes Old Town sell high-quality fur and leather coats and jackets. Made-to-measure items can be produced in just a few days.

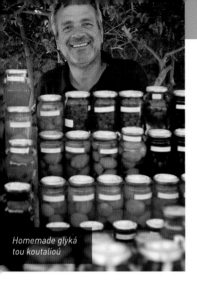

Homemade *glyká tou koutalioú*

Carpets. The oriental carpets sold locally are imported from Turkey. The indigenous coarse-weave carpet tradition of Rhodes has all but died out; most of the cotton rugs and bathmats on display, with Hellenic motifs such as deer or dolphins framed by a geometric pattern, are mass-produced and imported (usually from India). That said, such mats are cheap, hard-wearing and do not tend to shrink much.

Jewellery. You can choose as many carats in precious stones as your budget can handle. Gold and silver are sold by weight, with relatively little extra cost added for the workmanship. Ancient Greek designs – especially Minoan and Macedonian – are very much in evidence. In the lower price ranges there is plenty of everyday jewellery such as ankle chains, navel studs and rings.

Food and drink. Summer fruits – especially sour cherries, figs, plums and bitter oranges – have always been preserved as jars of *glyká tou koutalioú* or 'spoon sweets'. Bees frequent the island's aromatic hillside herbs, producing delicious honey to which fresh almonds and walnuts are added. Olives are preserved either in oil or brine, or made into 'extra virgin' (the first pressing) oil for cooking and making delicious salad dressings.

If you want to take a distinctively Greek drink home with you, then try *oúzo* – though Rhodian *oúzo* is not esteemed; the best comes from the islands of Sámos and Lésvos. Some of

⊙ THE GENUINE ICON

An icon (*ikóna* in Greek) is a religious image of a saint, arch-angel or apostle, or of a critical event in the life of Christ or the Virgin. They are descended from portraits of the dead on Egyptian mummy sarcophagi at Fayyum and are not neces-sarily meant to be a naturalistic depiction of the holy fig-ure. The visual attributes of each of them – hairstyle, beard length, instruments of martyrdom, clothing – were fixed early in Christianity, and do not vary between an ancient or a modern icon.

Icons lie at the heart of Orthodox worship, forming a focus for prayer, and a 'window' to the saint being peti-tioned. All are considered holy, and some are said to possess miraculous powers. The characteristic gold leaf used in their production symbolises the glory of God. The oldest surviving examples date from the latter part of the first millennium.

Icon-painters created works for private clients as well as for churches, and for centuries they were popular souvenirs for European Grand Tourists and religious pilgrims. How-ever, modern production methods, including the use of thin canvas and garish synthetic colours, saw them lose favour. Since the 1980sthere has been a revival of traditional icon-painting methods, both for church renovations and for com-mercial sale. Natural pigments and egg tempera (egg yolk and vinegar) binding are painstakingly mixed and applied to a sturdy canvas stretched over wood, or even a solid plank. Gold leaf is then applied, and the whole image is given a patina. Such time-consuming work is exquisite and corre-spondingly expensive.

the better Greek wines – and there are many – can be found at Marinos (www.marinossa.gr), in suitably cellar-like premises at Ermoú 23 in the Old Town, between the Marine and Arnáldou gates.

ENTERTAINMENT

MUSIC AND DANCE

For many, Greek music and dance is inexorably linked to the film *Zorba the Greek*, in which Anthony Quinn performed the *syrtáki* (in fact an amalgam of several different traditional dances) to the sound of the *bouzoúki*, a five-stringed fretted instrument with a haunting effect and a slightly metallic tone.

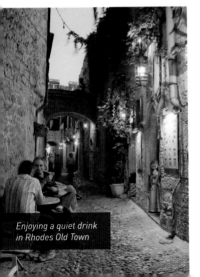

Enjoying a quiet drink in Rhodes Old Town

The rich and varied Greek musical tradition goes back hundreds of years, originally based on Byzantine chant but in modern times featuring wonderful settings of popular poetry to music. Rhythms are very different from those characterising Western music and so can be difficult to follow. Each region of Greece has its own particular songs and dances; those of the southern islands, including Rhodes, are called *nisiótika*.

It is now quite difficult to see genuine dance performances; the best way is at a private wedding or saint's day when the performances occur in their true context (see Calendar of Events on page 97). If this is not an option, most large hotels hold regular 'Greek nights', with live music and dancing. While not exactly authentic, they do allow you to get a feel for the passion and movement of Greek dance, and to get into the swing of things by joining in yourself.

If you develop a taste for authentic Greek music, there are two good record shops in Rhodes Town: Sakellaridis, in the Old Town just off Platía Mousíou, with a well-priced collection of quality music in the back (behind the tourist stock); or Manuel Music at Amerikís 93 in Neohóri, with a broader choice but slightly higher prices.

NIGHTLIFE

The best places for nightlife on the island are Neohóri in Rhodes Town, Rhodes Old Town (particularly Platía Aríonos and around the Ibrahim Pasha Mosque), Líndos and Faliráki, all of which have bars that stay open until around 3am. Hotspots change almost every year, though in Neohóri most of the bars are located on a 150m/yd stretch of Orfanídou. Of these, Colorado at Orfanídou 53 (www.facebook.com/ ColoradoClubRhodes) has three sound-stages for live acts, and Sticky Fingers at Anthoúla Zérvou 2–6 (a bit south on the hillside; www.facebook.com/groups/22700985859/about) hosts live rock acts several nights a week in high season. At the east end of Élli beach, the Italian-built Ronda bathing club has DJ-moderated party nights all summer. The Sound-and-Light Gardens off Platía Rímini are mostly used for performances of ancient drama and modern music, though Sound-and-Light shows may resume in 2019.

All-day beach bars with DJd music are also popular during summer, most notably at Faliráki, Kiotári and Gennádi. They generally get going around noon and keep on until the small hours.

CHILDREN'S RHODES

Rhodes is a great place to take children. Greek society is very family-orientated, and children will be indulged in cafés and restaurants. Most resort hotels have a range of child-friendly activities, including kids' clubs, designated swimming areas and playgrounds.

Since the Mediterranean has very little tide and the island has many gently shelving bays, there are lots of safe places for children to paddle. Sandy beaches are more fun than pebbly ones for castle-building and hole-digging, so bear that in mind when choosing your accommodation.

For older children the watersports on offer at most resorts across the island – pedalos, kayaks, windsurfing – provide an exciting challenge. For a fun day out, try Faliráki Water Park (June–Aug daily 9.30am–7pm, May, Sept–Oct daily 9.30am–6pm; tel: 22410 84403, www.water-park.gr), with its pools, lazy river and a dozen slides.

A trip to the shady Petaloúdes Valley to search for Jersey tiger moths is a great adventure for budding naturalists (see page 68). Another popular activity is riding a donkey from Líndos to its acropolis or a pony at one of the riding stables, while there are friendly ducks (and somewhat more menacing peacocks) to be seen at the Rodíni Park.

Gaily painted excursion boats ply between the main resorts and nearby beaches. Children love to watch the coastline go by and spy shoals of fish in the clear water.

CALENDAR OF EVENTS

1 January: *Protohroniá*, or St Basil's Day; the traditional greeting is *Kalí Hroniá*.

6 January: Epiphany; young men dive into the sea to recover a crucifix cast by the local bishop; the retriever is considered lucky for the year.

7 March: Union of the Dodecanese with Greece in 1948 – parades and folk dancing.

Clean Monday: 48 days before Easter, the first day of Lenten fasting (when no meat or cheese may be eaten), marked by kite-flying and outings to the countryside.

25 March: Greek Independence Day/Festival of the Annunciation.

Easter: the most important Orthodox holiday. On Maundy Thursday evening there is the moving Crucifixion Mass, while on Good Friday candlelit processions in each parish follow the flower-decked bier of Christ. The midnight Resurrection Mass on Holy Saturday is concluded with deafening fireworks and the relaying of the sacred flame from the officiating priests to the parishioners, who carefully take the lit candles home. On Sunday lambs are spit-roasted, signifying the end of the Lenten fast.

1 May: May Day or *Protomagiá*, marked by flower-gathering excursions to the country – and demonstrations by the political Left.

24 June: Birthday of St John the Baptist. On the night before, bonfires are lit and the young leap over them.

15 August: Dormition Day (*Kímisi tis Theotókou*, 'Falling Asleep of the God-Bearer' in Greek). Processions and festivals across the island.

8 September: Main pilgrimage day to Tsambíka Monastery and festival at Skiádi Monastery near Mesanagrós, both honouring the Birth of thePanagía [NB: Virgin (Mary) is a Western, Catholic concept. In Greek Orthodoxy she is the Panagía (All-Holy) or Theótokos (God-Birthing).

28 October: *Óhi* (No) Day, commemorating Greek defiance of the Italian invasion of 1940.

8 November: Festival of Archangel Michael at Panormítis, Sými.

New Year's Eve: Adults play cards for money, and a cake (the *vassilópita*) is baked with a coin hidden inside – bringing good luck to whoever gets that slice. Big parties at Rhodes Town bars and clubs.

EATING OUT

The backbone of Greek cuisine is local, seasonal ingredients at their peak of flavour and freshness, served raw, or cooked simply – on a grill, flash-fried or slow-baked. Greeks have relied for centuries on staples like olive oil, wild herbs, seafood and lamb or goat's meat, along with abundant fresh vegetables, fruit, pulses and nuts, accompanied by local wine. The traditional Greek diet is one of the healthiest in the world, and prices in our selected establishments offer reasonable value for money. The prevalence of vegetable and dairy dishes makes eating out a delight for non-meat-eaters.

WHERE TO EAT

On Rhodes you will find a range of eating establishments, often family-run, each type emphasising certain dishes; don't expect elaborate oven-cooked casseroles at a seaside grill, or European-style desserts at any eatery. However, many island restaurants offer bland fare aimed at the tourist palate; for more authentic cuisine, the best eating establishments are listed in the recommendations section (see page 108). Some may be in the backstreets away from the pretty views, but the food is superior.

Among establishment types, the *psistaría* offers charcoal-grilled meats, plus a limited selection of salads and *mezédes*. The *tavérna* (written TABEPNA in the Greek alphabet) is a more elaborate eatery, offering pre-cooked, steam-tray dishes known as *magireftá*, as well as a few grills and bulk wine.

An *ouzerí* purveys not just the famous aniseed-flavoured alcoholic drink, but also the *mezédes* dishes that complement it – thus the increasingly popular alias, *mezedopolío*. *Oúzo* is never drunk on an empty stomach: octopus, olives, a bit of

Relaxed drinks with a view over Anthony Quinn Bay

cheese or a platter of small fried fish are traditional accompaniments, but there are various other hot and cold vegetable and meat dishes to choose from.

The *kafenío* is the Greek coffee shop, traditionally an exclusively male domain, and still so in the Rhodian countryside. Usually very plainly decorated (though tables and chairs are smarter of late), they are the venues for political debate and serious backgammon games. In most cases, only drinks – alcoholic and soft – are served.

WHEN TO EAT

Rhodian resort tavernas open for breakfast, lunch and dinner (many offer a full English breakfast). Traditionally, Greeks don't eat breakfast – a coffee and *friganiés* (melba toast) or a baked pastry is about as much as they indulge in. English-style breakfasts are only available in the major resorts and fancier hotels. Lunch is taken between 2.30 and 4pm, followed by a siesta, before work begins again at around 5.30pm. Dinner is eaten late – usually from 9.30pm onwards, and some establishments will take last orders as late as midnight.

If you want to eat earlier, some tavernas begin their evening service at around 6.30pm. You will probably have your choice of table if you eat before 7.30pm, but the atmosphere is definitely better later on when locals come out to eat.

Some tavernas close on Sunday evening and part or all of Monday.

WHAT TO EAT

You will usually be given an extensive menu (often in both Greek and English), where available items have a price pencilled in beside them. The menu is most useful for checking that the taverna is in your price range (especially for more expensive items like meat or fish), and a more reliable account of what is actually available that day can be obtained from your waiter. A good way to familiarise yourself with the various dishes is to order straight from the steam trays or chiller case based on what looks most enticing.

All restaurants impose a cover charge. This includes a serving of bread and is rarely more than €1 per person.

Appetisers

Carefully selected appetisers (*mezédes*) can constitute a full meal in Greece. Shared by the whole table, they are a fun way to eat – you simply order as few or as many platters as you want. *Ouzerís/mezedopolía* have no qualms about taking orders for *mezédes*-only meals, bringing your choices out on a *dískos* or tray – though they also serve hot main courses.

The most common appetisers are *tzatzíki*, a yogurt dip flavoured with garlic, cucumber and mint; *yaprákia*, vine leaves

stuffed with rice and vegetables – sometimes mince
– which can be served hot
(with *avgolémono* sauce,
made of eggs and lemon)
or cold (with a dollop of
yogurt); *taramosaláta*,
cod-roe paste blended
with breadcrumbs, olive
oil and lemon juice; *gígandes*, large beans in tomato
sauce; *kalamarákia*, fried
small squid; *mavromátika*,
black-eyed peas; *tyrokafterí* or *kopanistí,* two kinds
of spicy cheese dips; and

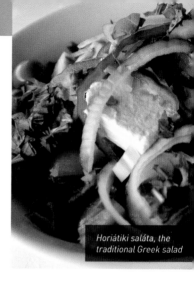

*Horiátiki saláta, the
traditional Greek salad*

hórta, boiled wild greens. *Saganáki* is yellow cheese coated
in breadcrumbs and then fried, while *féta psití* is feta cheese
wrapped in foil with garlic and herbs – often spicy ones – and
baked. A particularly Rhodian appetiser is a plate of pitaroúdia
– fried patties of flaked courgettes, chickpeas or mixtures of the
two, with flour, onions and mint; each village has its own recipe.

Greek salad or *horiátiki saláta* (usually translated as 'village
salad') consists of tomato, cucumber, onion, green peppers and
olives topped with feta cheese. Cruets of olive oil *(ládi)* and wine
vinegar *(xýdi)* are found with other condiments on the table.

Fish

At fish tavernas you choose from the day's catch, displayed on
ice inside a chiller case. This is then weighed, uncleaned, before
cooking – check the price as seafood is almost always a relatively
expensive option. If the seafood is frozen or farmed (very likely

A lunch of fresh fish

from June to September), this must be stated on the menu – though often rather cryptically, with an asterisk or a small 'k' for katepsygméno. The idiom for wild, free-range fish is *alaniáriko*.

Larger fish are usually grilled and smaller fish fried; all are served with fresh lemon and *ladolémono* (olive oil with lemon juice). Most common species are *barboúni* (red mullet), *xifías* (swordfish), *tsipoúra* (gilt-head bream) and *fangrí* (bream) – the latter two often farmed. *Drákena* (weever fish) is outstanding, either grilled or in soup. Another cheap Rhodian springtime speciality is *germanós* (leatherback), an exotic from the Indian Ocean, served fried. *Marídes* (picarel), *gávros* (anchovy) and *sardélles* (sardines) are also served crisp-fried. More elaborate seafood dishes include *ktapódi krasáto* (octopus in red wine and tomato sauce), *soupiá* (cuttlefish) with spinach rice, or *garídes* (prawns) in a cheese sauce *(saganáki)*.

Meat and Casserole Dishes

Meaty snacks include *gýros* (thin slices of pork cut from a vertical skewer and served with tomato, *tzatzíki* and lettuce in pitta bread), or *souvláki* (small chunks of meat cooked on a skewer). Rotisseried chickens, sides of lamb and pork are all cooked to perfection. *Brizóla* – either pork or veal – is a basic cutlet; lamb or goat chops, however, are *païdákia*. In these economically fraught times, *sykotariá arnísia* (lamb liver chunks) are inexpensive, tasty and increasingly common, as are *sykotákia* (chicken livers/giblets).

Greece's most famous slow-cooked oven dish is *moussakás* – layers of sliced potato, aubergine and minced lamb topped with a very generous layer of béchamel sauce. It should be firm but succulent, and aromatic with nutmeg. *Pastítsio* is another layered dish with macaroni, meat and cheese sauce. Other common casseroles include *giouvétsi* (meat baked in a clay pot with rice-shaped *kritharáki* pasta) and *stifádo* (braised beef with onions).

For a hot meatless dish, *gemistá* are tomatoes, peppers or aubergine stuffed with herb-flavoured rice; alternatively, *melitzánes imám* (aubergine stuffed richly with tomato, garlic and oil) is reliably vegetarian, as is *briám* or *tourloú* (ratatouille). *Yaprákia* (stuffed vine leaves) without meat are called *gialantzí* ('liar's', 'fake').

Cheeses

Greek cheeses *(tyriá)* are made from cow's, ewe's or goat's milk, or often blends of two. The best-known cheese is *féta*, popping up in every Greek salad or served alone garnished with olive oil and oregano. *Graviéra* is the most common hard cheese, varying in sharpness; there are also many sweet soft cheeses such as *manoúri*, *myzithra* and *anthótyro*.

Dessert

Most tavernas bring a plate of fresh seasonal fruit (*froúta*; see box) as a finale to your meal, or perhaps a serving of semolina halva *(simigdalísios halvás)* or *kormós* (chocolate loaf). For something more substantial, the *zaharoplastío* (sticky-cake shop) dishes out some of the more enduring legacies of the Ottomans, who introduced incredibly decadent sweets: *baklavás*, layers of honey-soaked flaky pastry with walnuts; *kataïfi*, shredded wheat

Favourite fruits

Fruit platters after meals typically include watermelon or Persian melon in summer, grapes or pears in autumn, sliced apples with cinnamon in winter and citrus fruits or maybe some luscious strawberries in early spring. Greece imports just a few temperate fruits from Italy, Argentina or Spain and relatively little tropical fruit, so this is pretty much the full repertoire.

filled with chopped almonds and honey; *galaktoboúreko*, custard pie; or *ravaní*, honey-soaked sponge cake. If you prefer dairy desserts, try yogurt with local honey or *ryzógalo*, cold rice pudding at a *galaktopolío* (dairy shop). A quality ice-cream *(pagotó)* cult is well established in the Dodecanese; on Rhodes, head for outlets of the Stani chain (central branch is at Agías Anastasías 28 in Neohóri), or to Gelato Punto, opposite the Néa Agorá bus stops at Avérof 6.

WHAT TO DRINK

Greek winemaking goes back at least three millennia; quality, especially at certain mainland vintners, has risen dramatically in recent decades, but owing to limited export – many boutique wineries produce fewer than 20,000 bottles annually – you are unlikely to have heard of even the best labels.

Rhodian wine (see box) is more than respectable, served mostly bottled, but also available more cheaply in bulk – *hýma* or *varelísio*. Bulk red, white or rosé are offered in full, half- or quarter-litre measures, either in pink or orange metal cups or glass flagons. Quality varies considerably; if in doubt, order a quarter-litre to start with as a test, plus a can of soda water to dilute it.

Retsína has been around since ancient times, when Greeks accidentally discovered the preservative properties of treating wine with pine resin. It complements the olive-oil base of oven-cooked dishes perfectly, but can be an acquired taste and should be served well chilled.

Oúzo is taken as an aperitif with ice and water; a compound in its anise flavouring makes the mixture cloudy. Although Rhodes makes its own *oúzo*, the most popular brands come from the islands of Lésvos or Sámos, or from the mainland. For a digestif, Metaxa is the most popular brand of Greek-produced brandy, sold (in ascending order of strength and aging) in 3-, 5- and 7-star grades.

There are nearly a dozen beers produced in Greece (mostly, however, by one brewing conglomerate), as well as imports from Britain, Germany, Belgium and Ireland. Foreign brands made under licence in Greece include Amstel, Kaiser and Heineken. Popular Greek beers include Alfa, Fix (reckoned the best), Mythos and Pils Hellas. Rhodes has two local breweries, the better by far being Magnus Magister.

Non-Alcoholic Drinks

Hot coffee *(kafés)* is offered *ellinikós* or 'Greek-style', freshly brewed in copper pots and served in small cups. It will probably arrive *glykós* (sweet) or even *varý glykós* (very sweet) unless you order it *métrios* (medium) or

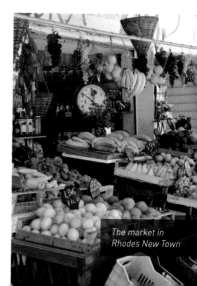

The market in Rhodes New Town

skétos (without sugar). Don't drink right to the bottom, as that is where the grounds settle. Instant coffee (called 'Nes' irrespective of brand) has made big inroads in Greece; more appetising is *frappé*, cold instant coffee whipped up in a blender with or without milk *(gála)*, especially refreshing on a summer's day. If you prefer a proper cappuccino or espresso, numerous Italian-style coffee bars will oblige you.

Soft drinks come in all the international varieties, while juices are usually from cartons rather than freshly squeezed. Bottled *(enfialoméno)* still mineral water is typically from Crete or the Greek mainland mountains. Souroti or Tuborg are the most widespread domestic sparkling brands.

⊙ RHODIAN WINE

Rhodian farmers always produced wine for domestic consumption, but under the Italians the local wine industry assumed commercial proportions. Today, there are some excellent producers and a good range of labels to choose from. The 1928-founded co-operative CAIR (www.cair.gr) and Emery (www.facebook.com/emery.rodos.wines/) in Émbona are the major players, but it's far preferable to seek out family-run micro-wineries like Alexandris (www.facebook.com/alexandriswinery), which makes the excellent Citizen of the World red and Apiro rosé; or Kounakis (www.kounakiwine.gr), which offers soúma (see box p.75) as well as wine. In Apóllona, 14km/8.5 miles east of Émbona. the Piperis winery (www.piperiswinery.com) produces a range of good labels. Triandafyllou, below Petaloúdes, makes a very good rosé (albeit from blends of grapes), as well as a semi-sweet white Muscat and a dry red Cabernet.

TO HELP YOU ORDER...

Could we have a table? **Bouroúme na éhoume éna trapézi?**
Could we order, please? **Na parangiloúme, parakaló?**
I'm a vegetarian **Íme hortofágos (m)/hortofági (f)**
The bill, please **To logariazmó, parakaló**
Cheers! **Giámas!**
Bon appetit! **Kalí órexi!**
Enjoy the rest of your meal! (literally 'Good continuation')
   Kalí synéhia!

plate **piáto**	butter **voútyro**
cutlery **maheropírouna**	salt **aláti**
glass **potíri**	black pepper **mávro pipéri**
bread **psomí**	

MENU READER

arní lamb
býra beer
eliés olives
Éna kiló/misó kilo A litre/
   half litre
fasolákia runner beans
garídes small shrimp
gemistó psári stuffed fish
hirinó pork
hórta boiled greens
katsíki goat
keftedákia meatballs
kotópoulo chicken
krasí wine
kréas meat
melitzána aubergine/
   eggplant

moskhári, vodinó beef
okhtapódi octopus
(pagoméno) neró (chilled)
   water
patátes potatoes
psitó roasted
revýthia chickpeas
rýzi, piláfi rice
saláta salad
soupiá cuttlefish
sta kárvouna grilled
sto foúrno baked
thrápsalo deep-water
   squid
tiganitó fried
xifías swordfish

PLACES TO EAT

Price categories refer to the cost of a meal per person with a modest intake of beer, wine or oúzo. Except where indicated, reservations are not necessary (or usually even possible) – one waits, or an extra table is fitted in.

€€€€€	over 55 euros
€€€€	40–55euros
€€€	30–40euros
€€	20–30euros
€	below 20 euros

RHODES OLD TOWN

Ergon €€€ *Platía Sofokléous 35, tel: 22410 77787,* www.ergonfoods.com/restaurants/rodos. Since moving in 2016 from the new town to a lovely plaza in the old town, the setting finally matches the food. The menu consists of traditional yet innovative Greek recipes prepared from the best available ingredients. Expect the likes of *fáva* with *sýnglino* (chunky bacon), caramelised onions and truffle oil, or *kritharáki* (orzo pasta) with seafood. Excellent house wine options. They also run delis in many locations in Greece, as well as in London, Singapore and Brussels. Daily 1pm–midnight.

Hatzikelis €€€ *Solomoú Alhadéf 9, tel: 22410 27215.* Upscale, seafood-strong taverna installed in a former Jewish school, from whose vast, professional kitchen issue fair portions of such delicacies as smoked eel and mullet *botárgo* from Misolóngi, crayfish nuggets, delicate *rozéttia* fish, *lakérda* (cured bonito),and *mermizéli* (Kalymnian-style salad). Their *soupiórizo* (cuttlefish risotto) with pine nuts is excellent. A conservatory terrace and fireplace permit year-round operation. Open daily, most of the year, lunch and dinner.

Polo Café €€€ *Agíou Fanouríou 42, tel: 22410 25562,* www.marcopolo mansion.gr. The idyllic courtyard of the *Marco Polo Mansion* hosts the Old

Town's most creative cooking. Platters change seasonally but might include grilled octopus on aubergine mousse, skewered lamb mince enlivened with pistachio chunks, or monkfish on saffron mash potatoes. Save room for decadent desserts like chocolate frozen with strawberries, or tiramisu in various flavours. Co-proprietor Spýros is a wine fanatic, so sample his cellar if the well-chosen Neméa bulk wine fails to appeal. Open mid-May to mid-October from 8pm; last orders 11pm. Reservations mandatory.

Mikes €€ *Alley behind Sokrátous 17, tel: 22410 74850*. This galley-like diner (the name is pronounced 'mee-kess') has just a few tables in the lane but serves some of the freshest and least expensive seafood on the island. Not much else other than surprisingly elaborate salads, a few token dips and wine. Open Apr–Nov. Cash only.

Nireas €€€€ *Sofokléous 22, tel: 22410 21703*. Atmospheric indoor/outdoor seating under vines or stone arches makes this a good choice for a romantic dinner or a last-night blowout. Fresh fish and shellfish plates – including smooth Venus clams, limpets, mussels and miniature Sými shrimps – are followed by Italian desserts like panna cotta and tiramisu. Open Apr–Nov.

Petaladika €€€ *Menekléous 8, tel: 22410 27319*. Lovely outdoor seating under a sprawling Indian fig is matched by the food which ranges from Armenian pastrami from Athens' Miran deli, through real rocket salad (no dilution with lettuce), flawlessly grilled skorpína fish (a variety usually stewed) and a dessert of the day (maybe treated by the house). A great selection of *soúma*, *tsípouro* and *oúzo*, and of course wine and beer. Off season, there's music two nights weekly inside. Open daily much of the year near noon to midnight.

Sea Star (Pizanias Kyriakos) €€ *Sofokléous 24, tel: 22410 22117*. This relatively inexpensive yet quality seafood outlet offers a limited menu of scaly fish (the seared June tuna is ace), shellfish and starters like *kápari* (pickled caper shoots), chunky grilled eggplant salad and *koliós pastós* (salt-cured mackerel). Seating is indoors during the cooler months (not open midwinter), otherwise outside on the little square. Open daily noon to midnight. Cash only.

RHODES NEW TOWN

Griniaris € *Platía Agíou Ioánnou 176, tel: 22410 34005.* Well-established *mezedopolío* at the heart of Ágios Ioánnis, one of the Orthodox Greek suburb villages outside the medieval walls. The name, translated in-house as 'Grumpy's', actually means 'The Whinger', but there should be no whinging about the strictly seafood menu with its competent shrimp risotto, *pínnes* and *foúskes* (marine molluscs served in their own li-queur) and octopus prepared several ways. Daily dinner all year but shut Sun high summer, Mon otherwise. Reservations suggested, particularly for tables outside. Cash only.

Koozina €€ *Georgíou Leóndou 19, tel: 6943 451450.* This cosy little place excels at fusion recipes like tuna burger with wasabe sauce, quinoa salad with beets and avocado, blueberry cheesecake. Contemporary decor. Daily 1pm–1am.

Koukos € *Nikifórou Mandilará 20–26, Neohóri, tel: 22410 73022.* From mod-est beginnings as a young peoples' coffee-bar and takeaway bakery, Koukos has evolved into one of the few genuine, and most popular, *mezedopolía* in otherwise touristy Neohóri. It's worth showing up just for the multi-level, Tardis-like interior, effectively a private folklore museum, though on fine days everyone is out on the terraces. The fare – seafood probably a better bet than meat – is decent. Open daily most of the day into the evening; cash only.

Locanda Demenagas € *Avstralías 16, Akandiá Bay, tel 22410 30060.* Long-considered the best *inomagerío* (wine-and-cook-shop) in town, ideally placed for a pre-ferry-ride lunch. You'll rub shoulders with half of the town here, from tradesmen to local mafiosi, all tucking into a daily-changing menu which might encompass *pastítsio* (baked macaroni pie), *fasoláda* (bean soup), fresh beets with their greens, or rooster with noodles. A fire-place burns in winter, though the window-girt premises acts as a sun-trap.

Meltemi €€ *Platía Koundourióti 8, Élli beach, tel: 22410 30480.* Classy and surprisingly well-priced *ouzerí* offering such delights as crayfish nuggets, octopus croquettes, grilled red peppers in balsamic vinegar, chunky *húmmus* and superb roast aubergine with beans and onions to a local crowd. There is a pleasant winter salon with old engravings inside. Open all day, all year; top lunch choice if you're at Élli beach. Cash only.

Mezes €€ *Aktí Kanári 9, Psaropoúla, tel: 22410 27962 or 6944 709693*. The interior may not have the quirky charm of *Koukos* but there's a small terrace facing the sea, and the food here is superior and portion sizes more generous. Tuck into starters like chickpea stew, breaded mastéllo cheese from Híos, oyster mushrooms or *lahmatzoún* (Armenian pizza); meat and seafood mains like chops by the kilo or grilled smoked macka-rel are even bigger. Save room for Efi's desserts, including tiramisu. Live music some Saturdays. Open daily noon–12.30am. Cash only.

Paragadi €€€ *Corner of Klavdíou Pépper and Avstralías, Zéfyros, tel: 22410 37775*. Seafood restaurant where reasonable prices for wine and a limited range of vegetarian starters is offset by somewhat bumped-up fish prices; their seafood risotto is excellent, though it won't satisfy pur-ists. Sea views during the day; large parties must book weekend nights. Closed Sun evening and (usually) Mon noon.

Perche'no/Giati Ohi €€ *Lazárou Tiliakoú 165, near Zéfyros Marina, tel: 22410 29866*. The name means 'Why Not', and there's no reason not to show up at this Italian-run bistro for thin-crust, wood-oven pizzas, pasta platters, salads (the dolce with pears, rocket, walnuts and parmesan never disap-points) and a limited choice of Italian desserts. Short but sweet wine list. Open daily except Tue from 7pm, also Sun lunch. Cash only.

Steno € *Agíon Anargýron 29, 300m/yds southwest of Ágios Athanásios Gate, tel: 22410 35914*. Long-running, cult *mezedopolío* with indoor/outdoor seating according to season, attracting a mix of locals, expats and savvy tourists. The proprietor, Ilías, is from Kárpathos, something reflected in the style of the chunky sausages, *pitaroúdia*, *hórta*, chickpea stew, stuffed squash flowers, green runner beans with garlic sauce and simple sea-food platters served here. Local bulk *soúma* by the 200ml carafe. Daily except 1 month in winter, dinner only. Reservations required. Cash only.

Wonder €€€€ *Eleftheríou Venizélou 16–18, tel: 22410 39805*, www.restaurantwonder.gr. Interesting mixture of Mediterranean, Scandinavian and Asian cuisines; the menu changes seasonally, but always has lots of seafood and salads. Excellent service. Reservations recommended. Daily 7pm–midnight.

AROUND THE ISLAND

Artemida €€ *Pastída road, 1km south of centre, Psínthos, tel 22410 50003.* This village is famous for its meat tavernas, grouped around the central spring-fed oasis. This one is exceptional for its remoter location and willingness to cater to vegetarians also with *pitaroúdia*, *dákos* salad, cheese recipes, *yaprákia* or stuffed squash blossoms. Of course they also have carnivorous countryside standards like goat with chickpeas and roast suckling pig. Open 11am–9pm daily, most of year.

To Fresko €€ *South end of Afándou beachfront road, then inland, tel: 22410 53077.* The fish here is advertised as straight off the family boat, and it tastes that way too, corroborating the taverna name ('The Fresh'). Per-kilo prices are very fair for Rhodes; succulent *fangrí* (red porgy), a premium species, was mid-priced. Beer is ice cold and fair priced, as were *karafákia* of *ouzo* and local *soúma*. The decor is maritime kitsch, in a pleasant way, and marine life, with Hellenic blue-and-white-checked tablecloths and friendly service. Reservations recommended at weekends. May–Sept daily noon until late, otherwise Sat/Sun only. Cash only.

Limeri tou Listi € *Profýlia centre, tel: 22440 61578.* It's not every taverna which has, like this one, a frescoed 16th-century chapel of Archangel Michael and St George on its terrace, plus fine views over the village rooftops and even a distant patch of sea. The lamb-strong grills and *mezédes* like cheese-stuffed aubergine have improved over recent years, the price is right and, since this place doubles as the main kafenío, it's open daily continuously 8am–11pm. Cash only.

Maria € *Access road to Tsambíka beach, tel: 6909 48543 16939 293280, www.taverna-maria.gr.* Presiding over the grill, Kyra Maria is the heart and soul of the most bucolic of a trio of tavernas in the olive groves and grazing goats here. Seating is under a shelter or out on the thick lawn, with a playground for kids. The menu includes chunky *tyrokafterí*, fried whole peppers, hand-cut chips, occasional seafood and a selection of meats or *magireftá* (casseroles). Open all day. Cash only.

Mavrikos €€€€–€€€€€ *Main taxi square, Líndos, tel: 22440 31232.* This family-run restaurant, in business since 1933, is rated as among the best on the island for its extensive menu of creative oven-cooked dishes and seafood (with less prominent meat dishes). Broad beans and wild greens in carob syrup, fennel root slow-cooked in wine, leeks casseroled with prunes, or beetroot in goat's-cheese sauce precede mains like cured tuna with grilled fennel, lamb-liver sautéed with chillis, or pork belly slabs in grape molasses. Excellent (and expensive) Greek wine list. Open noon–late, Apr–late Oct.

Oasis € *Kallithéa shoreline, tel 6948 174459.* This deceptively simple-lookin *kantína*, a friendly one-woman-and-kids operation, is much the best of several local snack-bars, each dominating its own patch of cove amidst the rock formations. The menu, like the gravel-floor decor, is simple but wholesome: heaping salads with pickled capers and *peperoncini*, perfectly grilled butterflied sardines, a very few meat dishes and *kolokythókeftedes* (courgette croquettes). Other bonuses include beer in iced steins and great views south towards Cape Ladikó. Open Apr–Oct. Cash only.

Paraga € *Apóllona village on hillside at east end of village, tel: 22460 91247, www.paraga-apollona.gr.* Parága is Greek for 'shack', but there's nothing shack-like about these sturdy wood, stone and tile premises, where honest, country cooking such as homemade bread, *yaprákia*, *sheftaliés* and chickpeas with goat is dished up by lovely folk who are very proud of what they do. A top lunch choice while touring the island. Open lunch and dinner most of the year; cash only.

Palios Monolithos €€ *Opposite the church, Monólithos Village, tel: 22460 61276.* A favourite weekend lunch venue that serves well-cooked grills, two dishes of the day, unusual starters like wild mushrooms, wild greens or *kopanistí*, and superior (homemade) wine. It has indoor/outdoor seating (and a distant sea view). Open all year, weekends only off-season.

Pelecanos €€ *Bypass road, Váti, tel: 22440 61100.* Sleek mock-traditional taverna which is best at weekends when it fills up and the full menu is guaranteed. A wide range of salads, good thick cheese pie amongst other *orektiká* (appetisers) and succulent meat grills. There is beer, bulk wine and *oúzo* for those wishing to steer clear of the stiffly priced bottled wine list. Open all year, noon until late (winter weekends only). Cash only.

Petalas €€€ *Kiotári Beach, mid-strip, tel: 22440 47265.* Long-established favourite here in blue-and-white Hellenic livery, doing creative Mediterranean fusion platters, especially seafood-based, as well as Greek staples like baked *gígandes* (haricot beans) and salads. Vegans and carnivores also catered for. Portions are on the small side but quality high. Unusually for the islands, they have decent rosé wine. Open noon–11pm, Apr–Oct.

Platanos € *Lower platía, Lahaniá village, tel: 6944 199991,* www.lachania-platanostaverna.com. Set in the most attractive village in Rhodes, bar none, beside two gushing Ottoman fountains. The indoor premises are housed in a sumptuous new building. The *mezédes* (*keftédes, hoummus* and *tyrokafterí*) are top-notch, as are mains like lemon lamb shank and goat stew. Good choice of desserts. Open all year (weekends only winter). Cash only.

Stegna Kozas €€–€€€ *Stegná coast road, north end, tel: 22440 22632,* www.stegnakozas.gr. Founded in 1932 and now in its third generation of management, this somewhat pricey but excellent, friendly seafood taverna scores for such delights as village bread with olive paste, chunky smoked aubergine salad with pine nuts and sweet red peppers, and linguine with urchin roe and coriander, as well as shellfish and scaly fish. A wide range of beers comes in iced mugs; retractable glazing on the water-level terrace permits year-round operation. Cash only.

KOS

Barbouni €€€ *Georgíou Avérof 26, tel: 22420 20170;* www.ilovebarbouni. com. Classier-than-normal waterside seafood spot, with vistas across to Turkey. All usual fish dishes plus novelties like risotto with cuttle-fish and its ink, shellfish linguine in dill white sauce, spinach salad with pine nuts and *krasotýri*, plus a surprisingly full dessert list. Thanks to its Turkish clientele, some quality *rakı* labels.

Pote tin Kyriaki € *Pisándrou 9, tel: 22420 48460.* Going since 1997, Kos' only genuine *mezedopolío* has signature platters like *marathópita* (fennel pie), mushroom sautée with vegies, *kavourdistí* (pork fry-up) and assorted seafood at encouraging prices, complemented by proprietress Stamatia's very strong bulk *tsikoudiá* (distilled spirit), and a soundtrack of Greek music for Greeks. Open late May–Oct Mon–Sat dinner only, winter Fri–Sat. Booking advisable; cash only.

SÝMI

Giorgos & Maria €€ *Near top of Kalí Stráta, Horió, tel: 22460 71984.* A local institution, working since the 1970s, with summer seating out on the *votsalotó* terrace. It has now adopted a largely *mezédes* format, with platters like lamb livers, stuffed squash blossoms, and rissoles made of spinach or eggplant. Their bulk wine, sadly, may be out of a supermarket carton, but live music sessions on Friday nights are a plus. Open all year for dinner; lunch in season by demand. Cash only.

To Spitiko €€ *south waterfront, Gialós, tel: 22460 72452.* Don't expect nouvelle cuisine here, but solid interpretations of all the Greek taverna standards – think lamb *kléftiko*, grilled fish, risotto, courgette rissoles – in big portions with ultra-friendly service. Deserved success means they expanded in 2018, without a drop in standards, however booking is still advisable.

HÁLKI

Taverna Lefkosia €€ *Emboriós quay, tel: 6946 978151.* For years, wherever Lefkosia Peraki was cooking was the top eatery on Hálki, and her recipes – for example *melitzanosaláta* (aubergine salad) – have been featured on the BBC. Since 2009 she's had her own restaurant, serving elaborate baked dishes like *soutzoukákia* (meat rissoles in sauce), grills including giant prawns, laboriously concocted *orektiká* (appetisers) and own-sourced ingredients – which means everything from her own livestock and olive oil to home-baked bread. Live music several nights weekly is a big bonus. Open Apr–Oct. Cash only.

A–Z TRAVEL TIPS

A SUMMARY OF PRACTICAL INFORMATION

A

ACCOMMODATION

Hotels. Hotels are now classified from five stars down to zero, this system having largely replaced the traditional categories of Luxury, A, B, C, D and E. Room rates for all categories other than luxury/five-star are theoretically government-controlled. Ratings are dictated primarily by the common facilities at the hotel, not the quality of the rooms, so a three-star room may be just as comfortable as a five-star room, but the hotel itself may not have a conference room, swimming pool or multiple restaurants on the premises.

Many hotels on Rhodes have contracts with EU, Russian and Israeli tour operators. This means that in peak season it may be difficult to find desirable accommodation. If you intend to arrive between mid-June and September it is wise to book in advance. At the beginning and end of the season (April to mid-June and October) the island becomes quieter and it is easier to get a good deal. Most hotels outside of Rhodes Town close from November to March.

In peak season there is often a minimum stay of three to five days. Quoted rates should include all applicable taxes.

Pensions, *enikiazómena domátia* and apartments. The main alternatives to hotels are *enikiazómena domátia* (rented rooms) or full-sized apartments; many of the 'pensions' found in Rhodes Old Town are technically *enikiazómena domátia*. Both licensed rooms and apartments are rated by the tourism authorities from one to three 'keys' based on their facilities. Arrivals by large catamaran at Kolóna Harbour or ferry at Akándia may be besieged by accommodation touts; it is unwise to follow them, as only proprietors of the most substandard, unlicensed lodgings resort to this tactic, and you will very likely have to move the next morning.

I'd like a single/double room with bath/shower **Tha íthela éna monó/dipló domátio me bánio/dous**

AIRPORT

Rhodes' Diagóras Airport (tel: 22410 88700, www.rhodes-airport.org) is on the west coast of the island, 14km (9 miles) south of Rhodes Town. The **north terminal** is for departures only; the adjacent **south terminal** still handles all arrivals and some domestic departures. They interconnect, handy if you discover your check-in counter (there are about 40) is at the other terminal.

From 6.30am to midnight in season there is a local bus connection (€2.50) into town. The bus stop is outside between the two terminals (turn left out of arrivals). Otherwise, a taxi into town will cost €25–30, depending on time of day, number of bags and exact destination.

B

BICYCLE AND MOTORCYCLE RENTAL

Cycling is popular during spring and autumn. In Neohóri, both Mike's Motor Club at Ioánni Kazoúli 23 (corner of Amarándou) and Bicycle Centre at Gríva 39 rent out a selection of bone-shakers and mountain-bikes.

Hiring a small motorbike is a popular way of cruising the resorts and immediate environs; rates are under €20 per day for a 50cc machine, lower if you hire it for three days or more. However, they're not really suitable for covering long distances on Rhodes, and every year there are numerous serious injuries and fatalities involving riders.

It is illegal in Greece to drive any scooter – even a 50cc one – without a full motorcycle licence (British provisional licenses with motorcycle entitlement may not be honoured), though many unscrupulous agencies ignore this law. If you hire a motorcycle without the appropriate licence, any insurance you have will be void if you are injured or involved in an accident. All riders must wear helmets.

BUDGETING FOR YOUR TRIP

Rhodes is a moderately expensive destination by EU standards – slightly more than Spain, still a bit less than Italy, Portugal or France, much dearer than Bulgaria.

Flight from Athens: €60–200 (one-way scheduled).

Boat ticket from Athens: €51 (one-way, deck class) to €78 (one-way, cheapest cabin).

Return boat trip to Sými: €23–30 depending on craft type.

Mid-range hotel: €120–200 (one night for two).

Mid-range restaurant: €20–33 (full meal for one).

Admission charges: €4–12 (most museums and archaeological sites).

Car rental: €35 per day, €210 per week (small car in peak season, walk-in rate).

Bus fare: €2.20–10.40. Rhodes to Líndos trips cost €5.50.

C

CAR RENTAL (see also Driving)

Several major rental chains have booths at the airport:

Alamo: tel: 22410 81600; www.alamo.com.

Avis: tel: 22410 82896; www.avis.com.

Hertz: tel: 22410 82902; www.hertz.com.

Sixt: tel: 22410 81995; www.sixt.com.

There are also many reputable local rental agencies that give reasonable service and keener pricing than the major international chains. One especially recommended company with several offices on the island, including at the airport, is **Drive Rent A Car**, tel: 22410 68243, 22410 81011 (airport office), www.driverentacar.gr, the local franchise of international chain Budget.

A national driving licence is accepted for EU/EEA nationals provided that it has been held for one full year and the driver is over 21 years of age. All other nationalities must carry an International Driving Permit in addition to their home licence. You will also need a credit card to avoid paying a large cash deposit upfront, or buying an overpriced insurance policy.

CLIMATE

It is claimed that Rhodes gets 300 sunny days each year – certainly from mid-May until mid-October you are almost guaranteed blue, rain-free skies. Midday temperatures reach a sweltering 38ºC (100ºF) in the summer months, with hot nights, although evenings become cooler early and late in the season.

The northerly *meltémi* wind that blows down from the Aegean buffets the northwest coast of the island, making it a little cooler throughout the year. The east coast has fewer breezes, and Líndos can be very oppressive on a hot, still summer afternoon.

Considerable rain falls between November and April, when the air feels damp, although temperatures are seldom very cold.

CLOTHING

In summer you require very little clothing on Rhodes. Shorts or lightweight trousers and T-shirts or lightweight dresses are fine for sightseeing. Remember to bring comfortable shoes for archaeological sites, as well as a hat and sunglasses. For evenings, very few places have a dress code, although smarter hotels require men to wear long trousers, and ban sandals. It can also get remarkably chilly after dark on the decks of ferries, when a jacket or fleece might be a good idea.

Appropriate dress is compulsory when visiting churches or monasteries. Both sexes should cover their shoulders; men should wear long trousers, and women a skirt that covers their knees.

CRIME AND SAFETY

Rhodes rates relatively well both in terms of personal safety and the safety of your belongings. Most visitor problems tend to involve motorbike accidents and over-indulgence in sun or alcohol. Break-ins are on the rise, but serious crime is rare. Don't accept rides from strangers when returning late from clubbing, and always use official taxis.

If you do fall victim to crime, you will need to contact the ordinary local police in the first instance – insurance claim forms will not be valid without their report.

All the obvious recreational drugs are illegal in Greece, and if you are arrested on narcotics charges you can spend up to 18 months on remand before a trial date is set. If you take any prescription painkillers or tranquillisers, carry your supply in the original pharmacy container.

D

DRIVING

Road conditions. Most roads and signs are adequate or better, with the main southeast coast highway two lanes in each direction from just south of Rhodes Town past Afándou to Kolýmbia. However, getting to the far south and back in one day can be arduous, and local driving habits leave much to be desired. Few parts of the island remain inaccessible to a normal rental car; however, most roads have no paved verges, only dust and gravel along the sides. Many asphalt surfaces are very slick when wet, a problem aggravated by most bends being banked the wrong way to save on installing culverts.

Are we on the right road for...? **Páme kalá giá...?**
Full tank, please. **Óso pérni, parakaló.**
super/lead-free/diesel soúper/**amólyvdis/dízel**
Check the oil/tires/battery. **Na elénxete ta ládia/ta lástiha/ti bataría.**
My car has broken down. **I amáxi mou éhi páthi vlávi.**
There's been an accident. **Égine éna atýhima.**

Rules and regulations. Traffic drives on the right and passes on the left, yielding to vehicles from the right except at roundabouts where one supposedly yields to the left (often countermanded by counterintuitive stop/yield sign schemes). Speed limits on open roads are 90kmh (55mph) and in towns 50kmh (30mph) unless otherwise stated, although most locals ignore these. Both speed-limit and distance signs are in kilometres.

Seat-belt use is compulsory (€350 fine for violations), as are crash helmets when riding a motorcycle (identical fine for non-compliance).

Drink-driving laws are strict – expect fines of €400–1200 and licence loss if caught – and police checkpoints proliferate at night and weekends.

Rhodes Town in particular is full of one-way systems, which many scooter-riders (and some car-drivers) routinely ignore. Many – especially young army recruits driving military trucks – are inexperienced and may not be properly insured. Give them a wide berth. Pedestrians – especially inebriated holidaymakers – also have their own agenda, and are likely to step out into the roadway without looking.

Breakdowns and accidents. If you have an accident or breakdown, put a red warning triangle some distance behind you to warn oncoming traffic. Always carry the telephone number of your rental office with you; they will be able to advise you if you have difficulties. Almost all agencies subscribe to one or other of the nationwide emergency roadside services (ELPA, Express Service, Ellas Service, Intersalonika); make sure you are given their local numbers.

If you have an accident involving another vehicle, do not admit fault or move either car until the police arrive and prepare a report; a copy will be given to you to present to the rental agency. It is an offence to leave the scene of an accident, or move vehicles before the police have attended.

Road signs. Most road signs are the standard pictographs used throughout Europe but you may also see some of these written signs:

Detour Παράκαμψη/**Parákampsi**
Parking Πάρκιγκ/**Párking**
No parking Απαγορεύεται/**Apagorévete to párking**
Be careful Προσοχή/**Prosohí**
Bus stop Στάση λεωφορείου/**Stási leoforíou**
Pedestrians Για πεζούς/**Gia pezoús**
Danger, dangerous Κίνδυνος, επικίνδυνος/**Kíndynos, epikíndynos**
No entry Απαγορεύεται η είσοδος/**Apagorévete i ísodos**

E

ELECTRICITY

The electric current is 220 volts/50 cycles. Electric plugs are two-prong Schuko Type F, CEE 7/7. Adaptor plugs are sold, but it is best to buy one at home before you leave – UK-to-Continental are much harder to find than North-American-to-Continental.

> A transformer **énas metaskhimatistís**
> an adapter **énas prosarmostís**

EMBASSIES AND CONSULATES

There is a British Vice-Consulate in Rhodes Town at Grigoríou Lambráki 29, Neohóri; tel: 22410 22005, and an Honorary Irish Consulate at Amerikís 111, Neohóri; tel: 22410 75655.

All other national embassies are located in Athens.

Australian Embassy and Consulate: Corner Kifissías and Alexándras avenues, Level 6, Thon Building, 115 23 Ambelókipi; tel: 210 87 04 000, www.greece.embassy.gov.au/athn/consular.html.

British Embassy and Consulate: Ploutárhou 1, 106 75 Athens; tel: 210 72 72 600, www.gov.uk/world/greece

Canadian Embassy: Ethnikís Andistáseos 48, 152 31 Athens; tel: 210 72 73 400, www.canadainternational.gc.ca/greece-grece.

Irish Embassy: Vassiléos Konstandínou 7, 106 74 Athens; tel: 210 72 32 771/2, www.dfa.ie/embassies/irish-embassies-abroad/europe/greece/

US Embassy and Consulate: Vassilísis Sofías 91, 101 60 Athens; tel: 210 72 12 951, https://gr.usembassy.gov

EMERGENCIES

The following emergency numbers are used on the island.

Police: 100

Ambulance: 166
Fire: 199
Traffic police: 22410 22346
Forest fire reporting: 191

G

GAY AND LESBIAN TRAVELLERS

Greece has historically been a very conservative country where traditional family relationships form the backbone of society. However, there is a natural courtesy towards visitors, and this, combined with the number of different types of international tourists, makes Rhodes an increasingly popular destination for gay and lesbian travellers. There is a recognised gay nudist lido near Pigés Kallithéas, on the rocks well to the left beyond the Oasis snack-bar. At Élli, known hangouts and cruising grounds are at the north tip, near the Aquarium, and around the Nautical Club beach-bar at the opposite end of the beach. The Old Town hamam men's section, if it ever resumes operation, has long been another gay pole of attraction.

GETTING THERE

By air. Literally dozens of charter flights carrying package patrons call daily in season from almost every country in Europe, as well as a few from Israel and Turkey.

Currently direct scheduled services from Britain, all from March to late October or early November, are with British Airways from Gatwick (www.ba.com), easyJet (www.easyjet.com) from Gatwick, Luton, Newcastle and Liverpool; Jet2 (www.jet2.com) from nine UK airports, including Belfast, two in Scotland, Stansted plus the North and Midlands; and Ryanair (www.ryanair.com) from Liverpool, Stansted, East Midlands and Manchester.

From North America, you will need to reach Athens first and then continue on one of three airlines currently serving the domestic route: Olympic Air (www.olympicair.com), now a subsidiary of Aegean, Ellinair (https://en.ellinair.com) and Sky Express (www.skyexpress.gr). All flights fill quickly in high summer – even business class sells out – and must be booked weeks in advance; June and September travel is easier.

Besides Aegean and Ellinair, numerous other carriers fly into Athens. These include Air France: www.airfrance.com; Alitalia: www.alitalia.com; Lufthansa: www.lufthansa.com; KLM: www.klm.com; Swiss: www.swiss.com; and British Airways: www.ba.com.

Direct flights from North America to Athens are provided only by Delta Airlines: www.delta.com, from JFK, Emirates: www.emirates.com, from Newark, and seasonally by American Airlines: www.aa.com, from Philadelphia and United: www.united.com, from Newark.

From Australia and New Zealand there are indirect flights only; the most reliable providers, besides European carriers, are Etihad Airways: www.etihad.com, Qatar Airways: www.qatarairways.com, and Emirates: www.emirates.com.

By boat. Rhodes is connected to Piraeus, the port for Athens, by almost daily car and passenger ferry. Sailings are most frequent from mid-June to mid-September. Boats can be very crowded at peak times, and it is advisable to buy tickets for cars or a cabin as far in advance as possible. A good online resource for checking schedules and prices is www.gtp.gr.

As of writing only two companies, Blue Star: www.bluestarferries.com and Aegeon Pelagos Sea Lines (ANEK): www.anek.gr, are providing service on this route. Journey time depends on boat and number of stops: 11–18 hours from Piraeus with modern craft calling at three to seven intermediate ports in the Cyclades and Dodecanese, up to 32 hours on ANEK's slower boats, stopping at certain Cylades, Crete and Kárpathos /Háli. There are also more rapid links with most of the other Dodecanese with the two catamarans *Dodekanisos Pride* and *Dodekanisos Express* (www.12ne.gr/EL).

GUIDES AND TOURS

Various companies offer organised guided tours to the major sites and attractions. These will be offered at a higher price compared with organising them yourself, but you may find it worth the extra cost for the convenience of being transported by coach.

In Rhodes Town, Triton Holidays (Plastíra 9; tel: 22410 21690; www.tritondmc.gr) offer tours, car rental and tickets to nearby islands and Turkey (Adriana handles all travel arrangements), as well as discounted quality accommodation across the Dodecanese.

H

HEALTH AND MEDICAL CARE

Emergency treatment is given free at hospital casualty wards (ask for the *thálamo epigón peristatiká*), but this covers only immediate treatment. EU residents will be able to get further free treatment, but must carry a European Health Insurance Card, obtainable in the UK online at www.ehic.org.uk.

Rhodes' main public hospital is 2km (1 mile) south of town, and despite relatively new premises still has a poor reputation. If you are privately insured for medical emergencies, go instead to the well-signed, expensive Euromedica clinic in Koskinoú, 6.5km (4 miles) south of Rhodes Town, (24hrs; English-speaking staff; tel: 22410 45000, www.euromedica-rhodes.gr).

If you have a minor problem, look for a pharmacy (*farmakío*), identified by a green cross, where you will be able to obtain basic advice. Most pharmacists will speak some English.

Rhodes has a few scorpions and snakes, which tend only to be found off the beaten track. Mosquitoes, especially in summer, are a more serious nuisance. Spiny sea urchins on submerged rocks can cause injury to inattentive swimmers. Avoidance is the best tactic, but if the worst should happen, dig out the spine tips with a sterilised sewing needle and olive oil.

Although Rhodes tap water is safe to drink, bottled water often tastes better and is universally available. Always carry water with you to the beach or when sightseeing to protect against dehydration.

There are no required vaccinations for Greece.

L

LANGUAGE

The sounds of the Greek language do not always correspond to exact equivalents in English, and the letters of the Greek alphabet do not always have a match in the Roman alphabet. This accounts for the divergent spellings of the same place name on road signs – for example, the word *ágios* is often also spelled *ághios* and *áyios* in the Roman alphabet, although it is always pronounced the same. Emphasis is also a vital element in pronouncing Greek. Throughout this book we have accented vowels within each Greek word to show which syllable to stress, except for one-syllable words.

Don't worry if you can't speak Greek. You will find that most people working anywhere near the tourist industry will have a basic English vocabulary, and many speak English very well.

The table lists the 24 letters of the Greek alphabet in their upper- and lower-case forms, followed by the closest individual or combined letters to which they correspond in English.

Α α	a	as in father
Β β	v	as in English
Γ γ	g	-as in go (except pronounced 'y' before 'e' and 'i' sounds)
Δ δ	d	like th in this
Ε ε	e	as in get
Ζ ζ	z	as in English
Η η	i	as in ski
Θ θ	th	like th in thin
Ι ι	i	as in ski
Κ κ	k	as in English
Λ λ	l	as in English
Μ μ	m	as in English

M μ	m	as in English
N v	n	as in English
Ξ ξ	x	as in box
O o	o	as in toad
Π π	p	as in English
Ρ ρ	r	as in English
Σ σ/ς	s	as in English, except sounds like z before m or g sounds
Τ τ	t	as in English
Υ υ	y	as in country
Φ φ	f	as in English
Χ χ	h	as in Scottish loch
Ψ ψ	ps	as in tipsy
Ω ω	o	as in bone

M

MAPS

You'll find a range of free maps at hotels, the airport and car-rental offices. These are adequate for exploring the island and Rhodes Town, though not precise enough to pinpoint attractions on smaller streets.

Most maps of Rhodes and the surrounding islands, especially those produced by Orama, are out of date or inaccurate; the Terrain (www.terrain-maps.gr) or Anavasi (www.anavasi.gr) maps of Rhodes, both at 1:75,000, are the best commercial maps available. The Old Town tourist office hands out an accurate street plan, based on the archaeological service's survey.

MEDIA

Newspapers. You will be able to buy all the major European newspapers, including the *International Herald Tribune*, which appears daily and includes the English-language version of top local paper *Kathimerini* (www.ekathimerini.com).

Television. Most hotels of three stars and above have a range of satellite channels, including CNN and BBC World. The Greek state channels ET1 and ET3 often have foreign films in the original language, especially late at night. SKAÏ is usually the best of the private channels.

MONEY

Currency. Greece uses the euro (abbreviated €), with notes of 5, 10, 20, 50, 100, 200and 500 euros; each euro comprises 100 leptá (euro-cents) and coins come in denominations of 1, 2, 5, 10, 20 and 50 leptá, as well as 1 and 2 euros.

Currency exchange. Most banks operate currency exchange for foreign notes, but commissions can be 3 percent and queues are long, so you may prefer to obtain cash from an ATM. Exchange rates, the same everywhere, are usually posted on a digital noticeboard inside the bank or in the window. Travel agencies no longer exchange foreign cash; go instead to the Bank of Greece, Platía Eleftherías 1, Mandráki, which should change notes with no commission at a decent rate.

ATMs. There are ATMs in all the major resort areas, and at least one in the larger settlements inland. These accept just about any type of debit card – look for your card's logo above the machine – although machines can run out of notes at weekends.

Travellers cheques: These are not recommended for use in Greece – expect severe delays or outright refusals in banks.

I want to change some pounds/dollars. **Thélo na alláxo merikéslíres/meriká dollária.**
How much commission do you take? **Póso promýthia pérnete?**
Have you a point of sale card machine? **Éhete mihánima pi oh ess?**

Credit cards. Many hotels, restaurants, travel agencies and shops accept credit cards, but there is still a sizeable minority that do not. Some may charge 3–5 percent extra for credit card payments, to cover their bank charges. Always ask about credit card acceptance before you sign the register or order your food, to avoid difficulties later. Usually there is a minimum spend at tavernas or shops. Encouraged by the government as a way to reduce the black economy, card machines are proliferating.

O

OPENING TIMES

Opening hours differ for official organisations and privately owned businesses. They also vary significantly between high and low season. To be sure of service or admission, it is best to visit any establishment between 9am and 1pm, Tue–Fri.

Banks operate Mon–Thur 8am–2.30pm, Fri 8am–2pm.

Most museums are open Tue–Sun 8.30am–3pm (this will vary). Most archaeological sites are open throughout the day but close on Mondays in winter. The last admission is 20 minutes before the official closing time; we cite the last admission time in 'Where to Go'.

Smaller shops are open Mon–Sat 9am–2.30pm, plus Tue, Thur and Fri 5.30pm–9pm (6–8.30pm in midsummer); supermarkets are open year-round Mon–Fri 8.30am–9pm, Sat 8.30am–8pm. A few (especially in major resorts) may also open 10am–4pm on Sunday. In peak season shops selling tourist-related items stay open until quite late.

P

POLICE

Ordinary police wear a two-tone blue uniform; the traffic police *(trohéa)* are part of the force. The tourist police is another branch that deals with tourist problems and complaints. They speak English and wear a dark grey uniform. **Emergency:** tel: 100

Non-emergency: tel: 22410 23849
Tourist police: tel: 22410 27423
Traffic police: tel: 22410 22346

> Where's the nearest police station? **Pou íne to kondinótero astynomikió tmíma?**

POST OFFICES

Post offices can be identified by a yellow-and-blue stylised Hermes head and the initials EΛTA. They are generally open 7.30am–2pm. The main, busy (take a number and wait) Neohóri post office on Mandráki west quay may also open Saturday, depending on staff availability. Post offices also have franchises of Western Union Moneygram.

> A stamp for this letter/postcard please **Éna grammatósimo giaftó to grámma/kart postál, parakaló.**

PUBLIC HOLIDAYS

Official holidays, when most things will be shut, are as follows:

1 January New Year's Day *(Protohroniá)*
6 January Epiphany *(Theofánia)*
25 March Greek Independence Day/Annunciation *(Evangelismós)*
1 May May Day *(Protomagiá)*
15 August Dormition of God's Mother *(Kímisis tis Theotókou)*
28 October 'No' or '*Ohi*' Day
25 December Christmas Day *(Hristoúgenna)*
26 December *Sýnaxis tis Panagías* (Gathering of God's Mother's Entourage)

Movable official holiday dates include the first day of Lent (Clean Monday; 48 days before Easter Sunday), Good Friday, Easter Monday and

Pentecost (Whit Monday, *Ágion Pnévma*; 50 days after Easter Sunday).

R

RELIGION

Most of the population belongs to the Greek Orthodox Church. There are two Roman Catholic churches and a synagogue in Rhodes Town, as well as two active mosques. Details of Catholic masses are posted outside both San Francisco/Ágios Frangískos (outside Ágios Athanásios Gate) and Santa Maria della Vittoria/Panagía tís Níkis (in Neohóri), also used by some Protestant denominations.

T

TELEPHONES

The international code for Greece is 30. All land-line numbers in Rhodes have 10 digits. Numbers in the north begin with 22410, while those in the south start with 22440 or 22460. Greek mobile numbers begin with 69 and, like land lines, have 10 digits.

Card-operated telephone booths are becoming rarer by the year, and invariably located at noisy intersections. Most people use prepaid calling cards with free access numbers prefixed 807 (reachable from any call box or private phone) and a 12-digit PIN.

Mobile users may roam on any of three local networks and EU-based phones get free roaming in Greece. Otherwise, if you are staying for more than a week, it is worth buying a Greek SIM. It (and the phone) must be registered at time of purchase, but the number remains valid for incoming calls for several months from each top-up.

TIME ZONES

Greece is two hours ahead of Greenwich Mean Time and also observes Daylight Saving Time – moving the clocks one hour forward at 3am on the last Sunday in March, one hour back at 3am on the last Sunday in October.

New York	London	Jo'burg	**Rhodes**	Sydney	Auckland
5am	10am	11am	**noon**	7pm	9pm

TIPPING

Service is notionally included in restaurant and bar bills, although it is customary to leave 5–10 percent of the bill in small change on the table for the waiting staff.

Taxi drivers are not tipped per se except at Easter week, but collect €0.43 extra per bag over 10 kilos in the boot, plus surcharges for entering the airport (€2.83) or harbour (€1.17).

Hotel chambermaids should be left a tip of around €1 per day. Bellhops and doormen should be tipped up to €2, depending on services provided.

TOILETS

Rhodes Town has public toilets at strategic locations across the old and new districts. Museums all have decent facilities.

Older sewage pipes in Greece are narrower than in most European countries and are easily clogged. Never put toilet paper into the bowl – always use the waste bin provided.

TOURIST INFORMATION

The moderately helpful Dodecanesian Tourism Directorate, part of the Greek National Tourism Organisation, tel: 22410 44335, www.ando.gr/eot, is found at the corner of Papágou and Makaríou in Neohóri (Mon–Fri 8.30am–2.45pm). The Municipal Tourist Office has two premises: one nearby on Rimini Square by the main taxi stand, tel: 22410 35945 (June–Oct Mon–Sat 9am–3pm), the other in the old city at the base of Odós Ippotón, opposite Panagía tou Kástrou (same hours).

For tourist information before you travel to Greece, you might contact one of the following overseas offices of the Greek National Tourism Organisation (www.visitgreece.gr):

UK and Ireland: 5th Floor East, Great Portland House, 4 Great Portland Street, London W1W 8QJ; tel: (020) 7495 9300.
USA: 800 3rd Avenue, 23rd Floor, New York, NY 10022; tel: (212) 421 5777.

TRANSPORT

Bus. The bus network links all the major settlements on the island with Rhodes Town and operates from early in the morning until 7–11pm depending on the destination. Photocopied timetables are available from tourist information offices, or just consult the placards at the stops. Buses for the east side of the island, run by KTEL, depart from the Papágou end of Odós Avérof, by the Néa Agorá (New Market); for the west side, southern suburb villages and the airport, RODA-run buses depart from 50m/yds further up Odós Avérof street, also outside the Néa Agorá.

Taxis. The island is well equipped with taxis, mostly midnight blue, but white on top. Prices to all destinations are regulated and posted outside the arrivals terminal at the airport, as well as being detailed on a sheet issued by the tourist authorities – though this does not entirely prevent fare-fiddling with foreigners, which can be brutal. Minimum fare is €3.69.

The basic charge structure also appears on a laminated sheet mounted on the dashboard. Meters must be set (to €1.29 at the start of each journey; '1' indicates regular fare, '2' indicates double tariff between midnight and 5am, and/or outside urban areas. All drivers are obliged to give receipts now, using dashboard-mounted apparatus.

Additionally, most taxi drivers refuse to enter the walled Old Town – resign yourself to walking in from the nearest gate.

Ferries and catamarans. In a move benefitting absolutely nobody except local taxi drivers (€10 flat fee from Rhodes Town to the dock), all main-line ferry docking was shifted to remote, shadeless, facility-less Akandiá harbour in 2011 – allow 20 minutes-plus if walking from town. Most ticket agencies, and the *Dodekanisos Express/Pride* catamarans, remain at the west quay of central Kólona harbour (the east quay is for international services to Turkey, and cruise ships). *See 'Getting There' for other typical destinations.*

V

VISAS, ENTRY REQUIREMENTS, CUSTOMS RULES

European Union (EU) citizens may enter Greece for an unlimited length of time. British citizens must have a valid passport, while citizens of Ireland can enter with a valid identity card or passport. Nationals of the US, Canada, Australia and New Zealand can stay for up to 90 days within any 180-day period upon production of a valid passport; no advance visas are needed. South Africans require a Schengen Visa, applied for in advance at a Greek embassy or consulate.

There are no limits on the amount of hard currency visitors can import or export, though amounts in excess of €10,000 or equivalent must be declared. All goods brought into Greece from within the EU must have duty paid on them. There are no limitations on the amount of duty-paid goods that can be brought into the country. If you are arriving from a non-EU country (eg Turkey), allowances for duty-free goods brought into Greece are as follows: 200 cigarettes or 50 cigars or 250g of tobacco; 1 litre of spirits or 4 litres of wine; 250ml of cologne or 50ml of perfume.

W

WEBSITES AND INTERNET ACCESS

www.visitgreece.gr useful information about what to do, where to go and what to see in Greece run by the Greek National Tourism Organisation
www.rodos.com allows you to book accommodation or car hire and visit resorts virtually
www.rhodes.gr is the municipality's site, but is not always up to date
www.rhodesguide.com has useful guides to the resorts and beaches
www.livinginrhodes.com targets resident expats, but has lots of info

The better hotels have Wi-fi zones (usually for a fee), a lobby computer or ethernet cables in the rooms; most modest hotels or old town inns offer free Wi-fi. Most tavernas or bars have free Wi-Fi access for their patrons.

RECOMMENDED HOTELS

The following recommendations include options for all budgets and cover Rhodes Town plus the rest of the island, as well as three popular excursion destinations. Most Rhodian beachside resort hotels have different types of room, including suites and bungalows, so be sure to confirm the type of accommodation that you are booking. Unless otherwise indicated, establishments operate only from April to October. Accommodation prices can vary significantly between high and low season. Tax and service charges should be included in quoted rates, though breakfast (typically €8–13 per person) may not be.

All recommendations accept credit or debit cards. The price categories indicated below are for a double room or suite per night in high season. Many establishments have minimum stays, indicated on their websites.

€€€€€	over 300 euros
€€€€	200–300 euros
€€€	120–200 euros
€€	80–120euros
€	below 80 euros

RHODES OLD TOWN

Allegory Boutique Hotel €€€€ doubles, €€€€€ suites *Andifánous 11, 851 00 Rhodes, tel: 22410 37470;* http://allegoryhotel.com or www.yadeshotels. gr. Named after Ovidian characters, six suites here have original wall art, USB/Bluetooth sound systems, big TVs and subdued lighting. At ground-floor doubles 'Danai' and 'Daphne', oval butler sinks and counters separate the rooms from a rain-shower and closed-off toilet. Bedding means double mattresses on box springs. Upstairs suites impress with imported Burgundy paving stone underfoot, and queen/king-size beds. 'Andromeda' has a Jacuzzi on the patio; 'Callisto' and 'Orpheus' have beech-plank flooring and hydromassage showers. 'Narcissus' sports a blue-domed hammam with rain and waterfall showers. Breakfast is excellent: fresh fruit, charcuterie, muesli, pastries, eggs and coffee your style. Open all year.

Andreas €€ *Omírou 28D, 851 00 Rhodes, tel: 22410 34156,* www.hotel andreas.com. At the quietest, highest point of the Old Town, occupying a former Turkish mansion, stands this exquisite little suite-hotel with just two suites and one room, although a fourth unit may emerge in 2020. Galleried Nessim has a fireplace; the Terrace Suite enjoys unbeatable views (though the bathroom is down the hall); while the two-storeyed Tower Suite makes a romantic eyrie. All units have air con, Wi-fi and offer a double bed plus a single (minimum child age 7). Common areas comprise a secluded patio garden where breakfast is served, and an indoor lounge/library. Open late June–late Sept only.

Avalon €€€€–€€€€€ *Háritos 9, 851 00 Rhodes, tel: 22410 31438,* www. avalonrhodes.gr. This 14th-century manor house, converted in 2007 with no expense spared, contains six luxury suites (some are suitable for smaller groups, four have original fireplaces, many are dark) with state-of-the-art bathrooms, plasma TV and Wi-fi signal. Breakfast is served in your suite, or down in the courtyard with its koi-stocked water feature, or in the vaulted bar where meals for guests are also available. Their frequent internet specials make it more affordable. Open all year.

In Camera €€€€ suites, €€€€€ villa *Sofokléous 35, 851 00 Rhodes, tel: 22410 77277,* www.incamera.gr. Photographer Nikos Kasseris and architect daughter Verolucy have restored this former rambling medieval ruin. One enters via a small courtyard where a jacuzzi lies below a Kütahya-tile-adorned wall fountain. The raised breakfast (fruit, cereal, cake, omelette, yoghurt) area looks to minarets and domes over a ficus-shaded plaza, a view shared by most of six suites and one villa. Multi-level 'Nymph of Helios' exhibits Nikos' working cameras; in the bathroom, the shower occupies the old hamam chimney, open to the sky. 'Forms of Light', also multi-level, has Belle Epoque tiles underfoot, rain-shower with hydromassage, plus private roof terrace. The Villa (capacity 6) offers two verandas and kitchen; the plank-floored living room has a working fireplace and adjoining formal diner. The bathroom sports a tub and Japanese toilet. Open all year.

Kokkini Porta Rosa €€€€ *Opposite Pródromos bastion church, inside the Koskinoú Gate (aka the Kókkini Pórta), 851 00 Rhodes, tel: 22410 75114,* www.kokkiniporta.com. Under the supervision of Nikos and Angela, superb hosts who know everything worth knowing about Rhodes, a crumbled medieval manor has become six unique, luxurious and sensitively restored suites – four up and two down – named for past inhabitants of the building. All have natural-fibre mattresses, Frette-brand bedding, and antique copper or textiles. Upstairs units may have galleried sleeping areas, conservatories or even a fireplace. Ground-floor 'Michalis', under a vaulted ceiling, opens onto a private patio-garden with plunge-pool. Daily changing breakfasts, prepared to order and served in the mulberry courtyard, are the most creative in town. Open 20 March–11 Nov.

Marco Polo Mansion €€€ *Agíou Fanouríou 42, 851 00 Rhodes, tel: 22410 25562,* www.marcopolomansion.gr. Hardly noticeable off the cobbled thoroughfare, this discreet inn, converted from a rambling old Ottoman mansion (the hamam survives, though no longer used), is stunning once inside. All en-suite rooms are furnished with antiques from the nearby eponymous gallery, plus natural-fibre, handmade bedding; the garden-side rooms are a bit cheaper (but also less airy). Buffet breakfasts (enhanced Continental style, with fruit and muesli) are served by the well in the courtyard, which becomes one of Rhodes Town's best restaurants after dark.

Nikos Takis €€€–€€€€ *Panetíou 26, near clock tower, 851 00 Rhodes, tel: 22410 70773,* www.nikostakishotel.com. You'll find just eight unique rooms or suites at this converted 1884 mansion. Designed by two of Greece's more flamboyant *haute couturiers*, with exposed stone pointing, wood floors and Indian-textile accents – plus a clothing boutique. A rich breakfast –probably walnut-carrot cake, omelettes, crepes, assorted turnovers – is served in the pebble-mosaic courtyard, also an ideal vantage for enjoying evening views over town to the harbour. Open all year.

Rhodes 4 Vacation €–€€€ *851 00 Rhodes, tel: 6976 009383,* www.rhodes-4vacation.com . A selection of six restored old houses, built for owner occupation and not as vacation villas, in Rhodes Old Town, plus over 30 modern villas scattered across the island. Flagship of the Old Town fleet is tasteful, three-bedroom, two-bath Villa Alexandra with huge garden; there are also smaller houses suitable for four sharing a large garden nearby, and a tall, narrow-fronted maisonette for three with roof terrace in the old Jewish Quarter.

RHODES NEW TOWN

Cactus €€ rooms, €€€ suites *Ko 14, 851 00 Rhodes, tel: 22410 26100,* www.
cactus-hotel.gr. Three-star hotel of 1970s vintage, partially renovated,
with a pool – though you are opposite the best, northern end of Élli beach.
Rooms are fair-sized if unexciting, with large, white-tile bathrooms; the
suites are by contrast more cutting-edge. The co-managed, four-star
Aquarium View (www.aquarium-hotel.gr), **€€,** across the way has more
rooms facing the square rather than the sea but shares the same decor.

Rodos Park Suites €€€€ standard double, €€€€€ all others *Ríga Fer-
eoú 12, 851 00 Rhodes, tel: 22410 89700,* www.rodospark.gr. Arguably the
highest-quality accommodation in the New Town, this boutique hotel offers three grades each of rooms and suites, with tasteful soft furnishings plus sleek modern fittings like rain-showers and high-tech air-con
and shutter controls; deluxe doubles are the minimum category to go for.
Rear units face a quiet hillside and archaeological dig, front ones overlook
the pool. A highlight is the wood-decked roof-bar, with unrivalled views.
The basement spa, free gym, sauna and hammam and two decent on-site
restaurants (one poolside) complete the picture. Open end Mar–end Oct.

AROUND THE ISLAND

Atrium Palace €€€€ rooms, €€€€€ villas *Kálathos beach, 851 02 Rhodes,
tel: 22440 31601,* www.atrium.gr. This family-friendly 'thalasso spa resort'
occupies vast, landscaped grounds extending down to the beach, with several novelty pools, thalasso-spa, gym, mini-golf, tennis courts and three
restaurants. Even the standard doubles have large bathrooms and parquet
floors, while the luxury villas down near the spa are the quietest.

Elafos € rooms, €€ suites *Profítis Ilías, 851 06 Rhodes, tel: 22460 22280,*
www.elafoshotel.gr. This Italian-built period piece from 1929 reopened
in 2006 as a rustic hotel popular with walking groups. The high-ceilinged
units (the three suites are worth the extra charge) have considerable
retro charm, and there are great views of the forest from the balconies. The à la carte ground-floor café makes a good rest stop if touring.
There's also a full menu of Greek standards. Open all year.

Esperos Palace €€€ rooms, €€€€€ suites *Faliráki, 851 00 Rhodes, tel: 22410 84300,* www.esperospalace.gr. While perhaps overrated as a five-star (adults only) resort, understated good taste is evident: from the white-and-beige lobby to four grades of rooms and suites with their subtle lighting, flat-screen TVs and miniature sound systems. Bathrooms are functional but small at the lower grade. Common areas, merging with those of the co-run Esperides Palace 'family' resort adjacent, include several pools set in mature gardens, a gym, sauna-spa and a good stretch of beach.

Lindian Village €€€ standard doubles, €€€€€ suites *851 09 Lárdos, tel: 22440 35900,* www.lindianvillage.gr. This ingeniously designed bungalow complex just beyond Glýstra cove has its own private beach, a spa with domed hammam, gym, outdoor yoga classes, a central 'lazy river' bubbling through, several restaurants (including three à la carte) and eight grades of units. Families are welcome, with larger suites fitting four to five, a crèche for toddlers and kids' club for older children up to 12.

Lindos Mare Hotel €€€€ rooms, €€€€€ suites *Vlýha, 851 07 Rhodes, tel: 22440 31130,* www.lindosmare.gr. Situated just 2km (1 mile) northwest of Líndos, this tiered hotel manages to feel low-key and intimate despite comprising 153 designer units (one-third suites; not all of them with sea views). A funicular (or shady walkway) brings you down through lush grounds from the larger of two pools to the beach with its sun-loungers and watersports franchise. There are also two full-service restaurants and a spa. Adjacent, the ultra-sleek adults-only **Lindos Blu €€€€€** *(tel: 22440 32110,* www.lindosblu.gr*)* is a five-star annexe, with only water features relieving visual starkness. Unlike its neighbour, its 74 units – in several grades, many with private pools – are often full with repeat clientele owing to exceptional customer service and gourmet on-site dining (advantageous half-board rates offered).

Melenos €€€€€ *851 07 Líndos, Rhodes, tel: 22440 32222,* www.melenos lindos.com. This boutique hotel in traditional style has the best location in the village. The 12 cedar-wood-trimmed units vary in plan, but all have big designer baths with glazed Kütahya tiles, and semi-private sea-view patios with pebble mosaics underfoot. Whether it is worth the price tag of up to €940 per night (for the best unit) is a personal matter. There is an equally pricey bar-restaurant with stunning views.

Paraktio Beach Apartments €€ *Kiotári, 851 09 Rhodes, tel: 22440 47350,* www.paraktio.com. Exceptionally well-appointed studios for couples and galleried four-person apartments with huge terraces, perched on a bluff just above a nice stretch of beach. The units are fully self-catering, but there is a small snack-and-breakfast bar on site. Friendly family management, no package bookings, free sunbeds.

Rodos Palace rooms €€€, suites €€€€€ *Triandón Avenue, Ixiá, 851 00 Rhodes, tel: 22410 97222,* www.rodos-palace.gr. As much a business and conference hotel as a five-star resort, the Rodos Palace offers 26 grades of accommodation. These range from standard rooms and suites in the ugly main tower to the myriad suites occupying prettier two- or three-storey villas in a landscaped hillside setting through which an artificial 'lazy river' runs – really the best reason to stay here. All have minimalist furnishings; some have private plunge pools. The centrepiece of the vast common areas is a greenhouse-domed pool, best in winter. Open mid-Apr–end Oct.

KOS

Afendoulis € *Evrypýlou 1, 853 00 Kos, tel: 22420 25321,* www.afendoulis hotel.com. The friendliest place to stay in Kos Town, the Zíkas family hotel has large air-conditioned rooms – their bathrooms redone in 2015 – with and without balconies. A loyal repeat clientele means advance booking is necessary. No frills aside from in-room fridges, but Wi-fi throughout, and delicious breakfasts (charged extra) available until 11.30am in the lobby or on the shady patio. Open late Mar–early Nov.

Aqua Blu €€€€€ *Near lighthouse, Lámbi, tel: 22420 22440,* www.aqua-bluhotel.gr. Dark-colour accents offset the usual lighter earth tones of Greek boutique hotels. All units have coffee-making kit and quality Apivita toiletries. The 'loft' suite, with brown-and-green palette, parquet flooring and combo rain shower-whirlpool tub, enjoys views to Turkey and Psérimos. The main pool laps decking and day-beds, or there's a charming patch of beach. Spa treatments are keenly priced, with couple's treatment rooms; naturally lit gym. The in-house restaurant does scallops with marsh samphire, veal cheeks under garbanzo purée, creative desserts; going à la carte is dear, though more affordable tasting menus exist.

SÝMI

Aliki €€–€€€ *Aktí Georgíou Gennimáta, Gialós, 856 00 Sými, tel: 22410 71665,* www.hotelaliki.gr. This 1895 mansion right on the quay is one of Sými's most exclusive hotels. The rooms all have wooden floors and antique furnishings, although only some (suites in the higher price category) have sea views and/ or balconies. An affiliated Italian restaurant is next door. Open Apr–mid-Oct.

Iapetos Village €€€ *Behind Gialós Platía, 856 00 Sými, tel: 22460 72777,* www.iapetos-village.gr. A complex of spacious, self-catering maison-ettes – some accommodate up to six – and studios. A generous breakfast is offered beside the only swimming pool on the island. Open Apr–Nov.

Sými Visitor Accommodation €€–€€€ *Head of Gialós Bay, tel: 22460 71785,* www.symivisitor-accommodation.com. Adriana offers a wide range of restored properties, ranging from simple studios to mansions suitable for large families. All are serviced second homes let in their owners' absence, so they come with fully equipped kitchens, libraries, music systems – and unpredictable quirks. Available Apr–Nov.

HÁLKI

The Admiral's House €€€ Waterfront, Emboriós, *851 10 Hálki, tel: 6937 181225,* www.admiralshouse.gr. Consisting of two large villas, upper Anna Maria, and ground-floor Marianthi Pasithea, the Admiral's House is a beautifully refurbished 19th-century mansion. With a sun terrace, pri-vate beach area and views to a private seafront garden or the sea, each villa offers accommodation for two: a sitting room, bedroom, bathroom, internet and fully equipped kitchen.One week minimum stay.

Aretanassa €€ *South quay, Emboriós, 851 10 Hálki, tel: 22460 70927,* www. aretanassa-hotel.gr. After a bumpy start, the municipally owned hotel oc-cupying an old sponge factory is under new, friendly, pro-active manage-ment since 2017. All rooms face the sea, entered via steps from a private lido; common areas include a gym and conference facilities. Copious buffet breakfast and snacks offered, though kitchen closes at 6pm. Reserve well in advance, as special-interest groups often book it out. Open Apr–Oct.

DICTIONARY

adj adjective **adv** adverb **BE** British English **n** noun **prep** preposition **v** verb

A

access n πρόσβαση
prohz•vah•see

accessory αξεσουάρ
ah•kseh•soo•ahr

accident ατύχημα
ah•tee•khee•mah

accompany συνοδεύω
see•oh•THeh•voh

account n λογαριασμός
loh•ghahr•yahz•mohs

adaptor προσαρμοστής
proh•sahr•moh•stees

address n διεύθυνση
THee•ehf•theen•see

admission είσοδος *ee•soh•THohs*

adult ενήλικας *eh•nee•lee•kahs*

advance προκαταβολή
proh•kah•tah•voh•lee

after μετά *meh•tah*

afternoon απόγευμα
ah•poh•yehv•mah

after-sun lotion λοσιόν μετά
την ηλιοθεραπεία *loh•siohn*
meh•tah teen ee•lioh•theh•
rah•pee•ah

age n ηλικία *ee•lee•kee•ah*

agree συμφωνώ *seem•foh•noh*

air conditioning κλιματισμός
klee•mah•teez•mohs

air pump n αντλία αέρος
ahn•dlee•ah ah•eh•rohs

airline αεροπορική εταιρία
ah•eh•roh•poh•ree•kee
eh•the•ree•ah

airmail αεροπορικώς
ah•eh•roh•poh•ree•kohs

airport αεροδρόμιο
ah•eh•roh•THroh•mee•oh

aisle seat διάδρομος
THee•ah•Throh•mohs

allergic αλλεργικός
ahl•ehr•yee•kohs

allergy αλλεργία *ah•lehr•yee•ah*

alone μόνος *moh•nohs*

aluminum foil αλουμινόχαρτο
ah•loo•mee•noh•khah•rtoh

amazing καταπληκτικός
kah•tahp•leek•tee•kohs

ambassador πρεσβευτής
prehz•vehf•tees

amber κεχριμπάρι
kehkh•reem•bah•ree

ambulance ασθενοφόρο
ahs•theh•noh•foh•roh

American adj αμερικάνικος
ah•meh•ree•kah•nee•kohs;
(nationality) Αμερικανός
ah•meh•ree•kah•nohs

amount n ποσό *poh•soh*

amusement park πάρκο
ψυχαγωγίας *pahr•koh*
psee•khah•ghoh•yee•ahs

animal ζώο *zoh•oh*

another άλλος *ah•lohs*

antibiotic αντιβιοτικό
ahn•dee•vee•oh•tee•koh

antiques store κατάστημα με
αντίκες *kah•tah•stee•mah meh*
ahn•tee•kehs

antiseptic cream αντισηπτική
κρέμα *ahn•dee•seep•tee•kee*
kreh•mah

anything οτιδήποτε

oh•tee•THee•poh•teh

apartment διαμέρισμα
THee•ah•meh•reez•mah

apologize ζητώ συγγνώμη
zee•toh seegh•noh•mee

appendix σκωληκοειδίτιδα
skoh•lee•koh•ee•
THee•tee•THah

appointment ραντεβού
rahn•deh•voo

architecture αρχιτεκτονική
ahr•khee•teh•ktoh•nee•kee

area code κωδικός
περιοχής *koh•THee•kohs*
peh•ree•oh•khees

arm n χέρι *kheh•ree*

arrange κανονίζω
kah•noh•nee•zoh

arrest v συλλαμβάνω
see•lahm•vah•noh

arrive φτάνω *ftah•noh*

art τέχνη *tekh•nee*

art gallery γκαλερί τέχνης
gah•leh•ree tekh•nees

ashtray σταχτοδοχείο
stakh•toh•THoh•khee•oh

ask ζητώ *zee•toh*

aspirin ασπιρίνη
ahs•pee•ree•nee

asthmatic ασθματικός
ahsth•mah•tee•kohs

ATM ATM *ehee•tee•ehm*

attack n επίθεση
eh•pee•theh•see; v επιτίθεμαι
eh•pee•tee•theh•meh

attractive ελκυστικός
ehl•kees•tee•kohs

authenticity αυθεντικότητα
ahf•thehn•dee•koh•tee•tah

B

baby μωρό *moh•roh*

baby food βρεφική τροφή
vreh•fee•kee troh•fee

baby seat καρέκλα μωρού
kah•reh•klah moh•roo

babysitter μπέιμπι σίτερ
beh•ee•bee see•tehr

back n πλάτη *plah•tee*

back ache πόνος στην πλάτη
poh•nohs steen plah•tee

backgammon τάβλι *tah•vlee*

bad κακός *kah•kohs*

baggage αποσκευές
ah•pohs•keh•vehs

baggage check φύλαξη
αποσκευών *fee•lah•ksee
ah•poh•skeh•vohn*

baggage reclaim παραλαβή
αποσκευών *pah•rah•lah•vee
ah•poh•skeh•vohn*

bakery αρτοποιείο
ah•rtoh•pee•ee•oh

balcony μπαλκόνι *bahl•koh•nee*

ballet μπαλέτο *bah•leh•toh*

bandage γάζα *ghah•zah*

bank τράπεζα *trah•peh•zah*

bank account λογαριασμός
τραπέζης *loh•ghahr•yahz•mohs
trah•peh•zees*

bank loan τραπεζικό δάνειο
trah•peh•zee•koh THah•nee•oh

bar μπαρ *bahr*

barber κουρείο *koo•ree•oh*

basket καλάθι *kah•lah•THee*

basketball μπάσκετ *bah•skeht*

bathing suit μαγιό *mah•yoh*

bathroom μπάνιο *bah•nioh*

battery μπαταρία
bah•tah•ree•ah

beach παραλία *pah•rah•lee•ah*

beautiful όμορφος *oh•mohr•fohs*

bed κρεβάτι *kreh•vah•tee*

bed and breakfast διαμονή με
πρωινό *THah•moh•nee meh
proh•ee•noh*

bedding σεντόνια *sehn•doh•niah*

bedroom υπνοδωμάτιο
eep•noh•THah•mah•tee•oh

before πριν *preen*

beginner αρχάριος
ahr•khah•ree•ohs

belong ανήκω *ah•nee•koh*

belt ζώνη *zoh•nee*

bicycle ποδήλατο
poh•THee•lah•toh

big μεγάλος *meh•ghah•lohs*

bikini μπικίνι *bee•kee•nee*

bird πουλί *poo•lee*

bite n (insect) τσίμπημα
tsee•bee•mah

bladder ουροδόχος κύστη
oo•roh•THoh•khohs kee•stee

blanket κουβέρτα *koo•veh•rtah*

bleed n αιμορραγία
eh•moh•rah•yee•ah; v
αιμορραγώ *eh•moh•rah•yoh*

blinds περσίδες *peh•rsee•THehs*

blister φουσκάλα *foo•skah•lah*

blood αίμα *eh•mah*

blood group ομάδα αίματος
oh•mah•THah eh•mah•tohs

blood pressure πίεση *pee•eh•see*

blouse μπλούζα *bloo•zah*

boarding card κάρτα επιβίβασης
kah•rtah eh•pee•vee•vah•sees

boat βάρκα *vah•rkah*

boat trip ταξίδι με πλοίο
tah•ksee•THee meh plee•oh

body σώμα *soh•mah*

bone οστό *oh•stoh*

book n βιβλίο *veev•lee•oh*;
v κάνω κράτηση *kah•noh
krah•tee•see*

bookstore βιβλιοπωλείο
veev•lee•oh•poh•lee•oh

boot μπότα *boh•tah*

border (country) σύνορο
see•noh•roh

boring βαρετός *vah•reh•tohs*

borrow δανείζομαι
THah•nee•zoh•meh

botanical garden βοτανικός
κήπος *voh•tah•nee•kohs
kee•pohs*

bottle μπουκάλι *boo•kah•lee*

bottle opener τιρμπουσόν
teer•boo•sohn

bowel έντερο *ehn•deh•roh*

box office ταχυδρομική θυρίδα
*tah•khee•THroh•mee•kee
THee•ree•THah*

boxing n μποξ *bohks*

boy αγόρι *ah•ghoh•ree*

boyfriend φίλος *fee•lohs*

bra σουτιέν *soo•tiehn*

break n διάλειμμα *THee•ah•
lee•mah*; v σπάω *spah•oh*

breakdown n (car) βλάβη
vlah•vee

breakfast πρωινό *proh•ee•noh*

break-in n διάρρηξη
THee•ah•ree•ksee

breast στήθος *stee•THohs*

breathe αναπνέω
ah•nahp•neh•oh

breathtaking φαντασμαγορικός
*fahn•dahz•mah•
ghoh•ree•kohs*

bridge n (over water) γέφυρα *yeh•
fee•rah*; (card game) μπριτζ
breetz

briefcase χαρτοφύλακας
khah•rtoh•fee•lah•kahs

briefs (men's, women's) σλιπ
sleep (women's); κυλοτάκι
kee•loh•tah•kee

bring φέρνω *fehr•noh*

Britain Βρετανία
vreh•tah•nee•ah

British adj βρετανικός
vreh•tah•nee•kohs; (nationality)
Βρετανός *vreh•tah•nohs*

brochure φυλλάδιο
fee•lah•THee•oh

broken σπασμένος
spahz•meh•nohs

broom n σκούπα *skoo•pah*

browse ξεφυλλίζω
kseh•fee•leez•oh

bruise n μελανιά *meh•lah•niah*

brush n βούρτσα *voor•tsah*; v
βουρτσίζω *voor•tsee•zoh*

build κτίζω *ktee•zoh*

building κτίριο *ktee•ree•oh*

burn n έγκαυμα *eh•gahv•mah*

bus λεωφορείο
leh•oh•foh•ree•oh

bus route διαδρομή λεωφορείων
*THee•ah•THroh•mee
leh•oh•foh•ree•ohn*

bus station σταθμός
λεωφορείων *stahTH•mohs*
leh•oh•foh•ree•ohn

bus stop στάση λεωφορείου
stah•see leh•oh•foh•ree•oo

business class μπίζνες θέση
bee•znehs theh•see

business trip επαγγελματικό
ταξίδι *eh•pah•gehl•mah•tee•
koh tah•ksee•THee*

busy (occupied)
απασχολημένος
ah•pahs•khoh•lee•meh•nohs

but αλλά *ah•lah*

butane gas υγραέριο
eegh•rah•eh•ree•oh

butcher shop κρεοπωλείο
kreh•oh•poh•lee•oh

button κουμπί *koo•bee*

buy αγοράζω *ah•ghoh•rah•zoh*

C

cabaret καμπαρέ *kah•bah•reh*

cabin καμπίνα *kah•bee•nah*

cable car τελεφερίκ
teh•leh•feh•reek

cafe καφετέρια
kah•feh•teh•ree•ah

calendar ημερολόγιο
ee•meh•rah•loh•yee•oh

call collect με χρέωση του
καλούμενου *meh khreh•oh•see
too kah•loo•meh•noo*

call n κλήση *klee•see*; v καλώ
kah•loh

camcorder φορητή
βιντεοκάμερα *foh•ree•tee
vee•deh•oh•kah•meh•rah*

camera φωτογραφική μηχανή
*foh•toh•ghrah•fee•kee
mee•khah•nee*

camera case θήκη μηχανής
thee•kee mee•khah•nees

camera store κατάστημα με
φωτογραφικά είδη *kah•tah•
stee•mah meh foh•tohgh•
rah•fee•kah ee•THee*

camp bed κρεβάτι
εκστρατείας *kreh•vah•tee
ehk•strah•tee•ahs*

camping κάμπινγκ *kah•mpeeng*

camping equipment εξοπλισμός
κάμπιγκ *eh•ksohp•leez•mohs
kah•mpeeng*

campsite χώρος κάμπινγκ
khoh•rohs kah•mpeeng

can opener ανοιχτήρι
ah•neekh•tee•ree

Canada Καναδάς *kah•nah•THahs*

canal κανάλι *kah•nah•lee*

cancel v ακυρώνω
ah•kee•roh•noh

cancer (disease) καρκίνος
kahr•kee•nohs

candle κερί *keh•ree*

canoe κανό *kah•noh*

car αυτοκίνητο
ahf•toh•kee•nee•toh

car park [BE] χώρος στάθμευσης
khoh•rohs stahth•mehf•sees

car rental ενοικίαση αυτοκινήτων
*eh•nee•kee•ah•see
ahf•toh•kee•nee•tohn*

car wash πλύσιμο
αυτοκινήτου *plee•see•moh
ahf•toh•kee•nee•too*

carafe καράφα *kah•rah•fah*

caravan τροχόσπιτο
troh•khohs•pee•toh

cards χαρτιά *khahr•tiah*

carpet (fitted) μοκέτα
moh•keh•tah

carton κουτί *koo•tee*

cash desk [BE] ταμείο
tah•mee•oh

cash n μετρητά *meht•ree•tah*;
v εξαργυρώνω
eh•ksahr•ghee•roh•noh

casino καζίνο *kah•see•noh*

castle κάστρο *kahs•troh*

catch v (bus) παίρνω *pehr•noh*

cathedral καθεδρικός ναός
kah•theh•THree•kohs nah•ohs

cave n σπήλαιο *spee•leh•oh*

CD σι ντι *see dee*

cell phone κινητό *kee•nee•toh*

change n αλλαγή *ah•lah•yee*; v
αλλάζω *ah•lah•zoh*

cheap φτηνός *ftee•nohs*

check n (bank) επιταγή *eh•pee•
tah•yee*; (bill) λογαριασμός
loh•ghahr•yahz•mohs

choose διαλέγω *THiah•leh•ghoh*

clean καθαρός *kah•thah•rohs*

cling film [BE] διαφανή
μεμβράνη *THee•ah•fah•nee
mehm•vrah•nee*

clothing store κατάστημα
ρούχων *kah•tahs•tee•mah
roo•khohn*

cold adj (temperature) κρύος
kree•ohs; n (chill) κρυολόγημα
kree•oh•loh•yee•mah

collapse v καταρρέω
kah•tah•reh•oh

collect v παίρνω *peh•rnoh*

color n χρώμα *khroh•mah*

comb n χτένα *khteh•nah*; v
χτενίζω *khteh•nee•zoh*

come έρχομαι *ehr•khoh•meh*

come back v (return) επιστρέφω
eh•pees•treh•foh

commission n (agent fee) προμήθεια proh•_mee_•thee•ah

company n (business) εταιρία eh•teh•_ree_•ah; (companionship) παρέα pah•_reh_•ah

complain παραπονιέμαι pah•rah•poh•nieh•meh

computer υπολογιστής ee•poh•loh•yee•_stees_

concert συναυλία see•nahv•_lee_•ah

concert hall αίθουσα συναυλιών _eh_•thoo•sah see•nahv•_lee_•_ohn_

conditioner (hair) γαλάκτωμα για τα μαλλιά ghah•_lah_•ktoh•mah yah tah mah•_liah_

condom προφυλακτικό proh•fee•lah•ktee•_koh_

conference συνέδριο see•_neh_•THree•oh

confirm επιβεβαιώνω eh•pee•veh•veh•_oh_•noh

constipation δυσκοιλιότητα thees•kee•lee•_oh_•tee•tah

Consulate Προξενείο proh•kseh•_nee_•oh

consult v συμβουλεύομαι seem•voo•_leh_•voh•meh

contact v επικοινωνώ eh•pee•kee•noh•_noh_

contact fluid υγρό για φακούς επαφής eegh•_roh_ yah fah•_koos_ eh•pah•_fees_

contact lens φακός επαφής fah•_kohs_ eh•pah•fees

contagious μεταδοτικός meh•tah•THoh•tee•_kohs_

contain περιέχω peh•ree•_eh_•khoh

contraceptive pill αντισυλληπτικό χάπι ahn•dee•see•lee•ptee•_koh_ khah•pee

cook n (chef) μάγειρας _mah_•yee•rahs; v μαγειρεύω mah•yee•_reh_•voh

---

copper χαλκός khahl•_kohs_

corkscrew τιρμπουσόν teer•boo•_sohn_

corner γωνία ghoh•_nee_•ah

correct v διορθώνω THee•ohr•_thoh_•noh

cosmetics καλλυντικά kah•leen•dee•_kah_

cot [BE] παιδικό κρεβάτι peh•THee•_koh_ kreh•_vah_•tee

cotton βαμβάκι vahm•_vah_•kee

cough n βήχας _vee_•khahs; v βήχω _vee_•khoh

counter ταμείο tah•_mee_•oh

country (nation) χώρα _khoh_•rah

countryside εξοχή eh•ksoh•_khee_

couple n (pair) ζευγάρι zehv•_ghah_•ree

courier n (messenger) κούριερ _koo_•ree•ehr

court house δικαστήριο THee•kahs•_tee_•ree•oh

cramp n κράμπα _krahm_•bah

credit card πιστωτική κάρτα pees•toh•tee•_kee_ _kahr_•tah

crib [cot BE] παιδικό κρεβάτι peh•THee•_koh_ kreh•_vah_•tee

crown n (dental, royal) κορώνα koh•_roh_•nah

cruise n κρουαζιέρα kroo•ahz•_yeh_•rah

crutch n (walking support) δεκανίκι THeh•kah•_nee_•kee

crystal n κρύσταλλο _kree_•stah•loh

cup φλυτζάνι flee•_jah_•nee

cupboard ντουλάπα doo•_lah_•pah

currency νόμισμα _noh_•meez•mah

currency exchange office γραφείο ανταλλαγής συναλλάγματος ghrah•_fee_•oh ahn•dah•lah•_yees_ see•nah•_lahgh_•mah•tohs

customs (tolls) τελωνείο teh•loh•_nee_•oh

customs declaration (tolls)

τελωνειακή δήλωση teh•loh•nee•ah•_kee_ THee•loh•see

cut n (wound) κόψιμο _koh_•psee•moh

cut glass n σκαλιστό γυαλί skah•lees•_toh_ yah•_lee_

cycle helmet κράνος ποδηλάτη _krah_•nohs poh•THee•_lah_•tee

cyclist ποδηλάτης poh•THee•_lah_•tees

Cypriot adj κυπριακός kee•pree•ah•_kohs_; (nationality) Κύπριος _kee_•pree•ohs

Cyprus Κύπρος _kee_•prohs

D

damage n ζημιά zee•_miah_; v καταστρέφω kah•tah•_streh_•foh

dance v χορεύω khoh•_reh_•voh

dangerous επικίνδυνος eh•pee•_keen_•THee•nohs

dark adj (color) σκούρος _skoo_•rohs

dawn n ξημερώματα ksee•meh•_roh_•mah•tah

day trip ημερήσια εκδρομή ee•meh•_ree_•see•ah ehk•THroh•_mee_

deaf κουφός koo•_fohs_

decide αποφασίζω ah•poh•fah•_see_•zoh

deck n κατάστρωμα kah•_tah_•stroh•mah

deck chair σεζ-λονγκ sehz _lohng_

declare δηλώνω THee•_loh_•noh

deduct (money) αφαιρώ ah•feh•_roh_

defrost ξεπαγώνω kseh•pah•_ghoh_•noh

degrees (temperature) βαθμοί vahth•_mee_

delay n καθυστέρηση kah•thee•_steh_•ree•see; v καθυστερώ kah•thee•steh•_roh_

delicious νόστιμος
nohs•tee•mohs

deliver παραδίδω
pah•rah•THee•THoh

dental floss οδοντικό νήμα
oh•THohn•dee•koh nee•mah

dentist οδοντίατρος
oh•THohn•dee•ah•trohs

deodorant αποσμητικό
ah•pohz•mee•tee•koh

department store πολυκατάστημα
poh•lee•kah•tahs•tee•mah

departure (travel) αναχώρηση
ah•nah•khoh•ree•see

departure lounge αίθουσα αναχωρήσεων _eh•thoo•sah ah•nah•khoh•ree•seh•ohn_

depend εξαρτώμαι
eh•ksahr•toh•meh

deposit n (down payment) προκαταβολή _proh•kah•tah•voh•lee_

describe περιγράφω
peh•reegh•rah•foh

designer σχεδιαστής
skheh•THee•ahs•tees

detergent απορρυπαντικό
ah•poh•ree•pahn•dee•koh

develop (photos) εμφανίζω
ehm•fah•nee•zoh

diabetes διαβήτης
THee•ah•vee•tees

diabetic διαβητικός
THee•ah•vee•tee•kohs

diagnosis διάγνωση
THee•ahgh•noh•see

dialing code κωδικός
koh•THee•kohs

diamond n διαμάντι
THiah•mahn•dee

diaper πάνα μωρού _pah•nah moh•roo_

diarrhea διάρροια
THee•ah•ree•ah

dice n ζάρια _zah•riah_

dictionary λεξικό _leh•ksee•koh_

diesel ντήζελ _dee•zehl_

diet n δίαιτα _THee•eh•tah_

difficult δύσκολος
THee•skoh•lohs

dining room τραπεζαρία
trah•peh•zah•ree•ah

dinner βραδινό _vrah•THee•noh_

direct v κατευθύνω
kah•tehf•thee•noh

direction n (instruction) οδηγία
oh•THee•yee•ah

dirty adj βρώμικος
vroh•mee•kohs

disabled άτομο με ειδικές ανάγκες _ah•toh•moh meh ee•_
•nahn THee•kehs ah•gehs

discounted ticket μειωμένο εισιτήριο _mee•oh•meh•noh_
ee•see•tee•ree•oh

dishwashing liquid λίγο υγρό πιάτων _lee•ghoh ee•ghroh_
piah•tohn

district περιφέρεια
peh•ree•feh•ree•ah

disturb ενοχλώ _ee•noh•khloh_

diving equipment καταδυτικός εξοπλισμός _kah•tah•THee•kohs_
eh•ksoh•pleez•mohs

divorced διαζευγμένος
THee•ah•zehv•ghmeh•nohs

dock προκυμαία
proh•kee•meh•ah

doctor γιατρός _yah•trohs_

doll κούκλα _kook•lah_

dollar δολάριο _THoh•lah•ree•oh_

door πόρτα _pohr•tah_

dosage δοσολογία
THoh•soh•loh•yee•ah

double adj διπλός _THee•plohs_

double bed διπλό κρεβάτι
THee•ploh kreh•vah•tee

double room δίκλινο δωμάτιο _THee•klee•noh_
THoh•mah•tee•oh

downtown area κέντρο της πόλης _kehn•droh tees poh•lees_

dozen ντουζίνα _doo•zee•nah_

dress n φόρεμα _foh•reh•mah_

drink n ποτό _poh•toh_; v πίνω
pee•noh

drive v οδηγώ _oh•THee•ghoh_

drugstore φαρμακείο
fahr•mah•kee•oh

dry cleaner καθαριστήριο
kah•thah•rees•tee•ree•oh

dubbed μεταγλωττισμένος _meh•tahgh•oh•tee•zmeh•nohs_

dusty σκονισμένος
skoh•neez•meh•nohs

duty (customs) φόρος
foh•rohs; (obligation) καθήκον
kah•thee•kohn

duty-free goods αφορολόγητα είδη _ah•foh•roh•loh•yee•tah_
ee•THee

duty-free shop κατάστημα αφορολόγητων _kah•tahs•tee•_
mah ah•foh•roh•loh•yee•tohn

E

each κάθε ένα _kah•theh eh•nah_

ear αυτί _ahf•tee_

earache πόνος στο αυτί _poh•nohs_
stoh ahf•tee

early νωρίς _noh•rees_

east ανατολικά
ah•nah•toh•lee•kah

easy adj εύκολος _ehf•koh•lohs_

eat τρώω _troh•oh_

economical οικονομικός
ee•koh•noh•mee•kohs

economy class τουριστική θέση
too•ree•stee•kee theh•see

elastic ελαστικός
eh•lah•stee•kohs

electrical outlet πρίζα _pree•zah_

e-mail ηλεκτρονικό ταχυδρομείο (e-mail) _ee•lehk•troh•nee•koh_
tah•hee•dro•mee•oh
(ee•meh•eel)

embassy πρεσβεία *prehz•vee•ah*

emerald σμαράγδι
zmah•raghTHee

emergency έκτακτη ανάγκη
ehk•tahk•tee ah•nah•gee

emergency exit έξοδος κινδύνου
eh•ksoh•THohs keen•THee•noo

empty *adj* άδειος *ah•THyohs*

end *n* τέλος *teh•lohs;* *v* τελειώνω
teh•lee•oh•noh

engine μηχανή *mee•khah•nee*

England Αγγλία *ahng•lee•ah*

English *adj* αγγλικός
ahng•lee•kohs; **(nationality)**
Άγγλος *ahng•lohs;* **(language)**
αγγλικά *ahng•lee•kah*

enjoy ευχαριστιέμαι
ehf•khah•rees•tieh•meh

enough αρκετά *ahr•keh•tah*

entertainment guide οδηγός
ψυχαγωγίας *oh•THee•ghohs*
psee•khah•ghoh•yee•ahs

entrance fee τιμή εισόδου
tee•mee ee•soh•THoo

epileptic επιληπτικός
eh•pee•leep•tee•kohs

error λάθος *lah•thohs*

escalator κυλιόμενες σκάλες *kee•lee•oh•meh•nehs skah•lehs*

essential απαραίτητος
ah•pah•reh•tee•tohs

e-ticket ηλεκτρονικό εισιτήριο
ee•leh•ktroh•nee•koh
ee•see•tee•ree•oh

European Union Ευρωπαϊκή
Ένωση *ehv•roh•pah•ee•kee*
eh•noh•see

euro ευρώ *ehv•roh*

evening βράδυ *vrah•THee*

examination (medical) ιατρική
εξέταση *ee•ah•tree•kee*
eh•kseh•tah•see

example παράδειγμα
pah•rah•THeegh•mah

excess baggage υπέρβαρο
ee•pehr•vah•roh

exchange *v (money)* αλλάζω
ah•lah•zoh

exchange rate τιμή
συναλλάγματος *tee•mee*
see•nah•lahgh•mah•tohs

excursion εκδρομή
ehk•THroh•mee

exhibition έκθεση *ehk•theh•see*

exit *n* έξοδος *eh•ksoh•THohs*

expensive ακριβός *ahk•ree•vohs*

expiration date ημερομηνία
λήξεως *ee•meh•roh•*
mee•nee•ah lee•kseh•ohs

exposure (photos) στάση
stah•see

express (mail) εξπρές
ehk•sprehs

extension (number) εσωτερική
γραμμή *eh•soh•theh•ree•kee*
ghrah•mee

extra (additional) άλλο ένα
ah•loh eh•nah

eye *n* μάτι *mah•tee*

F

fabric (cloth) ύφασμα
ee•fahs•mah

face *n* πρόσωπο *proh•soh•poh*

facial καθαρισμός προσώπου
kah•thah•reez•mohs
proh•soh•poo

facility εξυπηρέτηση
eh•ksee•pee•reh•tee•see

faint λιποθυμώ
lee•poh•thee•moh

fall *v* πέφτω *pehf•toh*

family οικογένεια
ee•koh•yeh•nee•ah

famous διάσημος
THee•ah•see•mohs

fan *n (air)* ανεμιστήρας
ah•neh•mees•tee•rahs

far *adv* μακριά *mahk•ree•ah*

fare εισιτήριο *ee•see•tee•ree•oh*

farm *n* φάρμα *fahr•mah*

fast *adv* γρήγορα *ghree•ghoh•rah*

fat *adj (person)* παχύς *pah•khees*

faucet βρύση *vree•see*

fault λάθος *lah•thohs*

favorite αγαπημένος
ah•ghah•pee•meh•nohs

fax facility υπηρεσία φαξ
ee•pee•reh•see•ah fahks

feed *v* ταΐζω *tah•ee•zoh*

female θηλυκός *thee•lee•kohs*

fence *n* φράχτης *frahkh•tees*

ferry φέρυ-μπωτ *feh•ree•boht*

festival φεστιβάλ *fehs•tee•vahl*

fever πυρετός *pee•reh•tohs*

fiancé αρραβωνιαστικός
ah•rah•voh•niahs•tee•kohs

fiancée αρραβωνιαστικιά
ah•rah•voh•niahs•tee•kiah

filling (dental) σφράγισμα
sfrah•yeez•mah

film *n (camera)* φιλμ *feelm*

filter *n* φίλτρο *feel•troh*

fine *adv* καλά *kah•lah;* *n*
πρόστιμο *prohs•tee•mah*

finger *n* δάχτυλο *THakh•tee•loh*

fire *n* φωτιά *foh•tiah*

fire brigade [BE] πυροσβεστική
pee•rohz•vehs•tee•kee

fire escape έξοδος
κινδύνου *eh•ksoh•THohs*
keen•THee•noo

fire extinguisher
πυροσβεστήρας
pee•rohz•vehs•tee•rahs

first class πρώτη θέση *proh•tee*
theh•see

first-aid kit κουτί πρώτων
βοηθειών *koo•tee proh•tohn*
voh•ee•thee•ohn

fishing ψάρεμα *psah•reh•mah*

flag *n* σημαία *see•meh•ah*

flashlight φακός *fah•kohs*

flat *adj* επίπεδος *eh•pee•*
peh•Thohs; *n* διαμέρισμα
THee•ah•mehr•eez•mah

flea ψύλλος *psee•lohs*

flight πτήση *ptee•see*

flight number αριθμός πτήσεως
ah•reeth•<u>mohs</u> ptee•seh•ohs

flip-flops σαγιονάρες
sah•yoh•<u>nah</u>•rehs

flood n πλημμύρα *plee•<u>mee</u>•rah*

florist ανθοπωλείο
ahn•thoh•poh•<u>lee</u>•oh

flower n λουλούδι *loo•<u>loo</u>•THee*

flu γρίππη *<u>ghree</u>•pee*

flush τραβώ το καζανάκι
trah•<u>voh</u> toh kah•zah•<u>nah</u>•kee

fly n μύγα *mee•ghah;* v πετάω
peh•<u>tah</u>•oh

follow v ακολουθώ
ah•koh•loo•<u>thoh</u>

foot πόδι *poh•THee*

football [BE] ποδόσφαιρο
poh•<u>THohs</u>•feh•roh

footpath μονοπάτι
moh•noh•<u>pah</u>•tee

forecast n πρόβλεψη
<u>prohv</u>•leh•psee

foreign ξένος *kseh•nohs*

foreign currency ξένο
συνάλλαγμα *kseh•noh
see•<u>nah</u>•lahgh•mah*

forest n δάσος *THah•sohs*

forget ξεχνώ *ksehkh•<u>noh</u>*

form n έντυπο *ehn•<u>dee</u>•poh*

fortunately ευτυχώς
ehf•tee•<u>khohs</u>

forward προωθώ *proh•oh•<u>thoh</u>*

fountain συντριβάνι
seen•dree•<u>vah</u>•nee

free adj (available) ελεύθερος
eh•<u>lehf</u>•theh•rohs

freezer κατάψυξη
kah•<u>tah</u>•psee•ksee

frequent adj συχνός *seekh•<u>nohs</u>*

fresh adj φρέσκος *frehs•kohs*

friend n φίλος *fee•lohs*

frightened φοβισμένος
foh•veez•<u>meh</u>•nohs

from από *ah•<u>poh</u>*

front n προκυμαία
proh•kee•<u>meh</u>•ah

full adj γεμάτος *yeh•<u>mah</u>•tohs*

furniture έπιπλα *eh•<u>peep</u>•lah*

fuse n ασφάλεια *ahs•<u>fah</u>•lee•ah*

G

gambling τζόγος *joh•ghohs*

game (toy) παιχνίδι
pehkh•<u>nee</u>•THee

garage γκαράζ *gah•<u>rahz</u>*

garden n κήπος *kee•pohs*

gas βενζίνη *vehn•<u>zee</u>•nee*

gas station βενζινάδικο
vehn•zee•<u>nah</u>•THee•koh

gastritis γαστρίτιδα
ghahs•<u>tree</u>•tee•THah

gate (airport) έξοδος
eh•ksohf•THohs

genuine αυθεντικός
ahf•thehn•dee•<u>kohs</u>

get off (transport) κατεβαίνω
kah•teh•<u>veh</u>•noh

get out (of vehicle) βγαίνω
vyeh•noh

gift δώρο *THoh•roh*

gift store κατάστημα με είδη
δώρων *kah•<u>tahs</u>•tee•mah meh
ee•THee THoh•rohn*

girl κορίτσι *koh•<u>ree</u>•tsee*

girlfriend φιλη *fee•lee*

give δίνω *THee•noh*

glass (container) ποτήρι
poh•<u>tee</u>•ree

glasses (optical) γυαλιά
yah•<u>liah</u>

glove n γάντι *ghahn•dee*

go πηγαίνω *pee•<u>yeh</u>•noh*

gold n χρυσός *khree•<u>sohs</u>*

golf γκόλφ *gohlf*

golf course γήπεδο γκολφ
<u>yee</u>•peh•THoh gohlf

good adj καλός *kah•lohs*

grass γρασίδι *ghrah•<u>see</u>•THee*

gratuity φιλοδώρημα
fee•loh•<u>THoh</u>•ree•mah

greasy (hair, skin) λιπαρός
lee•pah•<u>rohs</u>

Greece Ελλάδα *eh•<u>lah</u>•THah*

Greek adj ελληνικός
eh•lee•nee•<u>kohs</u>; (nationality) Έλληνας *eh•lee•nahs*

greengrocer [BE] οπωροπωλείο
oh•poh•roh•poh•<u>lee</u>•oh

ground (earth) έδαφος
eh•THah•fohs

group n γκρουπ *groop*

guarantee n εγγύηση
eh•<u>gee</u>•ee•see; see v εγγυώμαι
eh•gee•<u>oh</u>•meh

guide book τουριστικός
οδηγός *too•ree•stee•<u>kohs</u>
oh•THee•<u>ghohs</u>*

guided tour ξενάγηση
kseh•<u>nah</u>•yee•see

guitar κιθάρα *kee•<u>thah</u>•rah*

gynecologist γυναικολόγος
yee•neh•koh•<u>loh</u>•ghohs

H

hair μαλλιά *mah•<u>liah</u>*

hairbrush βούρτσα *<u>voor</u>•tsah*

hair dresser κομμωτήριο
koh•moh•<u>tee</u>•ree•oh

hair dryer σεσουάρ
seh•soo•<u>ahr</u>

half μισός *mee•<u>sohs</u>*

hammer σφυρί *sfee•<u>ree</u>*

hand n χέρι *kheh•ree*

hand luggage αποσκευές χειρός
ah•pohs•keh•<u>vehs</u> khee•<u>rohs</u>

handbag τσάντα *tsah•dah*

handicraft λαϊκή τέχνη
lah•ee•<u>kee</u> tehkh•nee

handicapped-accessible toilet
προσβάσιμη τουαλέτα για
ανάπηρους *prohs•<u>vah</u>•see•mee
too•ah•<u>leh</u>•tah yah
ah•<u>nah</u>•pee•rohs*

handkerchief χαρτομάντηλο
khahr•toh•<u>mahn</u>•dee•loh

handle n πόμολο *poh•moh•loh*

hanger κρεμάστρα
kreh•<u>mahs</u>•trah

harbor n λιμάνι lee•_mah_•nee

hat καπέλο kah•_peh_•loh

have (possession) έχω eh•khoh

have to (obligation) οφείλω
oh•_fee_•loh

head n κεφάλι keh•_fah_•lee

headache πονοκέφαλος
poh•noh•_keh_•fah•lohs

health food store κατάστημα
με υγιεινές τροφές
kah•_tahs_•tee•mah meh
ee•yee•ee•_nehs_ troh•_fehs_

health insurance ασφάλεια
υγείας ahs•_fah_•lee•ah
ee•_yee_•ahs

hearing aid ακουστικό
βαρυκοΐας ah•koo•stee•_koh_
vah•ree•_ko_•ee•ahs

heart n καρδιά kahr•_THee_•ah

heart attack καρδιακό
έμφραγμα kahr•_THee_•ah•_koh_
ehm•frahgh•mah

heat wave καύσωνας
kahf•soh•nahs

heater (water) θερμοσίφωνας
thehr•moh•_see_•foh•nahs

heating θέρμανση
thehr•mahn•see

heavy βαρύς vah•_rees_

height ύψος _ee_•psohs

helicopter ελικόπτερο
eh•lee•_kohp_•teh•roh

help n βοήθεια voh•_ee_•thee•ah;
v βοηθώ voh•ee•_thoh_

here εδώ eh•_THoh_

highway εθνική οδός
ehth•nee•_kee_ oh•_THohs_

hike v κάνω πεζοπορία _kah_•noh
peh•zoh•poh•_ree_•ah

hill λόφος _loh_•fohs

hire [BE] v νοικιάζω nee•_kiah_•zoh

history ιστορία ee•stoh•_ree_•ah

hitchhiking οτοστόπ
oh•toh•_stohp_

hobby (pastime) χόμπυ
khoh•bee

hold on περιμένω
peh•ree•_meh_•noh

hole (in clothes) τρύπα _tree_•pah

holiday [BE] διακοπές
THee•ah•koh•_pehs_

honeymoon μήνας του μέλιτος
mee•nahs too _meh_•lee•tohs

horse track ιπποδρόμιο
ee•poh•_THroh_•mee•oh

hospital νοσοκομείο
noh•soh•koh•_mee_•oh

hot (weather) ζεστός zehs•_tohs_

hot spring θερμή πηγή
thehr•_mee_ pee•_yee_

hotel ξενοδοχείο
kseh•noh•THoh•_khee_•oh

household articles είδη
οικιακής χρήσεως _ee_•THee
ee•kee•ah•_kees_ khree•_seh_•ohs

husband σύζυγος _see_•zee•ghohs

I

ice n πάγος _pah_•ghohs

identification ταυτότητα
tahf•_toh_•tee•tah

illegal παράνομος
pah•_rah_•noh•mohs

illness αρρώστεια
ahr•_ohs_•tee•ah

imitation απομίμηση
ah•poh•_mee_•mee•see

immediately αμέσως
ah•_meh_•sohs

impressive εντυπωσιακός
ehn•dee•poh•see•ah•_kohs_

included συμπεριλαμβάνεται
seem•beh•ree•lahm•_vah_•
neh•teh

indigestion δυσπεψία
THehs•peh•_psee_•ah

indoor εσωτερικός
eh•soh•teh•ree•_kohs_

indoor pool εσωτερική
πισίνα eh•soh•teh•ree•_kee_
pee•_see_•nah

inexpensive φτηνός ftee•_nohs_

infected μολυσμένος
moh•leez•_meh_•nohs

inflammation φλεγμονή
flegh•moh•_nee_

information πληροφορίες
plee•roh•foh•_ree_•ehs

information office γραφείο
πληροφοριών ghrah•_fee_•oh
plee•roh•foh•ree•_ohn_

injection ένεση _eh_•neh•see

injured τραυματισμένος
trahv•mah•teez•_meh_•nohs

innocent αθώος ah•_thoh_•ohs

insect bite τσίμπημα από έντομο
tseem•bee•mah ah•_poh_
ehn•doh•moh

insect repellent
εντομοαπωθητικό ehn•doh•
moh•ah•poh•thee•tee•_koh_

inside μέσα _meh_•sah

insist επιμένω eh•pee•_meh_•noh

insomnia αϋπνία
ah•eep•_nee_•ah

instruction οδηγία
oh•THee•_yee_•ah

insulin ινσουλίνη
een•soo•_lee_•nee

insurance ασφάλεια
ahs•_fah_•lee•ah

insurance certificate
πιστοποιητικό ασφάλειας
pees•toh•pee•ee•tee•_koh_
ahs•_fah_•lee•ahs

insurance claim ασφάλεια
αποζημίωση ahs•_fah_•lee•ah
ah•poh•zee•_mee_•oh•sees

**insurance com-
pany** ασφαλιστική εταιρία
ahs•fah•lees•tee•_kee_
eh•teh•ree•ah

interest rate επιτόκιο
eh•pee•_toh_•kee•oh

interesting ενδιαφέρων
ehn•THee•ah•_feh_•rohn

international διεθνής
THee•eth•_nees_

International Student Card διεθνής φοιτητική κάρτα *THee•ehth•nees fee•tee•tee•kee kahr•tah*

internet ίντερνετ *ee•nteh•rnet*

internet cafe ίντερνετ καφέ *ee•nteh•rnet kah•feh*

interpreter διερμηνέας *THee•ehr•mee•neh•ahs*

interval διάλειμμα *THee•ah•lee•mah*

introduce συστήνω *see•stee•noh*

introductions συστάσεις *see•stah•sees*

invitation πρόσκληση *prohs•klee•see*

invite v προσκαλώ *prohs•kah•loh*

iodine ιώδειο *ee•oh•THee•oh*

iron n σίδερο *see•THeh•roh; v* σιδερώνω *see•THeh•roh•noh*

itemized bill αναλυτικός λογαριασμός *ah•nah•lee•tee•kohs loh•ghahr•yahz•mohs*

J

jacket σακάκι *sah•kah•kee*

jammed σφηνωμένος *sfee•noh•meh•nohs*

jar n βάζο *vah•zoh*

jaw σαγόνι *sah•ghoh•nee*

jeans μπλου-τζην *bloo•jeen*

jellyfish μέδουσα *meh•THoo•sah*

jet-ski τζετ-σκι *jeht•skee*

jeweler κοσμηματοπωλείο *kohz•mee•mah•toh•poh•lee•oh*

job δουλειά *THoo•liah*

jogging τζόγκινγκ *joh•geeng*

joke n ανέκδοτο *ah•nehk•THoh•toh*

journey ταξίδι *tah•ksee•THee*

junction *(intersection)* κόμβος *kohm•vohs*

K

keep v κρατώ *krah•toh*

key n κλειδί *klee•THee*

key card κάρτα-κλειδί *kahr•tah•klee•dee*

key ring μπρελόκ *breh•lohk*

kidney νεφρό *nehf•roh*

kind είδος *ee•THohs*

king βασιλιάς *vah•see•liahs*

kiosk περίπτερο *peh•ree•pteh•roh*

kiss n φιλί *fee•lee; v* φιλώ *fee•loh*

kitchen χαρτί κουζίνας *khah•rtee koo•zee•nahs*

knapsack σάκκος *sah•kohs*

knee γόνατο *ghoh•nah•toh*

knife μαχαίρι *mah•kheh•ree*

know γνωρίζω *ghnoh•ree•zoh*

L

label n ετικέτα *eh•tee•keh•tah*

ladder σκάλα *skah•lah*

lake λίμνη *leem•nee*

lamp λάμπα *lahm•bah*

land n γη *ghee; v* προσγειώνομαι *prohz•yee•oh•noh•meh*

language course μάθημα ξένης γλώσσας *mah•thee•mah kseh•nees ghloh•sahs*

large *adj* μεγάλος *meh•ghah•lohs*

last τελευταίος *teh•lehf•teh•ohs*

late *adv* αργά *ahr•ghah*

laugh v γελώ *yeh•loh*

laundry facility πλυντήριο *pleen•dee•ree•oh*

lavatory μπάνιο *bah•nioh*

lawyer δικηγόρος *THee•kee•ghoh•rohs*

laxative καθαρτικό *kah•thahr•tee•koh*

learn μαθαίνω *mah•theh•noh*

leave v *(depart)* φεύγω *fehv•ghoh; (let go)* αφήνω *ah•fee•noh*

left *adj* αριστερός *ah•rees•teh•rohs; adv* αριστερά *ah•rees•teh•rah*

leg πόδι *poh•THee*

legal νόμιμος *noh•mee•mohs*

lend δανείζω *THah•nee•zoh*

length μήκος *mee•kohs*

lens φακός *fah•kohs*

lens cap κάλυμμα φακού *kah•lee•mah fah•koo*

less λιγότερο *lee•ghoh•teh•roh*

letter γράμμα *grah•mah*

level *(even)* επίπεδο *eh•pee•peh•THoh*

library βιβλιοθήκη *veev•lee•oh•thee•kee*

lie down ξαπλώνω *ksah•ploh•noh*

life boat ναυαγοσωστική λέμβος *nah•vah•ghoh•sohs•tee•kee lehm•vohs*

lifeguard ναυαγοσώστης *nah•vah•ghoh•sohs•tees*

life jacket σωσίβιο *soh•see•vee•oh*

lift [BE] n *(elevator)* ασανσέρ *ah•sahn•sehr*

lift pass άδεια σκι *ah•THee•ah skee*

light *adj (color)* ανοιχτός *ah•neekh•tohs; n (electric)* φως *fohs*

light bulb λάμπα *lahm•bah*

lighter *adj* ανοιχτότερος *ah•neekh•toh•teh•rohs; n* αναπτήρας *ah•nahp•tee•rahs*

lighthouse φάρος *fah•rohs*

lights (car) φώτα *foh•tah*

line n *(subway)* γραμμή *grah•mee*

lips χείλη *khee•lee*

lipstick κραγιόν *krah•yohn*

liter λίτρο *lee•troh*

little μικρός *meek•rohs*

liver συκώτι *see•koh•tee*

living room σαλόνι *sah•loh•nee*

local τοπικός *toh•pee•kohs*

location (space) θέση *theh•see*

lock n *(door)* κλειδαριά *klee•THahr•yah; (river, canal)* φράγμα *frahgh•mah; v* κλειδώνω *klee•THoh•noh*

long adj μακρύς mak•_rees_
long-distance bus
υπεραστικό λεωφορείο
ee•peh•rahs•tee•_koh_
leh•oh•foh•_ree_•oh
long-distance call
υπεραστικό τηλεφώνημα
ee•peh•rahs•tee•_koh_
tee•leh•_foh_•nee•mah
long-sighted [BE] πρεσβύωπας
prehz•_vee_•oh•pahs
look v κοιτάω kee•_tah_•oh
look for ψάχνω psahkh•noh
loose (fitting) φαρδύς
fahr•_THees_
loss n απώλεια ah•_poh_•lee•ah
lotion λοσιόν loh•_siohn_
loud adj δυνατός THee•nah•_tohs_
love v αγαπώ ah•ghah•_poh_
lower adj (berth) κάτω _kah_•toh
lubricant λιπαντικό
lee•pahn•dee•_koh_
luck τύχη _tee_•khee
luggage αποσκευές
ah•pohs•keh•_vehs_
luggage cart καροτσάκι
αποσκευών kah•roh•_tsah_•kee
ah•pohs•keh•_vohn_
luggage locker θυρίδα
thee•_ree_•THah
lukewarm χλιαρός khlee•ah•_rohs_
lump n σβώλος _svoh_•lohs;
(medical) εξόγκωμα
eh•_ksoh_•goh•mah
lunch n μεσημεριανό
meh•see•mehr•yah•_noh_
lung πνεύμονας _pnehv_•moh•nahs
luxury πολυτέλεια
poh•lee•_teh_•lee•ah

M

magazine περιοδικό
peh•ree•oh•THee•_koh_
magnificent μεγαλοπρεπής
meh•ghah•lohp•reh•_pees_
mailbox ταχυδρομικό κουτί tah•

mail n αλληλογραφία
ah•lee•lohgh•rah•_fee_•ah
main κύριος _kee_•ree•ohs
make-up μακιγιάζ mah•kee•_yahz_
man (male) άνδρας _ahn_•THrahs
manager διευθυντής
THee•ehf•theen•_dees_
manicure μανικιούρ
mah•nee•_kioor_
manual (car) χειροκίνητος
khee•roh•_kee_•nee•tohs
map n χάρτης _khahr_•tees
market n αγορά ah•ghoh•_rah_
married παντρεμένος
pahn•dreh•_meh_•nohs
mask n (diving) μάσκα _mahs_•kah
mass n (church) λειτουργία
lee•toor•_yee_•ah
massage n μασάζ mah•_sahz_
match n (sport) αγώνας
ah•_ghoh_•nahs; (fire starter)
σπίρτο _speer_•toh
maybe ίσως _ee_•sohs
meal γεύμα _yehv_•mah
mean v σημαίνω see•_meh_•noh
measure v μετρώ meht•_roh_
measurement μέτρηση
meh•tree•see
medication φάρμακα
fahr•mah•kah
meet συναντώ see•nahn•_doh_
memorial μνημείο mnee•_mee_•oh
mend διορθώνω
THee•ohr•_thoh_•noh
menstrual cramp πόνος
περιόδου _poh_•nohs
peh•ree•_oh_•THoo
mention αναφέρω
ah•nah•_feh_•roh
message n μήνυμα
mee•nee•mah
metal n μέταλλο _meh_•tah•loh
microwave (oven) φούρνος
μικροκυμάτων _foor_•nohs
mee•kroh•kee•_mah_•tohn

migraine ημικρανία
ee•mee•krah•_nee_•ah
mileage χιλιόμετρα
khee•_lioh_•meh•trah
mini-bar μίνι-μπαρ
mee•nee•bahr
minimart παντοπωλείο
pahn•doh•poh•_lee_•oh
minimum ελάχιστος
eh•_lah_•khees•tohs
minute n (time) λεπτό lehp•_toh_
mirror n καθρέφτης
kah•_threhf_•tees
mistake λάθος _lah_•thohs
misunderstanding παρεξήγηση
pah•reh•_ksee_•yee•see
mobile phone [BE] κινητό
kee•nee•_toh_
modern μοντέρνος
moh•_deh_•rnohs
moisturizer (cream) ενυδατική
κρέμα eh•nee•THah•tee•_kee_
kreh•mah
money χρήματα _khree_•mah•tah
money order
ταχυδρομική επιταγή
tah•kheeTH•roh•mee•_kee_
eh•pee•tah•_yee_
money-belt ζώνη για χρήματα
zoh•nee yah _khree_•mah•tah
monument μνημείο
mnee•_mee_•oh
moped μοτοποδήλατο
moh•toh•poh•_THee_•lah•toh
more παραπάνω
pah•rah•_pah_•noh
morning πρωί proh•_ee_
mosquito κουνούπι koo•_noo_•pee
mosquito bite τσίμπημα
κουνουπιού _tseem_•bee•mah
koo•noo•_piooh_
motorboat εξωλέμβιο
eh•ksoh•_lehm_•vee•oh
motorway [BE] εθνική οδός
ehth•nee•_kee_ oh•_THohs_
mountain βουνό voo•_noh_

moustache μουστάκι
moos•_tah_•kee

mouth n στόμα _stoh_•mah

move v (room) μετακομίζω
meh•tah•koh•_mee_•zoh

movie ταινία teh•_nee_•ah

movie theater κινηματογράφος
kee•nee•mah•tohgh•_rah_•fohs

much πολύ poh•_lee_

muscle n μυς mees

museum μουσείο moo•_see_•oh

music μουσική moo•see•_kee_

musician μουσικός
moo•see•_kohs_

must v πρέπει _preh_•pee

N

nail salon σαλόνι νυχιών
sah•_loh_•nee nee•_khiohn_

name n όνομα _oh_•noh•mah

napkin πετσέτα peh•_tseh_•tah

nappy [BE] πάνα μωρού _pah_•nah
moh•_roo_

narrow στενός steh•_nohs_

national εθνικός eth•nee•_kohs_

nationality υπηκοότητα
ee•pee•koh•_oh_•tee•tah

nature φύση _fee_•see

nature reserve εθνικός δρυμός
eth•nee•_kohs_ THree•_mohs_

nature trail μονοπάτι
moh•noh•_pah_•tee

nausea ναυτία naht•_tee_•ah

near adv κοντά koh•_dah_

nearby εδώ κοντά eh•_THoh_
kohn•_dah_

necessary απαραίτητος
ah•pah•_reh_•tee•tohs

necklace κολλιέ koh•_lieh_

need v χρειάζομαι
khree•_ah_•zoh•meh

neighbor n γείτονας
yee•toh•nahs

nerve νεύρο _nehv_•roh

never ποτέ poh•_teh_

new καινούργιος keh•_noor_•yohs

newspaper εφημερίδα
eh•fee•meh•_ree_•THah

newsstand περίπτερο
peh•_ree_•pteh•roh

next επόμενος eh•_poh_•meh•nohs

next to δίπλα THeep•lah

night νύχτα neekh•tah

night club νυχτερινό κέντρο
neekh•teh•ree•_noh kehn_•droh

noisy θορυβώδης
thoh•ree•_voh_•THees

none adj κανένας kah•_neh_•nahs

non-smoking μη καπνίζοντες
meh kap•_nee_•zohn•dehs

north βόρεια _voh_•ree•ah

nose n μύτη _mee_•tee

nudist beach παραλία
γυμνιστών pah•rah•_lee_•ah
yeem•nees•_tohn_

nurse n νοσοκόμα
noh•soh•_koh_•mah

O

occupied κατειλημένος
kah•tee•lee•_meh_•nohs

office γραφείο ghrah•_fee_•oh

old adj (thing) παλιός pah•_liohs_;
(person) γέρικος _yeh_•ree•kohs

old town παλιά πόλη pah•_liah_
poh•lee

old-fashioned ντεμοντέ
deh•mohn•_deh_

once μια φορά miah foh•_rah_

one-way ticket απλό εισιτήριο
ahp•_loh_ ee•see•_tee_•ree•oh

open adj ανοιχτός ah•neekh•_tohs_;
v ανοίγω ah•_nee_•ghoh

opening hours ώρες λειτουργίας
_oh_•rehs lee•toor•_yee_•ahs

opera όπερα _oh_•peh•rah

opposite απέναντι
ah•_peh_•nahn•dee

optician οφθαλμίατρος
ohf•thahl•_mee_•ah•trohs

orchestra ορχήστρα
ohr•_khees_•trah

order v παραγγέλνω
pah•rah•_gehl_•noh

organized οργανωμένος
ohr•ghah•_noh_•_meh_•nohs

others άλλα _ah_•lah

out adv έξω _eh_•ksoh

outdoor εξωτερικός
eh•ksoh•teh•ree•_kohs_

outside adj έξω _eh_•ksoh

oval οβάλ oh•_vahl_

oven φούρνος _foor_•nohs

over there εκεί eh•_kee_

overnight (package) ένα βράδυ
eh•_nah_ vrah•THee

owe χρωστώ khroh•_stoh_

owner κάτοχος _kah_•toh•khohs

P

pacifier πιπίλα pee•_pee_•lah

pack v (baggage) φτιάχνω τις
βαλίτσες ftee•_ahkh_•noh tees
vah•_lee_•tsehs

paddling pool [BE] ρηχή πισίνα
ree•_khee_ pee•_see_•nah

padlock λουκέτο loo•_keh_•toh

pain n πόνος poh•nohs

painkiller παυσίπονο
pahf•_see_•poh•noh

paint v ζωγραφίζω
zohgh•rah•_fee_•zoh

pair ζευγάρι zehv•_ghah_•ree

pajamas πυτζάμες pee•_jah_•mehs

palace ανάκτορα
ah•_nahk_•toh•rah

panorama πανόραμα
pah•_noh_•rah•mah

pants παντελόνι
pahn•deh•_loh_•nee

paper χαρτί khar•_tee_

paralysis παραλυσία
pah•rah•lee•_see_•ah

parcel πακέτο pah•_keh_•toh

parents γονείς ghoh•_nees_

park n πάρκο _pahr_•koh

parking lot χώρος στάθμευσης
khoh•rohs stahth•_mehf_•sees

parking meter παρκόμετρο
pahr•koh•meht•roh

party n (social gathering) πάρτυ
pah•rtee

pass v περνώ pehr•noh

passenger επιβάτης
eh•pee•vah•tees

passport διαβατήριο
THiah•vah•tee•ree•oh

pastry store ζαχαροπλαστείο
zah•khah•rohp•lahs•tee•oh

path n μονοπάτι moh•noh•pah•tee

pay v πληρώνω plee•roh•noh

payment πληρωμή plee•roh•mee

peak n κορυφή koh•ree•fee

pearl μαργαριτάρι
mahr•ghah•ree•tah•ree

pebbly (beach) με χαλίκια meh
khah•lee•kiah

pedestrian crossing διάβαση
πεζών THee•ah•vah•see
peh•zohn

pedestrian zone πεζόδρομος
peh•zohTH•roh•mohs

pen n στυλό stee•loh

per την teen

perhaps ίσως ee•sohs

period (menstrual) περίοδος
peh•ree•oh•THohs; (time)
χρονική περίοδος khroh•
nee•kee peh•ree•oh•Thohs

permit n άδεια ah•THee•ah

petrol [BE] βενζίνη
vehn•zee•nee

pewter κασσίτερος
kah•see•teh•rohs

phone n τηλέφωνο
tee•leh•foh•noh

phone call τηλεφώνημα
tee•leh•foh•nee•mah

phone card τηλεκάρτα
tee•leh•kahr•tah

photo v φωτογραφία
foh•tohgh•rah•fee•ah

photocopier φωτοτυπικό
foh•toh•tee•pee•koh

phrase n φράση frah•see

pick up v παίρνω pehr•noh

picnic area περιοχή για
πικνίκ peh•ree•oh•khee yah
peek•neek

piece τεμάχιο teh•mah•khee•oh

pillow μαξιλάρι
mah•ksee•lah•ree

pillow case μαξιλαροθήκη
mah•ksee•lah•roh•thee•kee

pipe (smoking) πίπα pee•pah

piste [BE] μονοπάτι
moh•noh•pah•tee

pizzeria πιτσαρία
pee•tsah•ree•ah

plan n σχέδιο skheh•THee•oh

plane n αεροπλάνο
ah•eh•rohp•lah•noh

plant n φυτό fee•toh

plastic wrap διαφανή
μεμβράνη THee•ah•fah•nee
mehm•vrah•nee

platform αποβάθρα
ah•poh•vahth•rah

platinum πλατίνα plah•tee•nah

play v (games) παίζω peh•zoh;
(music) παίζω peh•zoh

playground παιδική χαρά
peh•THee•kee khah•rah

pleasant ευχάριστος
ehf•khah•ree•tohs

plug n πρίζα pree•zah

point n σημείο see•mee•oh; v
δείχνω THeekh•noh

poison n δηλητήριο
THee•lee•tee•ree•oh

poisonous δηλητηριώδης
THee•lee•tee•ree•oh•THees

police n αστυνομία
ah•stee•noh•mee•ah

police station αστυνομικό
τμήμα ah•stee•noh•mee•koh
tmee•mah

pond n λιμνούλα leem•noo•lah

popular δημοφιλής
THee•moh•fee•lees

porter αχθοφόρος
ahkh•thoh•foh•rohs

portion n μερίδα meh•ree•THah

possible πιθανός pee•thah•nohs

postbox [BE] ταχυδρομικό κουτί
tah•kheeTH•roh•mee•koh
koo•tee

post card καρτποστάλ
kahrt•pohs•stahl

post office ταχυδρομείο
tah•kheeTH•roh•mee•oh

pottery αγγειοπλαστική
ahn•gee•ohp•lahs•tee•kee

pound (sterling) λίρα lee•rah

pregnant έγκυος eh•gee•ohs

prescribe συνταγογραφώ
seen•dah•ghoh•ghrah•foh

prescription συνταγή γιατρού
seen•dah•yee yiaht•roo

present δώρο THoh•roh

press v σιδερώνω
see•THeh•roh•noh

pretty adj όμορφος
oh•mohr•fohs

prison n φυλακή fee•lah•kee

private bathroom ιδιωτικό
μπάνιο ee•THee•oh•tee•koh
bah•nioh

problem πρόβλημα
prohv•lee•mah

program n πρόγραμμα
prohgh•rah•mah

program of events πρόγραμμα
θεαμάτων proh•ghrah•mah
theh•ah•mah•tohn

prohibited απαγορευμένος
ah•pah•ghoh•rehv•meh•nohs

pronounce προφέρω
proh•feh•roh

public δημόσιος
THee•moh•see•ohs

public holiday αργία
ahr•yee•ah

pump n τρόμπα troh•mbah

purpose σκοπός skoh•pohs

put v βάζω vah•zoh

Q

quality ποιότητα *pee•oh•tee•tah*

quantity ποσότητα *poh•soh•tee•tah*

quarantine *n* καραντίνα *kah•rahn•dee•nah*

quarter (quantity) ένα τέταρτο *eh•nah teh•tah•rtoh*

quay αποβάθρα *ah•poh•vath•rah*

question *n* ερώτηση *eh•roh•tee•see*

queue [BE] *v* περιμένω στην ουρά *peh•ree•meh•noh steen oo•rah*

quick γρήγορος *ghree•ghoh•rohs*

quiet *adj* ήσυχος *ee•see•khohs*

R

racket (tennis, squash) ρακέτα *rah•keh•tah*

radio *n* ραδιόφωνο *rah•THee•oh•foh•noh*

railway station [BE] σιδηροδρομικός σταθμός *see•THee•rohTH•roh•mee•kohs stahth•mohs*

rain *n* βροχή *vroh•khee*; *v* βρέχει *vreh•khee*

raincoat αδιάβροχο *ah•THee•ahv•roh•khoh*

rapids ρεύμα ποταμού *rehv•mah poh•tah•moo*

rare (unusual) σπάνιος *spah•nee•ohs*

rash *n* εξάνθημα *eh•ksahn•thee•mah*

ravine ρεματιά *reh•mah•tiah*

razor ξυραφάκι *ksee•rah•fah•kee*

razor blade ξυραφάκι *ksee•rah•fah•kee*

ready *adj* έτοιμος *eh•tee•mohs*

real (genuine) γνήσιος *ghee•see•ohs*; **(true)** αληθινός *ah•lee•thee•nohs*

receipt απόδειξη *ah•poh•THee•ksee*

reception (hotel) ρεσεψιόν *reh•seh•psiohn*

recommend συστήνω *sees•tee•noh*

reduction έκπτωση *ehk•ptoh•see*

refund *n* επιστροφή χρημάτων *eh•pees•troh•fee khree•mah•tohn*

region περιοχή *peh•ree•oh•khee*

registration number αριθμός κυκλοφορίας *ah•reeth•mohs kee•kloh•foh•ree•ahs*

religion θρησκεία *three•skee•ah*

remember θυμάμαι *thee•mah•meh*

rent *n* νοικιάζω *nee•kiah•zoh*

repair *n* επισκευή *eh•pee•skeh•vee*; *v* επισκευάζω *eh•pee•skeh•vah•zoh*

repeat *v* επαναλαμβάνω *eh•pah•nah•lahm•vah•noh*

replacement part ανταλλακτικό *ahn•dah•lahk•tee•koh*

report *v* αναφέρω *ah•nah•feh•roh*

restaurant εστιατόριο *ehs•tee•ah•toh•ree•oh*

restroom τουαλέτα *too•ah•leh•tah*

retired συνταξιούχος *seen•dah•ksee•oo•khohs*

return ticket [BE] εισιτήριο με επιστροφή *ee•see•tee•ree•oh meh eh•pee•stroh•fee*

reverse the charges με χρέωση του καλούμενου *meh khreh•oh•see too kah•loo•meh•noo*

revolting αηδιαστικός *ah•ee•THee•ah•stee•kohs*

rib πλευρό *plehv•roh*

right *adj* (**correct**) σωστός *soh•stohs*; (**side**) δεξιός *THeh•ksee•ohs*

river ποταμός *poh•tah•mohs*

road δρόμος *THroh•mohs*

road assistance οδική βοήθεια *oh•THee•kee voh•ee•thee•ah*

road sign πινακίδα *pee•nah•kee•Thah*

robbery ληστεία *lees•tee•ah*

rock *n* βράχος *vrah•khohs*

rock climbing αναρρίχηση *ah•nah•ree•khee•see*

romantic ρομαντικός *roh•mahn•dee•kohs*

roof *n* στέγη *steh•yee*

room *n* δωμάτιο *THoh•mah•tee•oh*

room service υπηρεσία δωματίου *ee•pee•reh•see•ah THoh•mah•tee•oo*

rope *n* σχοινί *skhee•nee*

round *adj* στρογγυλός *strohn•gkee•lohs*; *n* (**of golf**) παιχνίδι *pehkh•nee•THee*

round-trip ticket εισιτήριο με επιστροφή *ee•see•tee•ree•oh meh eh•pee•stroh•fee*

route *n* διαδρομή *THee•ahTH•roh•mee*

rowing κωπηλασία *koh•pee•lah•see•ah*

rubbish [BE] σκουπίδια *skoo•pee•THyah*

rude αγενής *ah•yeh•nees*

rug χαλί *khah•lee*

run *v* τρέχω *treh•khoh*

rush hour ώρα αιχμής *oh•rah ehkh•mees*

S

safe *adj* (**not dangerous**) ασφαλής *ahs•fah•lees*

sailing boat ιστιοπλοϊκό *ees•tee•oh•ploh•ee•koh*

sales tax ΦΠΑ *fee•pee•ah*

same ίδιος *ee•THee•ohs*

sand άμμος *ah•mohs*

sandals πέδιλα *peh•THee•lah*

sandy (beach) με άμμο *meh ah•moh*

sanitary napkin σερβιέτα
sehr•vee•eh•tah

satin σατέν *sah•tehn*

saucepan κατσαρόλα
kah•tsah•roh•lah

sauna σάουνα *sah•oo•nah*

scarf κασκόλ *kahs•kohl*

scissors ψαλίδι *psah•lee•THee*

scratch γρατζουνιά
ghrah•joo•niah

screw η βίδα *vee•THah*

screwdriver κατσαβίδι
kah•tsah•vee•THee

sea θάλασσα *thah•lah•sah*

seafront προκυμαία
proh•kee•meh•ah

seat η θέση *theh•see*

second-hand shop κατάστημα
μεταχειρισμένων ειδών *kah•
tah•stee•mah meh•tah•
kheee•reez•meh•nohn ee•THohn*

sedative ηρεμιστικό
ee•reh•mee•stee•koh

see βλέπω *vleh•poh*

send στέλνω *stehl•noh*

senior citizen ηλικιωμένος
ee•lee•kee•oh•meh•nohs

separately ξεχωριστά
kseh•khoh•ree•stah

service n (business) υπηρεσία
ee•pee•reh•see•ah; (mass)
λειτουργία *lee•toor•yee•ah*

service charge χρέωση
υπηρεσίας *khreh•oh•see
ee•pee•reh•see•ahs*

sewer υπόνομος
ee•poh•noh•mohs

shade (color) απόχρωση
ah•pohkh•roh•see; (darkness) σκιά *skee•ah*

shampoo n σαμπουάν
sahm•poo•ahn

shape n σχήμα *skhee•mah*

shaving cream κρέμα
ξυρίσματος *kreh•mah
kreez•mah•tohs*

shelf n ράφι *rah•fee*

ship n πλοίο *plee•oh*

shirt πουκάμισο
poo•kah•mee•soh

shock (electric)
ηλεκτροπληξία
ee•lehk•troh•plee•ksee•ah

shoe παπούτσι *pah•poo•tsee*

shoe polish βερνίκι
παπουτσιών *vehr•nee•kee
pah•poo•tsiohn*

shoe repair επισκευή
παπουτσιών *eh•pee•skeh•vee
pah•poo•tsiohn*

shoe store κατάστημα
υποδημάτων
*kah•tah•stee•mah
ee•poh•THee•mah•tohn*

shop (store) κατάστημα
kah•tah•stee•mah

shopping mall εμπορικό κέντρο
ehm•boh•ree•koh keh•ntroh

shore η ακτή *ahk•tee*

short adj κοντός *kohn•dohs*

shorts n σορτς *sohrts*

short-sighted [BE] μύωπας
mee•oh•pahs

shoulder n (anatomy) ώμος
oh•mohs

show δείχνω *THeekh•noh*

shower η ντους *dooz*

shower gel αφρόλουτρο για
ντους *ahf•roh•loot•roh
yah dooz*

shut adj κλειστός *klees•tohs*

sick adj άρρωστος *ah•rohs•tohs*

side (of road) μεριά *mehr•yah*

sightseeing sight αξιοθέατο
ah•ksee•oh•theh•ah•toh

sightseeing tour ξενάγηση στα
αξιοθέατα *kseh•nah•yee•see
stah ah•ksee•oh•theh•ah•tah*

sign (road) σήμα *see•mah*

silk μετάξι *meh•tah•ksee*

silver ασήμι *ah•see•mee*

simple απλός *ahp•lohs*

single (not married) ελεύθερος
eh•lehf•theh•rohs

single room μονόκλινο
δωμάτιο *moh•noh•klee•noh
THoh•mah•tee•oh*

single ticket [BE] απλό
εισιτήριο *ahp•loh
ee•see•tee•ree•oh*

sink (bathroom) νιπτήρας
nee•ptee•rahs

sit κάθομαι *kah•thoh•meh*

size n μέγεθος *meh•yeh•thohs*

skates παγοπέδιλα
pah•ghoh•peh•THee•lah

skating rink παγοδρόμιο
pah•ghohTH•roh•mee•oh

ski boots μπότες του σκι
boh•tehs too skee

ski poles μπαστούνια του σκι
bahs•too•niah too skee

ski school σχολή σκι *skhoh•lee
skee*

skiing σκι *skee*

skin n δέρμα *Thehr•mah*

skirt φούστα *foo•stah*

sleep v κοιμάμαι *kee•mah•meh*

sleeping bag υπνόσακκος
ee•pnoh•sah•kohs

sleeping car βαγκόν-λι
vah•gohn•lee

sleeping pill υπνωτικό χάπι
ee•pnoh•tee•koh khah•pee

slippers παντόφλες
pahn•dohf•lehs

slope (ski) πλαγιά *plah•yah*

slow adj αργός *ahr•ghohs*

small μικρός *meek•rohs*

smell v μυρίζω *mee•ree•zoh*

smoke v καπνίζω *kahp•nee•zoh*

smoking area περιοχή για
καπνίζοντες *peh•ree•oh•khee
yah kahp•nee•zoh•ndehs*

snack bar κυλικείο
kee•lee•kee•oh

sneakers αθλητικά παπούτσια
ath•lee•tee•kah pah•poo•tsiah

snorkeling equipment
εξοπλισμός για ελεύθερη
κατάδυση *eh•ksohp•leez•moh*
yah eh•<u>left</u>•theh•ree
kah•<u>tah</u>•THee•see

snow v χιονίζει *khioh•<u>nee</u>•zee*

soap n σαπούνι *sah•<u>poo</u>•nee*

soccer ποδόσφαιρο
poh•<u>THOhs</u>•feh•roh

socket πρίζα *<u>pree</u>•zah*

socks κάλτσες *<u>kahl</u>•tsehs*

sofa καναπές *kah•nah•<u>pehs</u>*

sole (shoes) σόλα *<u>soh</u>•lah*

something κάτι *<u>kah</u>•tee*

sometimes μερικές φορές
meh•ree•<u>kehs</u> foh•<u>rehs</u>

soon σύντομα *<u>seen</u>•doh•mah*

soother [BE] πιπίλα
pee•<u>pee</u>•lah

sore throat πονόλαιμος
poh•<u>noh</u>•leh•mohs

sort n είδος *<u>ee</u>•THohs*; v διαλέγω
THiah•<u>leh</u>•ghoh

south adj νότιος *<u>noh</u>•tee•ohs*

souvenir σουβενίρ *soo•veh•<u>neer</u>*

souvenir store κατάστημα
σουβενίρ *kah•<u>tahs</u>•tee•mah*
soo•veh•<u>neer</u>

spa σπα *spah*

space n (area) χώρος
<u>khoh</u>•rohs

spare (extra) επιπλέον
eh•<u>peep</u>•leh•ohn

speak μιλώ *mee•<u>loh</u>*

special requirement ειδική
ανάγκη *ee•THee•<u>kee</u>*
ah•<u>nahn</u>•gkee

specialist ειδικός *ee•THee•<u>kohs</u>*

specimen δείγμα *<u>THeegh</u>•mah*

speed v τρέχω *<u>treh</u>•khoh*

spend ξοδεύω *ksoh•<u>THeh</u>•voh*

spine σπονδυλική στήλη
spohn•THee•lee•<u>kee</u> <u>stee</u>•lee

spoon n κουτάλι *koo•<u>tah</u>•lee*

sport αθλητισμός
ahth•lee•teez•<u>mohs</u>

sporting goods store
κατάστημα αθλητικών
ειδών *kah•<u>tahs</u>•tee•mah*
ath•lee•tee•<u>kohn</u> ee•<u>THohn</u>

sports massage αθλητικό μασάζ
ahth•lee•tee•<u>koh</u> mah•<u>sahz</u>

sports stadium αθλητικό
στάδιο *ahth•lee•tee•<u>koh</u>*
<u>stah</u>•THee•oh

square τετράγωνος
teht•<u>rah</u>•ghoh•nohs

stadium στάδιο *<u>stah</u>•THee•oh*

stairs σκάλες *<u>skah</u>•lehs*

stale μπαγιάτικος
bah•<u>yah</u>•tee•kohs

stamp n (postage) γραμματόσημο
ghrah•mah•<u>toh</u>•see•moh

start v αρχίζω *ahr•<u>khee</u>•zoh*

statement (legal) δήλωση
<u>THee</u>•loh•see

statue άγαλμα *<u>ah</u>•ghahl•mah*

stay v μένω *<u>meh</u>•noh*

sterilizing solution
αποστειρωτικό διάλυμα
ah•pohs•tee•roh•<u>teh</u>•<u>koh</u>
THee•<u>ah</u>•lee•mah

sting n (insect) τσίμπημα
<u>tsee</u>•bee•mah

stolen κλεμένος *kleh•<u>meh</u>•nohs*

stomach n στομάχι
stoh•<u>mah</u>•khee

stomachache στομαχόπονος
stoh•mah•<u>khoh</u>•poh•nohs

stop n (bus) στάση *<u>stah</u>•see*; v
σταματώ *stah•mah•<u>toh</u>*

store guide [BE] οδηγός
καταστήματος *oh•THee•<u>ghohs</u>*
kah•tahs•<u>tee</u>•mah•tohs

stove κουζίνα *koo•<u>zee</u>•nah*

straight ahead ευθεία
ehf•<u>thee</u>•ah

strange παράξενος
pah•<u>rah</u>•kseh•nohs

straw (drinking) καλαμάκι
kah•lah•<u>mah</u>•kee

stream n ρυάκι *ree•<u>ah</u>•kee*

street δρόμος *<u>THroh</u>•mohs*

string n (cord) σπάγγος *<u>spah</u>•gohs*

student φοιτητής *fee•tee•<u>tees</u>*

study v σπουδάζω
spoo•<u>THah</u>•zoh

style n στυλ *steel*

subtitled με υπότιτλους *meh*
ee•<u>poh</u>•teet•loos

subway μετρό *meh•<u>troh</u>*

subway station σταθμός μετρό
stahth•<u>mohs</u> meh•<u>troh</u>

suggest προτείνω *proh•<u>tee</u>•noh*

suit (men's) κουστούμι
koos•<u>too</u>•mee; (women's)
ταγιέρ *tah•<u>yehr</u>*

suitable κατάλληλος
kah•<u>tah</u>•lee•lohs

sunburn n έγκαυμα ηλίου
ehn•gahv•mah ee•<u>lee</u>•oo

sunglasses γυαλιά ηλίου
yah•<u>liah</u> ee•<u>lee</u>•oo

sunshade [BE] ομπρέλλα
ohm•<u>breh</u>•lah

sunstroke ηλίαση *ee•<u>lee</u>•ah•see*

sun tan lotion λοσιόν
μαυρίσματος *loh•<u>siohn</u>*
mahv•<u>rees</u>•mah•tohs

sunscreen αντιηλιακό
ahn•dee•ee•lee•ah•<u>koh</u>

superb έξοχος *eh•<u>ksoh</u>•khohs*

supermarket σουπερμάρκετ
soo•pehr•<u>mahr</u>•keht

supervision επίβλεψη
eh•<u>peev</u>•leh•psee

surname επίθετο
eh•<u>pee</u>•theh•toh

sweatshirt φούτερ *<u>foo</u>•tehr*

swelling πρήξιμο *<u>pree</u>•ksee•moh*

swimming κολύμβηση
koh•<u>leem</u>•vee•see

swimming pool πισίνα
pee•<u>see</u>•nah

swimming trunks μαγιό
mah•<u>yoh</u>

swimsuit μαγιό *mah•<u>yoh</u>*

switch n διακόπτης
THiah•_koh_•ptees

swollen πρησμένος
preez•_meh_•nohs

symptom σύμπτωμα
seem•ptoh•mah

T

table τραπέζι trah•_peh_•zee

tablecloth τραπεζομάντηλο
trah•_peh_•zoh•_mahn_•dee•loh

tablet χάπι _khah_•pee

take παίρνω _pehr_•noh

take a photograph βγάζω
φωτογραφία vghah•_zoh_
foh•tohgh•rah•_fee_•ah

take away [BE] πακέτο για το
σπίτι pah•_keh_•toh yah toh
spee•tee

tall ψηλός psee•_lohs_

tampon ταμπόν tahm•_bohn_

tax n ο φόρος _foh_•rohs

taxi ταξί tah•_ksee_

taxi driver ταξιτζής
tah•ksee•_jees_

taxi rank [BE] πιάτσα ταξί
piah•tsah tah•_ksee_

teaspoon κουταλάκι
koo•tah•_lah_•kee

team n ομάδα oh•_mah_•THah

teenager έφηβος _eh_•fee•vohs

telephone n τηλέφωνο
tee•_leh_•foh•noh

telephone booth τηλεφωνικός
θάλαμος tee•leh•foh•nee•_kohs_
thah•lah•mohs

telephone call κλήση _klee_•see

telephone directory τηλεφωνικός
κατάλογος tee•leh•foh•
nee•_kohs_ kah•_tah_•loh•ghohs

telephone number αριθμός
τηλεφώνου ah•reeth•_mohs_
tee•_leh_•_foh_•noo

tell λέω _leh_•oh

temperature (body) θερμοκρασία
theh•rmohk•rah•_see_•ah

temple ναός nah•_ohs_

temporary προσωρινός
proh•soh•ree•_nohs_

tennis τέννις _teh_•nees

tennis court γήπεδο τέννις
yee•peh•THoh _teh_•nees

tent σκηνή skee•_nee_

terrible φοβερός foh•veh•_rohs_

theater θέατρο _theh_•aht•roh

theft κλοπή kloh•_pee_

there εκεί eh•_kee_

thermal bath ιαματικό λουτρό
ee•ah•mah•tee•_koh_ loot•roh

thermos flask θερμός thehr•_mohs_

thick χοντρός chohnt•_drohs_

thief κλέφτης _klehf_•tees

thin adj λεπτός lehp•_tohs_

think νομίζω noh•_mee_•zoh

thirsty διψάω THee•_psah_•oh

those εκείνα eh•_kee_•nah

throat λαιμός leh•_mohs_

thumb αντίχειρας
ahn•_dee_•khee•rahs

ticket εισιτήριο
ee•see•_tee_•ree•oh

ticket office γραφείο
εισιτηρίων ghrah•_fee_•oh
ee•see•tee•_ree_•ohn

tie n γραβάτα ghrah•_vah_•tah

tight adj στενός steh•_nohs_

tights [BE] n καλσόν kahl•_sohn_

timetable [BE] δρομολόγιο
THroh•moh•_loh_•yee•oh

tire λάστιχο _lahs_•tee•khoh

tired κουρασμένος
koo•rahz•_meh_•nohs

tissue χαρτομάντηλο
khahr•toh•_mahn_•dee•loh

toaster τοστιέρα toh•_stieh_•rah

tobacco καπνός kahp•_nohs_

tobacconist καπνοπωλείο
kahp•noh•poh•_lee_•oh

toilet [BE] τουαλέτα
too•ah•_leh_•tah

toilet paper χαρτί υγείας
khahr•_tee_ ee•_yee_•ahs

toiletries καλλυντικά
kah•leen•dee•_kah_

tongue γλώσσα _ghloh_•sah

too (extreme) πάρα πολύ
pah•rah poh•_lee_

tooth δόντι _THohn_•dee

toothache πονόδοντος
poh•_noh_•THohn•dohs

toothbrush οδοντόβουρτσα
oh•THohn•_doh_•voor•tsah

toothpaste οδοντόπαστα
oh•THohn•_doh_•pahs•tah

top adj πάνω _pah_•noh

torn σχισμένος skheez•_meh_•nohs

tour guide ξεναγός
kseh•nah•_ghohs_

tourist τουρίστας too•_rees_•tahs

towards προς prohs

tower πύργος _peer_•ghohs

town πόλη _poh_•lee

town hall δημαρχείο
THee•mahr•_khee_•oh

toy store κατάστημα
παιχνιδιών kah•_tahs_•tee•mah
peh•khnee•_THiohn_

traditional παραδοσιακός
pah•rah•THoh•see•ah•_kohs_

traffic κίνηση _kee_•nee•see

trail μονοπάτι moh•noh•_pah_•tee

trailer τροχόσπιτο
troh•_khohs_•pee•toh

train τρένο _treh_•noh

train station σταθμός των
τρένων stahth•_mohs_ tohn
treh•nohn

tram τραμ trahm

transfer μεταφέρω
meh•tah•_feh_•roh

transit n μεταφορά
meh•tah•foh•_rah_

translate μεταφράζω
meh•tah•_frah_•zoh

translation μετάφραση
meh•_tah_•frah•see

translator μεταφραστής
meh•tah•frah•_stees_

trash σκουπίδια *skoo•peeTH•yah*

trash can κάδος απορριμμάτων *kah•THohs ah•poh•ree•mah•tohn*

travel agency ταξιδιωτικό γραφείο *tah•ksee•THyoh• tee•koh ghrah fee•oh*

travel sickness [BE] ναυτία *nahf•tee•ah*

traveler's check ταξιδιωτική επιταγή *tah•ksee•THee•oh• tee•kee eh•pee•tah•yee*

tray δίσκος *THees•kohs*

tree δέντρο *THEhn•droh*

trim *n* διόρθωμα *THee•ghr•thoh•mah*

trolley [BE] (cart) καροτσάκι *kah•roh•tsah•kee*

trolley-bus τρόλλεϋ *troh•leh•ee*

trousers [BE] παντελόνι *pahn•deh•loh•nee*

try on δοκιμάζω *THoh•kee•mah•zoh*

T-shirt μπλουζάκι *bloo•zah•kee*

tunnel τούνελ *too•nehl*

turn *v* γυρίζω *yee•ree•zoh*

turn down *v (volume, heat)* χαμηλώνω *khah•mee•loh•noh*

turn off *v* σβήνω *svee•noh*

turn on *v* ανάβω *ah•nah•voh*

turn up *v (volume, heat)* ανεβάζω *ah•neh•vah•zoh*

TV τηλεόραση *tee•leh•oh•rah•see*

twin bed διπλό κρεβάτι *THeep•loh kreh•vah•tee*

typical τυπικός *tee•pee•kohs*

U

ugly άσχημος *ahs•khee•mohs*

unconscious αναίσθητος *ah•nehs•thee•tohs*

underground [BE] υπόγειος *ee•poh•ghee•ohs*

underpants [BE] κυλοτάκι *kee•loh•tah•kee*

understand καταλαβαίνω *kah•tah•lah•veh•noh*

uneven (ground) ανώμαλος *ah•noh•mah•lohs*

unfortunately δυστυχώς *THees•tee•khohs*

uniform *n* στολή *stoh•lee*

unique μοναδικός *moh•nah•THee•kohs*

unit μονάδα *moh•nah•THah*

United Kingdom Ηνωμένο Βασίλειο *ee•noh•meh•noh vah•see•lee•oh*

United States Ηνωμένες Πολιτείες *ee•noh•meh•nehs poh•lee•tee•ehs*

university Πανεπιστήμιο *pah•neh•pees•tee•mee•oh*

unlimited mileage απεριόριστα χιλιόμετρα *ah•peh•ree•ohr•ees•tah khee•lioh•meht•rah*

unpleasant δυσάρεστος *THee•sah•rehs•tohs*

upper (berth) πάνω (κουκέτα) *pah•noh (koo•keh•tah)*

upstairs επάνω *eh•pah•noh*

urgent επείγον *eh•pee•ghohn*

use *v* χρησιμοποιώ *khree•see•moh•pee•oh*

useful χρήσιμος *khree•see•mohs*

V

vacancy ελεύθερο δωμάτιο *eh•lehf•theh•roh THoh•mah•tee•oh*

vacant ελεύθερος *eh•lehf•theh•rohs*

vacation διακοπές *THee•ah•koh•pehs*

vacation resort θέρετρο διακοπών *theh•reh•troh THee•ah•koh•pohn*

vaccination εμβόλιο *ehm•voh•lee•oh*

valid ισχύει *ee•skhee•ee*

valley κοιλάδα *kee•lah•THah*

valuable πολύτιμος *poh•lee•tee•mohs*

value *n* αξία *ah•ksee•ah*

VAT [BE] ΦΠΑ *fee•pee•ah*

vegetarian χορτοφάγος *khohr•toh•fah•ghohs*

vein φλέβα *fleh•vah*

velvet βελούδο *veh•loo•THoh*

very πολύ *poh•lee*

video βιντεοκασέτα *vee•deh•oh•kah•seh•tah*

video game παιχνίδι βίντεο *pehkh•nee•THee vee•deh•oh*

village χωριό *khohr•yoh*

visa βίζα *vee•zah*

visit *n* επίσκεψη *eh•pees•keh•psee*

volleyball βόλεϋ *voh•leh•ee*

vomit *v* κάνω εμετό *kah•noh eh•meh•toh*

W

wait *v* περιμένω *peh•ree•meh•noh*

waiter ο γκαρσόν *gahr•sohn*

waitress δεσποινίς *THehs•pee•nees*

wake *v* ξυπνώ *kseep•noh*

walk *v* περπατώ *pehr•pah•toh*

walking route διαδρομή περιήγησης *THee•ah•THroh•mee peh•ree•ee•gee•sees*

wall τοίχος *tee•khohs*

wallet πορτοφόλι *pohr•toh•foh•lee*

want θέλω *theh•loh*

warm ζεστός *zehs•tohs*

washing machine πλυντήριο *pleen•dee•ree•oh*

watch *n* ρολόι *roh•loh•ee*

watch strap λουρί ρολογιού *loo•ree roh•loh•yioo*

water ν νερό *neh•roh*

waterfall καταρράχτης *kah•tah•rahkh•tees*

waterproof αδιάβροχος
ah•THee•ahv•roh•khohs

wave *n* κύμα *kee•mah*

way δρόμος *THroh•mohs*

wear *v* φορώ *foh•roh*

weather καιρός *keh•rohs*

weather forecast πρόβλεψη καιρού *prohv•leh•psee keh•roo*

wedding γάμος *ghah•mohs*

west δυτικά *THee•tee•kah*

wetsuit στολή δύτη *stoh•lee THee•tee*

wheelchair αναπηρική καρέκλα *ah•nah•pee•ree•kee kah•rehk•lah*

wide φαρδύς *fahr•THees*

wife σύζυγος *see•zee•ghohs*

window παράθυρο
pah•rah•thee•roh

window seat θέση δίπλα στο παράθυρο *theh•see THeep•lah stoh pah•rah•thee•roh*

winery οινοποιείο
ee•noh•pee•ee•oh

wireless internet ασύρματο ίντερνετ *ah•see•rmah•toh ee•nteh•rnet*

with με *meh*

withdraw κάνω ανάληψη
kah•noh ah•nah•lee•psee

without χωρίς *khoh•rees*

witness μάρτυρας *mahr•tee•rahs*

wood (forest) δάσος *THAh•sohs;* **(material)** ξύλο *ksee•loh*

work δουλεύω *THoo•leh•voh*

worry ανησυχώ *ah•nee•see•khoh*

worse χειρότερος
khee•roh•teh•rohs

wound (cut) πληγή *plee•yee*

write (down) γράφω *ghrah•foh*

wrong λάθος *lah•thohs*

X

x-ray ακτινογραφία
ahk•tee•nohgh•rah•fee•ah

Y

yacht γιωτ *yoht*

yellow κίτρινος *keet•ree•nohs*

young νέος *neh•ohs*

youth hostel ξενώνας νεότητας *kseh•noh•nahs neh•oh•tee•tahs*

Z

zoo ζωολογικός κήπος
zoh•oh•loh•yee•kohs kee•pohs

A

ATM *ehee•tee•ehm* ATM

άγαλμα *ah•ghahl•mah* statue

αγαπημένος *ah•ghah•pee•meh•nohs* favorite

αγαπώ *ah•ghah•poh v* love

αγγειοπλαστική *ahn•gee•ohp•lahs•tee•kee* pottery

Αγγλία *ahng•lee•ah* England

αγγλικά *ahng•lee•kah* English language

αγγλικός *ahng•lee•kohs adj* English

Άγγλος *ahng•lohs* English (nationality)

αγενής *ah•yeh•nees* rude

αγορά *ah•ghoh•rah n* market

αγοράζω *ah•ghoh•rah•zoh* buy

αγόρι *ah•ghoh•ree* boy

αγώνας *ah•ghoh•nahs n* match (sport)

άδεια *ah•THee•ah n* permit

άδεια σκι *ah•THee•ah skee* lift pass

άδειος *ahTH•yohs adj* empty

αδιάβροχο *ah•THee•ahv•roh•khoh* raincoat

αδιάβροχος *ah•THee•ahv•roh•khohs* waterproof

αδύναμος *ah•THee•nah•mohs* weak

αεροδρόμιο *ah•eh•roh•THroh•mee•oh* airport

αεροπλάνο *ah•eh•rohp•lah•noh n* plane

αεροπορική εταιρία *ah•eh•roh•poh•ree•kee eh•teh•ree•ah* airline

αεροπορικώς *ah•eh•roh•poh•ree•kohs* airmail

αηδιαστικός *ah•ee•THee•ah•stee•kohs* revolting

αθλητικά παπούτσια *ath•lee•tee•kah pah•poo•tsiah* sneakers

αθλητικό στάδιο *ahth•lee•tee•koh stah•THee•oh* sports stadium

αθλητικός όμιλος *ahth•lee•tee•kohs oh•mee•lohs* sports club

αθλητισμός *ahth•lee•teez•mohs* sport

αθώος *ah•thoh•ohs* innocent

αιμορραγία *eh•moh•rah•yee•ah n* bleed

αιμορραγώ *eh•moh•rah•yoh v* bleed

αίθουσα συναυλιών *eh•thoo•sah see•nahv•lee•ohn* concert hall

ακολουθώ *ah•koh•loo•thoh v* follow

ακουστικό βαρυκοΐας ah•koo•stee•<u>koh</u> vah•ree•<u>koh</u>•<u>ee</u>•ahs hearing aid

ακριβός ahk•ree•<u>vohs</u> expensive

ακτή ahk•<u>tee</u> n shore

ακτινογραφία ahk•tee•nohgh•rah•<u>fee</u>•ah x-ray

ακυρώνω ah•kee•<u>roh</u>•noh v cancel

αληθινός ah•lee•thee•<u>nohs</u> real (genuine)

αλλά ah•<u>lah</u> conj but

άλλα <u>ah</u>•lah others

αλλαγή ah•lah•<u>yee</u> n change

αλλάζω ah•<u>lah</u>•zoh v exchange (money)

αλλεργικός ahl•ehr•yee•<u>kohs</u> allergic

αλληλογραφία ah•lee•lohgh•rah•<u>fee</u>•ah n mail

άλλο ένα <u>ah</u>•loh eh•nah extra (additional)

άλλος <u>ah</u>•lohs another

αλουμινόχαρτο ah•loo•mee•<u>noh</u>•khar•rtoh aluminum foil

Αμερικανός ah•meh•ree•kah•<u>nohs</u> n American

αμέσως ah•<u>meh</u>•sohs immediately

άμμος <u>ah</u>•mohs sand

ανάβω ah•<u>nah</u>•voh v turn on

αναίσθητος ah•<u>nehs</u>•thee•tohs unconscious

ανάκτορα ah•<u>nahk</u>•toh•rah palace

αναλυτικός λογαριασμός ah•nah•lee•tee•<u>kohs</u> loh•ghahr•yahz•<u>mohs</u> itemized bill

αναπηρική καρέκλα ah•nah•pee•ree•<u>kee</u> kah•<u>rehk</u>•lah wheelchair

αναπνευστήρας ah•nahp•nehf•<u>stee</u>•rahs snorkel

αναπνέω ah•nahp•<u>neh</u>•oh breathe

αναπτήρας ah•nahp•<u>tee</u>•rahs n lighter (cigarette)

αναρρίχηση ah•nah•<u>ree</u>•khee•see rock climbing

ανατολικά ah•nah•toh•lee•<u>kah</u> east

αναφέρω ah•nah•<u>feh</u>•roh mention (report)

αναχώρηση ah•nah•<u>khoh</u>•ree•see departure (travel)

άνδρας <u>ahn</u>•THrahs n male (man)

ανεμιστήρας ah•neh•mees•<u>tee</u>•rahs n fan (air)

ανεβάζω ah•neh•<u>vah</u>•zoh v turn up (volume, heat)

ανέκδοτο ah•<u>nehk</u>•THoh•toh n joke

ανησυχώ ah•nee•see•<u>khoh</u> worry

ανθοπωλείο ahn•thoh•poh•<u>lee</u>•oh florist

ανοίγω ah•<u>nee</u>•ghoh v open

ανοιχτήρι ah•neekh•<u>tee</u>•ree can opener

ανοιχτός ah•neekh•<u>tohs</u> adj light (color), open

ανοιχτότερος ah•neekh•<u>toh</u>•teh•rohs adj lighter (color)

ανταλλακτικό ahn•dah•lahk•tee•<u>koh</u> replacement part

αντιβιοτικό ahn•dee•vee•oh•tee•<u>koh</u> antibiotic

αντιηλιακό ahn•dee•ee•lee•ah•<u>koh</u> sunscreen

αντισηπτική κρέμα ahn•dee•seep•tee•<u>kee</u> <u>kreh</u>•mah antiseptic cream

αντίχειρας ahn•<u>dee</u>•khee•rahs thumb

ανώμαλος ah•<u>noh</u>•mah•lohs uneven (ground)

αξεσουάρ ah•kseh•soo•<u>ahr</u> accessory

αξία ah•<u>ksee</u>•ah n value

αξιοθέατο ah•ksee•oh•<u>theh</u>•ah•tah sightseeing sight

απαγορευμένος ah•pah•ghoh•rehv•<u>meh</u>•nohs prohibited

απαραίτητος ah•pah•<u>reh</u>•tee•tohs essential, necessary

απασχολημένος ah•pahs•khoh•lee•<u>meh</u>•nohs adj busy (occupied)

απέναντι ah•<u>peh</u>•nahn•dee opposite

απεριόριστα χιλιόμετρα ah•peh•ree•<u>ohr</u>•ees•tah khee•<u>lioh</u>•meht•rah unlimited mileage

απλό εισιτήριο ap•<u>loh</u> ee•see•<u>tee</u>•ree•oh one-way (single BE) ticket

απλός ahp•<u>lohs</u> simple

από ah•<u>poh</u> from

απομίμηση ah•poh•<u>mee</u>•mee•see imitation

αποβάθρα ah•poh•<u>vahth</u>•rah platform, quay

απόγευμα ah•poh•<u>yehv</u>•mah afternoon

απόδειξη ah•<u>poh</u>•THee•ksee receipt

απορρυπαντικό ah•poh•ree•pahn•dee•<u>koh</u> detergent

αποσμητικό ah•pohz•mee•tee•<u>koh</u> deodorant

αποσκευές ah•pohs•keh•<u>vehs</u> baggage [BE]

αποσκευές χειρός ah•pohs•keh•<u>vehs</u> khee•<u>rohs</u> hand luggage

αποστειρωτικό διάλυμα ah•pohs•tee•roh•tee•<u>koh</u> THee•<u>ah</u>•lee•mah sterilizing solution

απόχρωση ah•<u>pohkh</u>•roh•see shade (color)

απώλεια ah•<u>poh</u>•lee•ah n loss

αργά ahr•<u>ghah</u> adv late

αργία ahr•<u>yee</u>•ah public holiday

αργός ahr•<u>ghohs</u> adj slow

αριθμός κυκλοφορίας ah•reeth•<u>mohs</u> kee•kloh•foh•<u>ree</u>•ahs registration number

αριθμός πτήσεως
ah•reeth•_mohs_ ptee•seh•ohs
flight number

αριθμός τηλεφώνου ah•reeth•
mohs tee•leh•_foh_•noo
telephone number

αριστερός ah•rees•teh•_rohs_
left (adj)

αριστερά ah•rees•teh•_rah_
left (adv)

αρκετά ahr•keh•_tah_ enough

αρραβωνιαστικιά ah•rah•voh•
niahs•tee•_kiah_ fiancée

αρραβωνιαστικός ah•rah•voh•
niahs•tee•_kohs_ fiancé

αρρώστεια ahr•_ohs_•tee•ah
illness

άρρωστος ah•_rohs_•tohs adj sick

αρτοποιείο ah•rtoh•pee•_ee_•oh
bakery

αρχάριος ahr•_khah_•ree•ohs
beginner

αρχίζω v ahr•_khee_•zoh start

ασανσέρ ah•sahn•_sehr_ n lift
(elevator)

ασήμι ah•_see_•mee silver

ασύρματο ίντερνετ ah•_see_•
rmah•toh ee•nteh•rnet wireless
internet

ασθενοφόρο ahs•theh•
noh•_foh_•roh ambulance

ασθματικός ahsth•mah•
tee•_kohs_ asthmatic

ασπιρίνη ahs•pee•_ree_•nee aspirin

αστυνομία ah•stee•noh•_mee_•ah
n police

αστυνομικό τμήμα
ah•stee•noh•mee•_koh_
tmee•mah police station

ασφάλεια ah•_fah_•lee•ah n
fuse; insurance

ασφάλεια αποζημίωσης
ahs•fah•lee•ah ah•poh•zee•
mee•oh•sees insurance claim

ασφάλεια υγείας ahs•_fah_•lee•
ah ee•_yee_•ahs health insurance

ασφαλής ahs•fah•_lees_ adj safe
(not dangerous)

ασφαλιστική εταιρία ahs•fah•
lees•tee•_kee_ eh•teh•_ree_•ah
insurance company

άσχημος _ahs_•khee•mohs ugly

άτομο με ειδικές ανάγκες
ah•toh•moh meh eh•_THee_•kehs
ah•_nahn_•gehs disabled

ατύχημα ah•_tee_•khee•mah
accident

αυθεντικός ahf•thehn•dee•_kohs_
genuine

αυθεντικότητα ahf•thehn•
dee•_koh_•tee•tah authenticity

αϋπνία ah•eep•_nee_•ah insomnia

αυτοκίνητο
ahf•toh•_kee_•nee•toh car

αυχένας ahf•_kheh_•nahs neck
(part of body)

αφήνω ah•_fee_•noh v leave (let go)

αφορολόγητα είδη
ah•foh•roh•_loh_•yee•tah
ee•_THee_ duty-free goods

αφρόλουτρο για ντουζ ahf•_roh_•
loot•roh yah dooz shower gel

αχθοφόρος ahkh•thoh•_foh_•rohs
porter

B

βαμβάκι vahm•_vah_•kee cotton

βαγκόν-λι vah•_gohn_•lee
sleeping car

βάζο _vah_•zoh n jar

βάζω _vah_•zoh v put

βαλές vah•_lehs_ jack

βαρετός vah•reh•_tohs_ boring

βάρκα _vah_•kah boat

βαρύς vah•_rees_ heavy

βασιλιάς vah•see•_liahs_ king

βγαίνω _vyeh_•noh get out (of
vehicle)

βελούδο veh•_loo_•THoh velvet

βενζινάδικο
vehn•zee•_nah_•THee•koh gas
[petrol BE] station

βενζίνη vehn•_zee_•nee gasoline
[petrol BE]

βερνίκι παπουτσιών vehr•_nee_•
kee pah•poo•_tsiohn_ shoe polish

βήχας _vee_•khahs n cough

βήχω _vee_•khoh v cough

βιβλίο veev•_lee_•oh n book

βιβλιοθήκη
veev•lee•oh•_thee_•kee library

βιβλιοπωλείο veev•lee•
oh•poh•_lee_•oh bookstore

βίδα _vee_•THah n screw

βίζα _vee_•zah visa

βιντεοκασέτα vee•deh•
oh•kah•_seh_•tah video

βλάβη _vlah_•vee breakdown n (car)

βλέπω _vleh_•poh see

βοήθεια voh•_ee_•thee•ah n help

βοηθώ voh•ee•_thoh_ v help

βόλεϊ _voh_•leh•ee volleyball

βόρεια _voh_•ree•ah north

βοτανικός κήπος
voh•tah•nee•_kohs_ kee•_pohs_
botanical garden

βουνό voo•_noh_ mountain

βουρτσίζω voor•_tsee_•zoh v brush

βραδινό vrah•THee•_noh_ dinner

βράδυ _vrah_•THee evening

βράζω _vrah_•zoh boil

βράχος _vrah_•khohs n rock

Βρετανικός vreh•tah•nee•_kohs_
British adj

Βρετανός vreh•tah•_nohs_ British
(nationality)

βρέχει _vreh_•khee v rain

βροχή vroh•_khee_ n rain

βρύση _vree_•see faucet

βρώμικος _vroh_•mee•kohs adj dirty

Γ

γάμος _ghah_•mohs wedding

γάζα _ghah_•zah bandage

γαλάκτωμα για τα μαλλιά
ghah•_lah_•ktoh•mah yah tah
mah•_liah_ conditioner (hair)

γάντι _ghahn_•dee n glove

γαστρίτιδα ghahs•_tree_•tee•THah gastritis

γεματός yeh•_mah_•tohs adj full

γείτονας _yee_•toh•nahs n neighbor

γελώ yeh•_loh_ v laugh

γεμιστή yeh•mees•_tee_ stuffed olive

γέρικος _yeh_•ree•kohs old (person)

γεύμα _yehv_•mah meal

γέφυρα _yeh_•fee•rah n bridge (over water)

γη ghee n land

γήπεδο γκολφ _yee_•peh•THoh gohlf golf course

γήπεδο τέννις _yee_•peh•THoh teh•nees tennis court

γιατρός yah•_trohs_ doctor

γιωτ yoht yacht

γκαράζ gah•_rahz_ garage

γκαρσόν gahr•_sohn_ waiter

γκολφ gohlf golf

γκρουπ groop n group

γλώσσα _ghloh_•sah tongue

γνωρίζω ghnoh•_ree_•zoh know

γόνατο _ghoh_•nah•toh knee

γονείς ghoh•_nees_ parents

γράμμα _ghrah_•mah letter

γραμματόσημο ghrah•_mah_• toh•_see_•moh n stamp (postage)

γραμμή ghrah•_mee_ n line (subway)

γραβάτα ghrah•_vah_•tah n tie

γρασίδι ghrah•_see_•THee grass

γραφείο ghrah•_fee_•oh office

γραφείο ανταλλαγής συναλλάγματος ghrah•_fee_•oh ahn•dah•lah•_yees_ see•nah•_lahgh_•mah•tohs currency exchange office

γραφείο εισιτηρίων ghrah•_fee_•oh ee•see•_tee_•ree•ohn ticket office

γραφείο πληροφοριών ghrah•_fee_•oh plee•roh•foh•ree•_ohn_ information office

γράφω _ghrah_•foh write (down)

γρήγορα _ghree_•ghoh•rah adv fast

γρήγορος _ghree_•ghoh•rohs quick

γρίππη _ghree_•pee flu

γυαλιά yah•_liah_ glasses (optical)

γυαλιά ηλίου yah•_liah_ ee•_lee_•oo sun glasses

γυναικολόγος yee•neh•koh•_loh_•ghohs gynecologist

γυρίζω yee•_ree_•zoh v turn

γωνία ghoh•_nee_•ah corner

Δ

δανείζω THah•_nee_•zoh lend

δάσος _THah_•sohs n forest (wood)

δάχτυλο THakh•tee•loh n finger

δείγμα _THeegh_•mah specimen

δείχνω _THeekh_•noh v point (show)

δέντρο _THehn_•droh tree

δεξιός THeh•ksee•_ohs_ adj right (not left)

δέρμα _THehr_•mah n skin

δημαρχείο THee•mahr•_khee_•oh town hall

δημοφιλής THee•moh•fee•_lees_ popular

δηλητήριο THee•lee•_tee_•ree•oh n poison

δηλητηριώδης THee•lee•tee•ree•_oh_•THees poisonous

δηλώνω THee•_loh_•noh declare

δήλωση THee•_loh_•see statement (legal)

δημόσιος THee•_moh_•see•ohs public

διαμάντι THiah•_mahn_•dee n diamond

διαμέρισμα THee•ah•_meh_• reez•mah apartment

διάβαση πεζών THee•_ah_•vah•see peh•_zohn_ pedestrian crossing

διαβατήριο THiah•vah•_tee_•ree•oh passport

διαβητικός THee•ah•vee•tee•_kohs_ diabetic

διαδρομή THee•ahTH•roh•_mee_ n route

διάδρομος THee•_ah_•THroh•mohs aisle seat

διαζευγμένος THee•ah•zehv•_ghmeh_•nohs divorced

διακοπές THee•ah•koh•_pehs_ vacation [holiday BE]

διακόπτης THiah•_koh_•ptees n switch

διαμέρισμα THee•ah•mehr•ees•mah n flat

διάρροια THee•_ah_•ree•ah diarrhea

διάσημος THee•_ah_•see•mohs famous

διεθνής THee•eth•_nees_ international

διεθνής φοιτητική κάρτα THee•ehth•_nees_ fee•tee•tee•_kee_ kahr•tah International Student Card

διερμηνέας THee•ehr•mee•_neh_•ahs interpreter

διεύθυνση THee•_ehf_•theen•see n address

διευθυντής THee•ehf•theen•_dees_ manager

δικηγόρος THee•kee•_ghoh_•rohs lawyer

δίκλινο δωμάτιο THeek•lee•noh THoh•_mah_•tee•oh double room

δίνω THee•noh give

διόρθωμα THee•ohr•thoh•mah n trim

δίπλα _THeep_•lah next to

διπλό κρεβάτι THeep•_loh_ kreh•_vah_•tee twin bed

δίσκος _THees_•kohs tray

διψάω THee•_psah_•oh thirsty

δοκιμάζω THoh•kee•_mah_•zoh try on

δολάριο _THoh•lah•ree•oh_ dollar

δόντι _THohn•dee_ tooth

δοσολογία _THoh•soh•loh•yee•ah_ dosage

δουλειά _THoo•liah_ job

δουλεύω _THoo•leh•voh_ work

δρομολόγιο _THroh•moh•loh•yee•oh_ time table

δρόμος _THroh•mohs_ road, street, way

δυνατός _THee•nah•tohs adj_ loud

δυσάρεστος _THee•sah•reh stohs_ unpleasant

δύσκολος _THee•skoh•lohs_ difficult

δυσπεψία _THes•peh•psee•ah_ indigestion

δυστυχώς _THees•tee•khohs_ unfortunately

δυτικά _THee•tee•kah_ west

δωμάτιο _THoh•mah•tee•oh_ n room

δώρο _THoh•roh_ gift

Ε

ελιά _eh•liah_ olive

εμβόλιο _ehm•voh•lee•oh_ vaccination

εμπορικό κέντρο _ehm•boh•ree•koh keh•ntroh_ shopping mall [centre BE]

εγγύηση _eh•gee•ee•see n_ guarantee

εγγυώμαι _eh•gee•oh•meh v_ guarantee

έγκαυμα ηλίου _ehn•gahv•mah ee•lee•oo n_ sun burn

έγκυος _eh•gee•ohs_ pregnant

έδαφος _eh•THah•fohs_ ground (earth)

εδώ _eh•THoh_ here

εδώ κοντά _eh•THoh kohn•dah_ nearby

εθνική οδός _ehth•nee•kee oh•THohs_ highway, motorway

εθνικός _eth•nee•kohs_ national

εθνικός δρυμός _eth•nee•kohs THree•mohs_ nature reserve

είμαι _ee•meh_ be

είμαι κουφός _koo•fohs_ deaf

είδη οικιακής χρήσεως _ee•THee ee•kee•ah•kees khree•seh•ohs_ household articles

ειδική ανάγκη _ee•THee•kee ah•nahn•gkee_ special requirement

ειδικός _ee•THee•kohs_ specialist

είδος _ee•THohs_ kind (sort)

εισιτήριο _ee•see•tee•ree•oh_ fare (ticket)

εισιτήριο με επιστροφή _ee•see•tee•ree•oh meh eh•pee•stroh•fee_ roundtrip [return BE] ticket

εκδρομή _ehk•THroh•mee_ excursion

εκεί _eh•kee_ there, over there

εκείνα _eh•kee•nah_ those

έκθεση _ehk•theh•see_ exhibition

έκπτωση _ehk•ptoh•see_ reduction

έκτακτη ανάγκη _ehk•tahk•tee ah•nah•gee_ emergency

ελάχιστος _eh•lah•khees•tohs_ minimum

ελεύθερο δωμάτιο _eh•lehf•theh•roh THoh•mah•tee•oh_ vacancy

ελεύθερος _eh•lehf•theh•rohs adj_ free, single, vacant

ελικόπτερο _eh•lee•kohp•teh•roh_ helicopter

Ελλάδα _eh•lah•THah_ Greece

Έλληνας _eh•lee•nahs_ Greek (nationality)

ελληνικός _eh•lee•nee•kohs adj_ Greek

ένα βράδυ _eh•nah vrah•THee_ overnight

ένα τέταρτο _eh•nah teh•tah•rtoh_ quarter (quantity)

ενδιαφέρων _en•THee•ah•feh•rohn_ interesting

ένεση _eh•neh•see_ injection

ενήλικας _eh•nee•lee•kahs_ adult

ενοχλώ _eh•noh•khloh_ disturb

έντομο _ehn•doh•moh_ insect

εντομοαπωθητικό _ehn•doh•moh•ah•poh•thee•tee•koh_ insect repellent

έντυπο _ehn•dee•poh n_ form

εντυπωσιακός _ehn•dee•poh•see•ah•kohs_ impressive

ενυδατική κρέμα _eh•nee•THah•tee•kee kreh•mah_ moisturizer (cream)

εξάνθημα _eh•ksahn•thee•mah_ n rash

εξαργυρώνω _eh•ksahr•ghee•roh•noh v_ cash

εξόγκωμα _eh•ksoh•goh•mah n_ lump (medical)

έξοδος _eh•ksoh•THohs n_ gate (airport); exit

έξοδος κινδύνου _eh•ksoh•THohs keen•THee•noo_ emergency, fire exit

εξοχή _eh•ksoh•khee_ countryside

έξοχος _eh•ksoh•khohs_ superb

εξπρές _ehk•sprehs_ express (mail)

εξυπηρέτηση _eh•ksee•pee•reh•tee•see_ facility

έξω _eh•ksoh adv_ out

έξω _eh•ksoh adj_ outside

εξωλέμβιο _eh•ksoh•lehm•vee•oh_ motorboat

εξωτερικός _eh•ksoh•teh•ree•kohs_ outdoor

επαναλαμβάνω _eh•pah•nah•lahm•vah•noh v_ repeat

επάνω _eh•pah•noh_ upstairs

επείγον _eh•pee•ghohn_ urgent

επιμένω _eh•pee•meh•noh v_ insist

επιβάτης _eh•pee•vah•tees_ passenger

επιβεβαιώνω eh•pee•veh•veh•<u>oh</u>•noh confirm

επίβλεψη eh•<u>peev</u>•leh•psee supervision

επίθεση eh•<u>pee</u>•theh•see n attack

επίθετο eh•<u>pee</u>•theh•toh surname

επικοινωνώ eh•pee•kee•noh•<u>noh</u> v contact

επιληπτικός eh•pee•leep•tee•<u>kohs</u> epileptic

επίπεδο eh•<u>pee</u>•peh•THoh level (even)

επίπεδος eh•<u>pee</u>•peh•THohs adj flat

έπιπλα <u>eh</u>•peep•lah furniture

επιπλέον eh•peep•<u>leh</u>•ohn spare (extra)

επισκευάζω eh•pee•skeh•<u>vah</u>•zoh v repair

επισκευή eh•pee•skeh•<u>vee</u> n repair

επισκευή παπουτσιών eh•pee•skeh•<u>vee</u> pah•poo•<u>tsiohn</u> shoe repair

επίσκεψη eh•<u>pees</u>•keh•psee n visit

επιστροφή χρημάτων eh•pees•troh•<u>fee</u> khree•<u>mah</u>•tohn n refund

επιταγή eh•pee•tah•<u>yee</u> n check [cheque BE] (bank)

επιτίθεμαι eh•pee•<u>tee</u>•theh•meh v attack

επιτόκιο eh•pee•<u>toh</u>•kee•oh interest rate

επόμενος eh•<u>poh</u>•meh•nohs next

έρχομαι <u>ehr</u>•khoh•meh come

ερώτηση eh•<u>roh</u>•tee•see n question

εστιατόριο ehs•tee•ah•<u>toh</u>•ree•oh restaurant

εσωτερική γραμμή eh•soh•teh•ree•<u>kee</u> ghrah•<u>mee</u> extension (number)

εσωτερική πισίνα eh•soh•teh•ree•<u>kee</u> pee•<u>see</u>•nah indoor pool

εσωτερικός eh•soh•teh•ree•<u>kohs</u> indoor

ετικέτα eh•tee•<u>keh</u>•tah n label

έτοιμος <u>eh</u>•tee•mohs adj ready

ευθεία ehf•<u>thee</u>•ah straight ahead

εύκολος <u>ehf</u>•koh•lohs adj easy

ευρώ ehv•<u>roh</u> euro

Ευρωπαϊκή Ένωση ehv•roh•pah•ee•<u>kee</u> <u>eh</u>•noh•see European Union

ευτυχώς ehf•tee•<u>khohs</u> fortunately

ευχαριστιέμαι ehf•khah•rees•<u>tieh</u>•meh enjoy

ευχάριστος ehf•<u>khah</u>•rees•tohs pleasant

εφημερίδα eh•fee•<u>mehree</u>•THah newspaper

έφηβος <u>eh</u>•fee•vohs teenager

έχω <u>eh</u>•khoh have (possession)

Z

ζαχαροπλαστείο zah•khah•roh•plahs•<u>tee</u>•oh pastry store

ζεστός zes•<u>tohs</u> hot, warm (weather)

ζημιά zee•<u>miah</u> n damage

ζητώ zee•<u>toh</u> ask

ζωγραφίζω zohgh•rah•<u>fee</u>•zoh v paint

ζωγράφος zohgh•<u>rah</u>•fohs painter

ζώνη <u>zoh</u>•nee belt

ζώνη για χρήματα <u>zoh</u>•nee yah <u>khree</u>•mah•tah money-belt

H

ημερομηνία λήξεως ee•meh•roh•mee•<u>nee</u>•ah <u>lee</u>•kseh•ohs expiration date

ημερολόγιο ee•meh•roh•<u>loh</u>•yee•oh calendar

ημικρανία ee•mee•krah•<u>nee</u>•ah migraine

ηλεκτρικός ee•lehk•tree•<u>kohs</u> electric

ηλεκτρονικό εισιτήριο ee•lehk•troh•nee•<u>koh</u> ee•see•<u>tee</u>•ree•oh e-ticket

ηλεκτρονικό ταχυδρομείο ee•lehk•troh•nee•<u>koh</u> tah•hee•dro•<u>mee</u>•oh (ee•meh•eel) e-mail

ηλεκτροπληξία ee•leh•ktroh•plee•<u>ksee</u>•ah shock (electric)

ηλίαση ee•<u>lee</u>•ah•see sun stroke

ηλικιωμένος ee•lee•kee•oh•<u>meh</u>•nohs senior citizen

Ηνωμένες Πολιτείες ee•noh•<u>meh</u>•nehs poh•lee•<u>tee</u>•ehs United States

Ηνωμένο Βασίλειο ee•noh•<u>meh</u>•noh vah•<u>see</u>•lee•oh United Kingdom

ηρεμιστικό ee•reh•mee•stee•<u>koh</u> sedative

ήσυχος <u>ee</u>•see•khohs adj quiet

Θ

θάλασσα <u>thah</u>•lah•sah sea

θέατρο <u>theh</u>•aht•roh theater

θέλω <u>theh</u>•loh want

θέρμανση <u>thehr</u>•mahn•see heating

θερμή πηγή thehr•<u>mee</u> pee•<u>yee</u> hot spring

θερμόμετρο thehr•<u>moh</u>•meht•roh thermometer

θερμοκρασία theh•rmohk•rah•<u>see</u>•ah temperature (body)

θερμός thehr•<u>mohs</u> thermos flask

θέρετρο διακοπών <u>theh</u>•reh•troh THee•ah•koh•<u>pohn</u> vacation resort

θέση <u>theh</u>•see n location (space), seat

θέση δίπλα στο παράθυρο
_theh•see THeep•lah stoh
pah•rah•thee•roh_ window seat
θηλυκός _thee•lee•kohs_ female
θορυβώδης _thoh•ree•voh•THees_
noisy
θρησκεία _three•skee•ah_ religion
θυμάμαι _thee•mah•meh_
remember
θυρίδα _thee•ree•THah_ luggage
locker (lock-up)

I

ιατρική εξέταση _ee•ah•tree•
kee eh•kseh•tah•see_ examination
(medical)
ίδιος _ee•THee•ohs_ same
ιδιωτικό μπάνιο
ee•THee•oh•tee•koh bah•nioh
private bathroom
ιερέας _ee•eh•reh•ahs_ priest
ινσουλίνη _een•soo•lee•nee_
insulin
ίντερνετ _een•nteh•rnet_ internet
ίντερνετ καφέ _ee•nteh•rnet
kah•feh_ internet cafe
ιπποδρομία
ee•poh•THroh•mee•ah horse
racing
ιστιοπλοϊκό _ees•tee•oh•
ploh•ee•koh_ sailing boat
ιστορία _ee•stoh•ree•ah_ history
ισχύει _ee•skhee•ee_ valid
ίσως _ee•sohs_ maybe, perhaps
ιώδειο _ee•oh•THee•oh_ iodine

K

κάδος απορριμμάτων
_kah•THohs ah•poh•ree•
mah•tohn_ trash can
καθαρισμός προσώπου
_kah•thah•reez•mohs
proh•soh•poo_ facial
καθαρός _kah•thah•rohs_ clean
καθαρτικό _kah•thahr•tee•koh_
laxative

καθεδρικός ναός _kah•theh•
THree•kohs nah•ohs_ cathedral
καθήκον _kah•thee•kohn_ duty
(obligation)
κάθομαι _kah•thoh•meh_ sit
καθρέφτης _kah•threhf•tees_
n mirror
καθυστέρηση _kah•thee•
steh•ree•see_ n delay
καθυστερώ _kah•thee•steh•roh_
v delay
καινούργιος _keh•noor•yohs_ new
καιρός _keh•rohs_ weather
καλά _kah•lah_ adv fine (well)
καλαμάκι _kah•lah•mah•kee_
straw (drinking)
καλάθι _kah•lah•THee_ basket
καλός _kah•lohs_ good
καλσόν _kahl•sohn_ n tights
κάλτσες _kahl•tsehs_ socks
κάλυμμα φακού _kah•lee•mah
fah•koo_ lens cap
καλώ _kah•loh_ v call
κάμπινγκ _kah•mpeeng_ camping
καναπές _kah•nah•pehs_ sofa
κανένας _kah•neh•nahs_ adj none
κάνω ανάληψη _kah•noh
ah•nah•lee•psee_ withdraw
κάνω εμετό _kah•noh
eh•meh•toh_ v vomit
κάνω κράτηση _kah•noh
krah•tee•see_ v book
κάνω πεζοπορία _kah•noh
peh•zoh•poh•ree•ah_ v hike
καπέλο _kah•peh•loh_ hat
καπνίζω _kahp•nee•zoh_ v smoke
καπνοπωλείο _kahp•noh•
poh•lee•oh_ tobacconist
καπνός _kahp•nohs_ tobacco
καραντίνα _kah•rahn•dee•nah_ n
quarantine
καράφα _kah•rah•fah_ carafe
καρδιά _kahr•THee•ah_ v heart
καρδιακό έμφραγμα
_kahr•THee•ah•koh
ehm•frahgh•mah_ heart attack

καροτσάκι _kah•roh•tsah•kee_
trolley (cart)
καροτσάκια αποσκευών
_kah•roh•tsah•kiah
ah•pohs•keh•vohn_ baggage
[BE] carts [trolleys]
κάρτα-κλειδί _kahr•tah klee•dee_
key card
καρτποστάλ _kahrt•poh•stahl_
post card
κασκόλ _kahs•kohl_ scarf
κασσίτερος _kah•see•teh•rohs_
pewter
κάστρο _kahs•troh_ castle
καταδυτικός εξοπλισμός _kah•
tah•THee•tee•kohs eh•ksoh•
pleez•mohs_ diving equipment
καταλαβαίνω _kah•tah•lah•
veh•noh_ understand
κατάλληλος _kah•tah•lee•lohs_
suitable
καταρράχτης
kah•tah•rahkh•tees waterfall
κατάστημα _kah•tah•stee•mah_
shop (store)
κατάστημα με αντίκες
_kah•tah•stee•mah meh
ahn•tee•kehs_ antiques store
κατάστημα με είδη δώρων
_kah•tahs•tee•mah meh
ee•THee THoh•rohn_ gift store
**κατάστημα με υγιεινές
τροφές** _kah•tahs•tee•mah
meh eh•yee•ee•nehs troh•fehs_
health food store
**κατάστημα μεταχειρισμένων
ειδών** _kah•tahs•tee•mah
meh•tah•khee•reez•meh•nohn
ee•THohn_ second-hand shop
**κατάστημα αθλητικών
ειδών** _kah•tahs•tee•mah
ath•lee•tee•kohn ee•THohn_
sporting goods store
κατάστημα ρούχων
kah•tahs•tee•mah roo•khohn
clothing store

κατάστημα σουβενίρ kah•_tahs_•tee•mah soo•veh•_neer_ souvenir store

κατάστημα υποδημάτων kah•_tah_•stee•mah ee•poh•THee•_mah_•tohn shoe store

καταστρέφω kah•tah•_streh_•foh v damage

κατάψυξη kah•_tah_•psee•ksee freezer

κατεβαίνω kah•teh•_veh_•noh get off (transport)

κατειλημένος kah•tee•lee•_meh_•nohs occupied

κάτι _kah_•tee something

κάτοχος _kah_•toh•khohs owner

κατσαβίδι kah•tsah•_vee_•THee screwdriver

κατσαρόλα kah•tsah•_roh_•lah saucepan

κάτω _kah_•toh adj lower (berth)

καύσωνας _kahf_•soh•nahs heat wave

καφετέρια kah•feh•_teh_•ree•ah cafe

κέντρο της πόλης _kehn_•droh tees poh•lees downtown area

κεφάλι keh•_fah_•lee n head

κήπος _kee_•pohs n garden

κιθάρα kee•_thah_•rah guitar

κινηματογράφος kee•nee•mah•tohgh•_rah_•fohs movie theater

κίνηση _kee_•nee•see traffic

κινητό kee•nee•_toh_ cell phone [mobile phone BE]

κίτρινος _keet_•ree•nohs yellow

κλειδαριά klee•THah•_ryah_ n lock (door)

κλειδί klee•_THee_ n key

κλειδώνω klee•_THoh_•noh v lock (door)

κλειστός klees•_tohs_ adj shut

κλεμένος kleh•_meh_•nos stolen

κλέφτης _klehf_•tees thief

κλήση _klee_•see n call

κλιματισμός klee•mah•_teez_•_mohs_ air conditioning

κλοπή kloh•_pee_ theft

κομμωτήριο koh•moh•_tee_•ree•oh hair dresser

κόμβος _kohm_•vohs junction (intersection)

κοιμάμαι kee•_mah_•meh v sleep

κοιλάδα kee•_lah_•THah valley

κοιτάω kee•_tah_•oh v look

κολύμβηση koh•_leem_•vee•see swimming

κοντά kohn•_dah_ adv near

κοντός kohn•_dohs_ adj short

κορίτσι koh•_ree_•tsee girl

κορυφή koh•ree•_fee_ n peak

κοσμηματοπωλείο kohz•mee•mah•toh•poh•_lee_•oh jeweler

κουβέρτα koo•_veh_•rtah blanket

κουζίνα koo•_zee_•nah stove

κουνούπι koo•_noo_•pee mosquito

κουρασμένος koo•rahz•_meh_•nohs tired

κουστούμι koos•_too_•mee men's suit

κουταλάκι koo•tah•_lah_•kee teaspoon

κουτάλι koo•_tah_•lee n spoon

κουτί koo•_tee_ carton

κουτί πρώτων βοηθειών koo•_tee_ proh•tohn voh•ee•thee•_ohn_ first-aid kit

κράμπα _krahm_•bah n cramp

κραγιόν krah•_yohn_ lipstick

κρατώ krah•_toh_ v keep

κρέμα ξυρίσματος _kreh_•mah ksee•_ree_•smah•tohs shaving cream

κρεμάστρα kreh•_mahs_•trah hanger

κρεβάτι kreh•_vah_•tee bed

κρυολόγημα kree•oh•_loh_•yee•mah n cold (flu)

κρύος _kree_•ohs adj cold (temperature)

κρύσταλλο _kree_•stah•loh n crystal

κύμα _kee_•mah n wave

κυλικείο kee•lee•_kee_•oh snack bar

κυλιόμενες σκάλες kee•_lee_•_oh_•meh•nehs _skah_•lehs escalator

Κύπρος _kee_•prohs Cyprus

κύριος _kee_•ree•ohs main

κωδικός περιοχής koh•THee•_kohs_ peh•ree•oh•_khees_ area code

κωπηλασία koh•pee•lah•_see_•ah rowing

Λ

λάμπα _lahm_•bah lamp, light bulb

λάθος _lah_•thohs error, wrong

λαιμόκοψη leh•_moh_•koh•psee neck (shirt)

λαιμός leh•_mohs_ throat

λάστιχο _lahs_•tee•khoh tire [tyre BE]

λειτουργία lee•toor•_yee_•ah n mass (church)

λεκές leh•_kehs_ n stain

λεξικό leh•ksee•_koh_ dictionary

λεπτό lehp•_toh_ n minute (time)

λεπτός lehp•_tohs_ adj thin

λέω _leh_•oh tell

λεωφορείο leh•oh•foh•_ree_•oh bus

ληστεία lees•_tee_•ah robbery

λιμάνι lee•_mah_•nee n harbor

λίμνη _leem_•nee lake

λιμνούλα leem•_noo_•lah n pond

λιγότερο lee•_ghoh_•teh•roh less

λιπαντικό lee•pahn•dee•_koh_ lubricant

λιπαρός lee•pah•_rohs_ greasy (hair, skin)

λιποθυμώ lee•poh•thee•_moh_ faint

λίρα _lee_•rah pound (sterling)

λίτρο _lee_•troh liter

λογαριασμός loh•ghahr•yahz•
mohs n check (bill), account
λοσιόν loh•_siohn_ lotion
λοσιόν μαυρίσματος loh•_siohn_
mahv•_rees_•mah•tohs sun
tan lotion
λουκέτο loo•_keh_•toh padlock
λουλούδι loo•_loo_•THee n flower
λουρί ρολογιού loo•_ree_
roh•loh•_yioo_ watch strap
λόφος loh•fohs hill

M

μαγιό mah•_yoh_ swimming trunks,
swimsuit
μαθαίνω mah•_theh_•noh learn
μάθημα ξένης γλώσσας
mah•thee mah kseh•nees
ghloh•sahs language course
μακιγιάζ mah•kee•_yahz_ make-up
μακριά mahk•ree•_ah_ adv far
μακρύς mak•_rees_ adj long
μαλλιά mah•_liah_ hair
μανικιούρ mah•nee•_kioor_
manicure
μαξιλαροθήκη mah•ksee•
lah•roh•_thee_•kee pillow case
μαργαριτάρι
mahr•ghah•ree•_tah_•ree pearl
μάρτυρας _mahr_•tee•rahs witness
μας mahs our
μασάζ mah•_sahz_ n massage
μάσκα _mahs_•kah n mask (diving)
μάτι _mah_•tee n eye
μαχαίρι mah•_kheh_•ree knife
με meh with
με άμμο meh _ah_•moh sandy
(beach)
με υπότιτλους meh
ee•_poh_•teet•loos subtitled
με χαλίκια meh khah•_lee_•kiah
pebbly (beach)
μεγαλοπρεπής meh•ghah•
lohp•reh•_pees_ magnificent
μεγάλος meh•_ghah_•lohs adj
big, large

μέγεθος _meh_•yeh•thohs n size
μέδουσα meh•THoo•sah jellyfish
μένω _meh_•noh v stay
μεριά mehr•_yah_ side (of road)
μερίδα meh•_ree_•THah n portion
μερικές φορές meh•ree•_kehs_
foh•_rehs_ sometimes
μέσα _meh_•sah inside
μεσημεριανό
meh•see•mehr•yah•_noh_ n lunch
μετά meh•_tah_ after
μετακομίζω meh•tah•koh•
mee•zoh v move (room)
μέταλλο _meh_•tah•loh n metal
μετάξι meh•_tah_•ksee silk
μεταφέρω meh•tah•_feh_•roh
transfer
μεταφορά meh•tah•foh•_rah_
n transit
μεταφράζω meh•tah•_frah_•zoh
translate
μετάφραση meh•_tah_•frah•see
translation
μεταφραστής
meh•tah•frah•_stees_ translator
μέτρηση meh•tree•see measurement
μετρητά meht•ree•_tah_ n cash
μετρό meh•_troh_ subway
μετρώ meht•_roh_ v measure
μη καπνίζοντες mee
kap•nee•_zon_•des non-smoking
μήκος _mee_•kohs length
μήνας του μέλιτος _mee_•nahs
too mee•lee•tohs honeymoon
μήνυμα _mee_•nee•mah n
message
μηχανή mee•khah•_nee_ engine
μια φορά miah foh•_rah_ once
μικρός meek•_rohs_ little, small
μιλώ mee•_loh_ speak
μίνι-μπαρ _mee_•nee bahr
mini-bar
μισός mee•_sohs_ half
μνημείο mnee•_mee_•oh memorial, monument

μολυσμένος
moh•leez•_meh_•nohs infected
μονάδα moh•_nah_•THah unit
μοναδικός moh•nah•THee•_kohs_
unique
μονόκλινο δωμάτιο
moh•_nohk_•klee•noh
THoh•_mah_•tee•oh single room
μονοπάτι moh•noh•_pah_•tee
path, trail
μοντέρνος moh•_deh_•rnohs
modern
μοτοποδήλατο moh•toh•poh•
THee•lah•toh moped
μουσείο moo•_see_•oh museum
μουσική moo•see•_kee_ music
μουσικός moo•see•_kohs_
musician
μουστάκι moos•_tah_•kee
moustache
μπαγιάτικος bah•yah•tee•kohs
stale
μπάνιο _bah_•nioh bathroom,
lavatory
μπαρ bahr bar
μπάσκετ _bah_•skeht basketball
μπαστούνια του σκι
bahs•_too_•niah too skee ski
poles
μπαταρία bah•tah•_ree_•ah
battery
μπέιμπι σίτερ beh•ee•bee
see•tehr babysitter
μπικίνι bee•_kee_•nee bikini
μπλούζα _bloo_•zah blouse
μπλουζάκι bloo•_zah_•kee T-shirt
μπλου-τζην bloo•_jeen_ jeans
μποξ bohks n boxing
μπότα _boh_•tah boot
μπότες πεζοπορίας _boh_•tehs
peh•zoh•poh•_ree_•ahs walking
boots
μπότες του σκι _boh_•tehs too
skee ski boots
μπουκάλι boo•_kah_•lee bottle
μπρελόκ breh•_lohk_ key ring

μύγα _mee•ghah_ n fly (insect)
μυρίζω _mee•ree•zoh_ v smell
μυς _mees_ n muscle
μύτη _mee•tee_ n nose
μύωπας _mee•oh•pahs_ short-sighted [BE]
μωρό _moh•roh_ baby

N

ναός _nah•ohs_ temple
ναυαγοσώστης _nah•vah•ghoh•sohs•tees_ lifeguard
ναυαγοσωστική λέμβος _nah•vah•ghoh•sohs•tee•kee lehm•vohs_ lifeboat
ναυτία _nahf•tee•ah_ nausea, travel sickness
νέος _neh•ohs_ young
νερό _neh•roh_ n water
νεύρο _nehv•roh_ nerve
νεφρό _nehf•roh_ kidney
νιπτήρας _nee•ptee•rahs_ sink (bathroom)
νόμιμος _noh•mee•mohs_ legal
νομίζω _noh•mee•zoh_ think
νόμισμα _noh•meez•mah_ currency
νοικιάζω _nee•kiah•zoh_ v hire, rent
νοσοκόμα _noh•soh•koh•mah_ n nurse
νοσοκομείο _noh•soh•koh•mee•oh_ hospital
νόστιμος _nohs•tee•mohs_ delicious
Νοτιοαφρικανός _noh•tee•oh•ahf•ree•kah•nohs_ South African (nationality)
νότιος _noh•tee•os_ adj south
ντεμοντέ _deh•mohn•deh_ old-fashioned
ντήζελ _dee•zehl_ diesel
ντουζ _dooz_ n shower
ντουζίνα _doo•zee•nah_ dozen
νύχι _nee•khee_ n nail
νύχτα _neekh•tah_ night

νυχτερινό κέντρο _neekh•teh•ree•noh kehn•droh_ night club
νωρίς _noh•rees_ early

Ξ

ξαπλώνω _ksah•ploh•noh_ lie down
ξενάγηση _kseh•nah•yee•see_ guided tour
ξενάγηση στα αξιοθέατα _kseh•nah•yee•see stah ah•ksee•oh•theh•ah•tah_ sightseeing tour
ξεναγός _kseh•nah•ghos_ tour guide
ξένο συνάλλαγμα _kseh•noh see•nah•lahgh•mah_ foreign currency
ξενοδοχείο _kseh•noh•THoh•khee•oh_ hotel
ξένος _kseh•nohs_ foreign
ξενώνας νεότητας _kseh•noh•nahs neh•oh•tee•tahs_ youth hostel
ξεχνώ _ksehkh•noh_ forget
ξεχωριστά _kseh•khoh•ree•stah_ separately
ξινός _ksee•nohs_ sour
ξοδεύω _ksoh•THeh•voh_ spend
ξύλο _ksee•loh_ wood (material)
ξυπνώ _kseep•noh_ v wake
ξυραφάκι _ksee•rah•fah•kee_ razor, razor blade

O

ομάδα _oh•mah•THah_ n team
όμορφος _oh•mohr•fohs_ adj beautiful, pretty
ομπρέλλα _ohm•breh•lah_ sun shade
οβάλ _oh•vahl_ oval
οδηγία _oh•THee•yee•ah_ instruction
οδηγός καταστήματος _oh•THee•ghohs kah•tahs•tee•mah•tohs_ store guide

οδηγός ψυχαγωγίας _oh•THee•ghohs psee•khah•ghoh•yee•ahs_ entertainment guide
οδηγώ _oh•THee•ghoh_ v drive
οδική βοήθεια _oh•THee•kee voh•ee•thee•ah_ road assistance
οδοντίατρος _oh•THohn•dee•ah•trohs_ dentist
οδοντόβουρτσα _oh•THohn•doh•voor•tsah_ tooth brush
οδοντόπαστα _oh•THohn•doh•pahs•tah_ tooth paste
οικογένεια _ee•koh•yeh•nee•ah_ family
οινοποιείο _ee•noh•pee•ee•oh_ winery
όνομα _oh•noh•mah_ n name
όπερα _oh•peh•rah_ opera
οπωροπωλείο _oh•poh•roh•poh•lee•oh_ greengrocer [BE]
οργανωμένος _ohr•ghah•noh•meh•nohs_ organized
ορχήστρα _ohr•khees•trah_ orchestra
οτιδήποτε _oh•tee•THee•poh•teh_ anything
οτοστόπ _oh•toh•stohp_ hitchhiking
οφείλω _oh•fee•loh_ have to (obligation)
οφθαλμίατρος _ohf•thahl•mee•aht•rohs_ optician

Π

παγοπέδιλα _pah•ghoh•peh•THee•lah_ skates
πάγος _pah•ghohs_ n ice
παιδική χαρά _peh•THee•kee khah•rah_ playground
παιδικό κρεβάτι _peh•THee•koh kreh•vah•tee_ crib [cot BE]
παίζω _peh•zoh_ v play (games, music)
παιχνίδι _pehkh•nee•THee_ n game (toy), round

παιχνίδι βίντεο pehkh•_nee_•THee _vee_•deh•oh video game

πακέτο pah•_keh_•toh parcel

πακέτο για το σπίτι pah•_keh_• toh yah toh _spee_•tee take away

παλιά πόλη pah•_liah_ poh•lee old town

παλιός pah•_liohs_ old (thing)

πάνα μωρού _pah_•nah moh•_roo_ diaper

Πανεπιστήμιο pah•neh•pees•_tee_•mee•oh university

πάνες μωρού _pah_•nehs moh•_roo_ nappies

πανόραμα pah•_noh_•rah•mah panorama

παντελόνι pahn•deh•_loh_•nee pants (trousers BE)

παντοπωλείο pahn•doh•poh•_lee_•oh minimart

παντόφλες pahn•_dohf_•lehs slippers

παντρεμένος pahn•dreh•_meh_•nohs married

πάνω _pah_•noh adj top, upper (berth)

παπούτσι pah•_poo_•tsee shoe

πάρα πολύ _pah_•rah poh•_lee_ too (extreme)

παραγγέλνω pah•rah•_gehl_•noh v order

παράδειγμα pah•_rah_•THeegh•mah example

παραδοσιακός pah•rah•THoh•see•ah•_kohs_ traditional

παράθυρο pah•_rah_•thee•roh window

παραλαβή αποσκευών pah•rah•lah•_vee_ ah•poh•skeh•_vohn_ baggage (BE) claim

παραλία pah•rah•_lee_•ah beach

παραλία γυμνιστών pah•rah•_lee_•ah yeem•nees•_tohn_ nudist beach

παραλυσία pah•rah•lee•_see_•ah paralysis

παράνομος pah•_rah_•noh•mohs illegal

παράξενος pah•_rah_•kseh•nohs strange

παραπάνω pah•rah•_pah_•noh more

παρεξήγηση pah•reh•_ksee_• yee•see misunderstanding

πάρκο _pahr_•koh n park

παρκόμετρο pahr•_koh_•meht•roh parking meter

πάρτυ _pahr_•tee n party (social gathering)

παυσίπονο pahf•_see_•poh•noh painkiller

παχύς pah•_khees_ adj fat (person)

πέδιλα _peh_•THee•lah sandals

πεζόδρομος peh•_zohTH_•roh•mohs pedestrian zone

περιμένω peh•ree•_meh_•noh v hold on, wait

περιμένω στην ουρά peh•ree•_meh_•noh steen oo•_rah_ v queue (BE)

περιέχω peh•ree•_eh_•khoh contain

περιοδικό peh•ree•oh•THee•_koh_ magazine

περίοδος peh•_ree_•oh•THohs period (menstrual)

περιοχή peh•ree•oh•_khee_ region

περιοχή για καπνίζοντες peh•ree•oh•_khee_ yah kahp•_nee_•zohn•dehs smoking area

περιοχή για πικνίκ peh•ree•oh•_khee_ yah peek•neek picnic area

περίπτερο peh•_ree_•pteh•roh newsstand, kiosk

περνώ pehr•_noh_ v pass

περπατώ pehr•pah•_toh_ v walk

περσίδες pehr•_see_•THehs blinds

πετάω peh•_tah_•oh v fly

πετσέτα peh•_tseh_•tah napkin

πέφτω _pehf_•toh v fall

πηγαίνω pee•_yeh_•noh go

πιάτσα ταξί _piah_•tsah tah•_ksee_ taxi rank (BE)

πίεση pee•_eh_•see blood pressure

πιθανός pee•thah•_nohs_ possible

πινακίδα pee•nah•_kee_•THah road sign

πίνω _pee_•noh v drink

πίπα _pee_•pah pipe (smoking)

πιπίλα pee•_pee_•lah pacifier [soother BE]

πισίνα pee•_see_•nah swimming pool

πιστοποιητικό ασφάλειας pees•toh•pee•ee•tee•_koh_ ahs•_fah_•lee•ahs insurance certificate

πιστωτική κάρτα pees•toh•tee• kee _kahr_•tah credit card

πιτσαρία pee•tsah•_ree_•ah pizzeria

πλαγιά plah•_yah_ slope (ski)

πλαστική σακούλα plahs•tee•_kee_ sah•_koo_•lah plastic bag

πλατίνα plah•_tee_•nah platinum

πλευρό plehv•_roh_ rib

πλημμύρα plee•_mee_•rah n flood

πληγή plee•_yee_ wound (cut)

πληροφορίες plee•roh•foh•_ree_•ehs information

πληρωμή plee•roh•_mee_ payment

πληρώνω plee•_roh_•noh v pay

πλοίο _plee_•oh n ship

πλυντήριο pleen•_deer_•ee•oh washing machine

πνεύμονας _pnehv_•moh•nahs lung

πόμολο _poh_•moh•loh n handle

ποδήλατο poh•_THee_•lah•toh bicycle

πόδι _poh_•THee foot, leg

ποδόσφαιρο poh•_THohs_•feh•roh soccer [football BE]

ποιότητα *pee•oh•tee•tah* quality

πόλη *poh•lee* town

πολυκατάστημα *poh•lee•kah•tahs•tee•mah* department store

πολυτέλεια *poh•lee•teh•lee•ah* luxury

πολύτιμος *poh•lee•tee•mohs* valuable

πονόδοντος *poh•noh•THon•dohs* toothache

πονοκέφαλος *poh•noh•keh•fah•lohs* headache

πονόλαιμος *poh•noh•leh•mohs* sore throat

πόνος *poh•nohs* n pain

πόνος στο αυτί *poh•nohs stoh ahf•tee* earache

πόρτα *pohr•tah* door

πορτοφόλι *pohr•toh•foh•lee* wallet

ποσό *poh•soh* n amount

ποσότητα *poh•soh•tee•tah* quantity

ποταμός *poh•tah•mohs* river

ποτέ *poh•teh* never

ποτήρι *poh•tee•ree* glass (container)

ποτό *poh•toh* n drink

πουκάμισο *poo•kah•mee•soh* shirt

πράσινος *prah•see•nohs* green

πρέπει *preh•pee* v must

πρεσβεία *prehz•vee•ah* embassy

πρεσβύωπας *prehz•vee•oh•pahs* long-sighted [BE]

πρήξιμο *pree•ksee•moh* swelling

πρησμένος *preez•meh•nohs* swollen

πρίζα *pree•zah* n plug, socket

πριν *preen* before

πρόβλεψη *prohv•leh•psee* n forecast

πρόβλεψη καιρού *prohv•leh•psee keh•roo* weather forecast

πρόβλημα *prohv•lee•mah* problem

πρόγραμμα *prohgh•rah•mah* n program

πρόγραμμα θεαμάτων *proh•ghrah•mah theh•ah•mah•tohn* program of events

προς *prohs* towards

προσαρμοστής *proh•sahr•moh•stees* adaptor

πρόσβαση *prohz•vah•see* n access

προσγειώνομαι *prohz•yee•oh•noh•meh* v land

προσκαλώ *prohs•kah•loh* v invite

πρόσκληση *prohs•klee•see* invitation

πρόστιμο *prohs•tee•moh* n fine (penalty)

πρόσωπο *proh•soh•poh* n face

προσωρινός *proh•soh•ree•nohs* temporary

προτείνω *proh•tee•noh* suggest

προφέρω *proh•feh•roh* pronounce

προφυλακτικό *proh•fee•lah•ktee•koh* condom

προωθώ *proh•oh•thoh* forward

πρωί *proh•ee* morning

πρωινό *proh•ee•noh* breakfast

πρώτη θέση *proh•tee theh•see* first class

πτήση *ptee•see* flight

πυρετός *pee•reh•tohs* fever

πυροσβεστήρας *pee•rohz•vehs•tee•rahs* fire extinguisher

πυροσβεστική *pee•rohz•vehs•tee•kee* fire brigade [BE]

πυτζάμες *pee•jah•mehs* pajamas

Ρ

ραδιόφωνο *rah•THee•oh•foh•noh* n radio

ρακέτα *rah•keh•tah* racket (tennis, squash)

ραντεβού *rahn•deh•voo* appointment

ράφι *rah•fee* n shelf

ρεματιά *reh•mah•tiah* ravine

ρεσεψιόν *reh•seh•psiohn* reception (hotel)

ρεύμα ποταμού *rehv•mah poh•tah•moo* rapids

ρηχή πισίνα *ree•khee pee•see•nah* paddling pool

ρομαντικός *roh•mahn•dee•kohs* romantic

ρολόι *roh•loh•ee* n watch

ρυάκι *ree•ah•kee* n stream

Σ

σμαράγδι *zmah•rahgh•THee* emerald

σαμπουάν *sahm•poo•ahn* n shampoo

σαγιονάρες *sah•yoh•nah•rehs* flip-flops

σαγόνι *sah•ghoh•nee* jaw

σάκκος *sah•kohs* knapsack

σαλόνι *sah•loh•nee* living room

σάουνα *sah•oo•nah* sauna

σαπούνι *sah•poo•nee* n soap

σατέν *sah•tehn* satin

σβήνω *svee•noh* v turn off

σβώλος *svoh•lohs* n lump

σεζ-λονγκ *sehz lohng* deck chair

σενιάν *seh•niahn* rare (steak)

σερβιέτες *sehr•vee•eh•tehs* sanitary towels

σεσουάρ *seh•soo•ahr* hair dryer

σήμα *see•mah* sign (road)

σημαία *see•meh•ah* n flag

σημαίνω *see•meh•noh* v mean

σημείο *see•mee•oh* n point

σίδερο *see•THeh•roh* n iron

σιδερώνω see•THeh•_roh_•noh v iron, press

σιδηροδρομικός σταθμός see•THee•rohTH•roh•mee•_kohs_ stahth•_mohs_ rail station

σκάλα _skah_•lah ladder

σκάλες _skah_•lehs stairs

σκηνή skee•_nee_ tent

σκι skee skiing

σκιά skee•_ah_ shade (darkness)

σκοπός skoh•_pohs_ purpose

σκούπα _skoo_•pah n broom

σκουπίδια skoo•_peeTH_•yah trash [rubbish BE]

σκούρος _skoo_•rohs adj dark (color)

σλιπ sleep briefs

σόλα soh•_lah_ sole (shoes)

σορτς sohrts n shorts

σουβενίρ soo•veh•_neer_ souvenir

σουπερμάρκετ soo•pehr•_mahr_•keht supermarket

σουτιέν soo•_tiehn_ bra

σπα spah spa

σπάγγος _spah_•gohs n string (cord)

σπάνιος _spah_•nee•ohs rare (unusual)

σπασμένος spahz•_meh_•nohs broken

σπάω _spah_•oh v break

σπήλαιο _spee_•leh•oh n cave

σπίρτο _speer_•toh n match (to start fire)

σπονδυλική στήλη spohn•THee•lee•_kee_ stee•lee spine

σπουδάζω spoo•_THah_•zoh v study

σταματώ stah•mah•_toh_ v stop

στάδιο _stah_•THee•oh stadium

σταθμός μετρό stahth•_mohs_ meh•_troh_ subway [underground BE] station

σταθμός λεωφορείων stahTH•_mohs_ leh•oh•_foh_•_ree_•ohn bus station

στάση _stah_•see exposure (photos), stop (bus)

στάση λεωφορείου _stah_•see leh•oh•_foh_•_ree_•oo bus stop

στέγη _steh_•yee n roof

στέλνω _steh_•noh send

στενός steh•_nohs_ adj narrow, tight

στήθος _stee_•THohs breast

στόμα _stoh_•mah n mouth

στομάχι stoh•_mah_•khee n stomach

στομαχόπονος stoh•mah•_khoh_•poh•_nohs_ stomach ache

στολή stoh•_lee_ n uniform

στολή δύτη stoh•_lee_ THee•tee wetsuit

στρογγυλός strohn•gkee•_lohs_ adj round

στυλ steel n style

στυλό stee•_loh_ n pen

συμπεριλαμβάνεται seem•beh•ree•lahm•_vah_•neh•teh included

σύζυγος see•zee•_ghohs_ husband, wife

συκώτι see•_koh_•tee liver

σύμπτωμα _seem_•ptoh•mah symptom

συναγερμός πυρκαγιάς see•nah•yehr•_mohs_ peer•kah•_yahs_ fire alarm

συναντώ see•nahn•_doh_ meet

συνέδριο see•_neh_•THree•oh conference

συνταγή γιατρού seen•dah•_yee_ yaht•_roo_ prescription

συνταγογραφώ seen•dah•ghoh•ghrah•_foh_ prescribe

συνταξιούχος seen•dah•ksee•_oo_•khohs retired

σύντομα _seen_•doh•mah soon

συντριβάνι seen•dree•_vah_•nee fountain

συστάσεις see•_stah_•sees introductions

συστήνω see•_stee_•noh introduce, recommend

συχνός seekh•_nohs_ adj frequent

σφηνωμένος sfee•noh•_meh_•nohs jammed

σφράγισμα _sfrah_•yeez•mah filling (dental)

σφυρί sfee•_ree_ hammer

σχέδιο _skheh_•THee•oh n plan

σχήμα _skhee_•mah n shape

σχισμένος skheez•_meh_•nohs torn

σχοινί skhee•_nee_ n rope

σχολή σκι skhoh•_lee_ skee ski school

σωσίβιο soh•_see_•vee•oh lifejacket

σωστός sohs•_stohs_ adj right (correct)

T

ταμπόν tahm•_bohn_ tampon

τάβλι _tah_•vlee backgammon

ταγιέρ tah•_yehr_ women's suit

ταΐζω tah•_ee_•zoh v feed

ταινία tah•_nee_•ah movie

ταξί tah•_ksee_ taxi

ταξίδι tah•_ksee_•THee journey

ταξίδι με πλοίο tah•_ksee_•THee meh plee•oh boat trip

ταξιδιωτική επιταγή tah•ksee•THee•oh•tee•_kee_ eh•pee•tah•_yee_ traveler's check [traveller's cheque BE]

ταξιδιωτικό γραφείο tah•ksee•THyoh•tee•_koh_ ghrah•_fee_•oh travel agency

ταξιτζής tah•ksee•_jees_ taxi driver

ταυτότητα tahf•_toh_•tee•tah identification

ταχυδρομείο tah•khee•THrom•_mee_•oh post office

ταχυδρομική επιταγή tah•khee•THrom•mee•_kee_ eh•pee•tah•_yee_ money order

ταχυδρομικό κουτί *tah•kheeTH•roh•mee•koh koo•tee* mailbox [postbox BE]

τεμάχιο *teh•mah•khee•oh* piece

τελειώνω *teh•lee•oh•noh* v end

τελευταί ος *teh•lehf•teh•ohs* last

τελεφερίκ *teh•leh•feh•reek* cablecar

τέλος *teh•lohs* n end

τελωνειακή δήλωση *teh•loh•nee•ah•kee THee•loh•see* customs declaration (tolls)

τελωνείο *teh•loh•nee•oh* customs (tolls)

τέννις *teh•nees* tennis

τετράγωνος *teht•rah•ghoh•nohs* square

τζετ-σκι *jeht skee* jet-ski

τζόγκιγκ *joh•geeng* jogging

τζόγος *joh•ghohs* gambling

τηλεκάρτα *tee•leh•kahr•tah* phone card

τηλεόραση *tee•leh•oh•rah•see* TV

τηλεφώνημα *tee•leh•foh•nee•mah* phone call

τηλεφωνικός θάλαμος *tee•leh•foh•nee•kohs thah•lah•mohs* telephone booth

τηλεφωνικός κατάλογος *tee•leh•foh•nee•kohs kah•tah•loh•ghohs* telephone directory

τηλέφωνο *tee•leh•foh•noh* n phone

την *teen* per

τιμή συναλλάγματος *tee•mee see•nah•lahgh•mah•tohs* exchange rate

τιμή εισόδου *tee•mee ee•soh•THoo* entrance fee

τιρμπουσόν *teer•boo•sohn* corkscrew

τοίχος *tee•khohs* wall

τοπικός *toh•pee•kohs* local

τοστιέρα *toh•stieh•rah* toaster

τουαλέτα *too•ah•leh•tah* restroom [toilet BE]

τούνελ *too•nehl* tunnel

τουρίστας *too•rees•tahs* tourist

τουριστική θέση *too•ree•stee•kee theh•see* economy class

τουριστικός οδηγός *too•ree•stee•kohs oh•THee•ghohs* guide book

τραβώ το καζανάκι *trah•voh toh kah•zah•nah•kee* flush

τραμ *trahm* tram

τράπεζα *trah•peh•zah* bank

τραπέζι *trah•peh•zee* table

τραπεζομάντηλο *trah•peh•zoh•mahn•dee•loh* tablecloth

τραυματισμένος *trahv•mah•teez•meh•nohs* injured

τρένο *treh•noh* train

τρέχω *treh•khoh* v run, speed

τρόμπα *trohm•bah* n pump

τρόλλεϋ *troh•leh•ee* trolley-bus

τρύπα *tree•pah* hole (in clothes)

τρώω *troh•oh* eat

τσάντα *tsahn•dah* handbag

τσίμπημα *tsee•bee•mah* n bite, sting (insect)

τσίμπημα κουνουπιού *tseem•bee•mah koo•noo•piooh* mosquito bite

τυπικός *tee•pee•kohs* typical

τύχη *tee•khee* luck

Υ

υγρό πιάτων *eegh•roh piah•tohn* dishwashing detergent

υπεραστικό λεωφορείο *ee•pehr•ah•stee•koh leh•oh•foh•ree•oh* long-distance bus

υπεραστικό τηλεφώνημα *ee•pehr•ah•stee•koh tee•leh•foh•nee•mah* long-distance call

υπέρβαρο *ee•pehr•vah•roh* excess baggage [BE]

υπηκοότητα *ee•pee•koh•oh•tee•tah* nationality

υπηρεσία *ee•pee•reh•see•ah* n service (administration, business)

υπηρεσία δωματίου *ee•pee•reh•see•ah THoh•mah•tee•oo* room service

υπηρεσία πλυντηρίου *ee•pee•reh•see•ah pleen•dee•ree•oo* laundry service

υπνόσακκος *ee•pnoh•sah•kohs* sleeping bag

υπνωτικό χάπι *eep•noh•tee•koh khah•pee* sleeping pill

υπόγειος *ee•poh•ghee•ohs* underground [BE]

υπολογιστής *ee•poh•loh•yee•stees* computer

υπόνομος *ee•poh•noh•mohs* sewer

ύφασμα *ee•fahs•mah* fabric (cloth)

ύψος *ee•psohs* height

Φ

φακός *fah•kohs* flashlight, lens

φακός επαφής *fah•kohs eh•pah•fees* contact lens

υπηρεσία φαξ *ee•pee•reh•see•ah fahks* fax facility

φάρμα *fahr•mah* n farm

φάρμακα *fahr•mah•kah* medication

φαρδύς *fahr•THees* loose (fitting), wide

φάρος *fah•rohs* lighthouse

φέρνω *fehr•noh* bring

φέρυ-μπωτ *feh•ree boht* ferry

φεστιβάλ *fehs•tee•<u>vahl</u>* festival

φεύγω *<u>fehv</u>•ghoh* v leave (depart)

φιλμ *feelm* n film (camera)

φίλη *<u>fee</u>•lee* girlfriend

φιλί *fee•<u>lee</u>* n kiss

φιλοδώρημα
fee•loh•<u>THoh</u>•ree•mah gratuity

φίλος *<u>fee</u>•lohs* friend, boyfriend

φίλτρο *<u>feel</u>•troh* n filter

φιλώ *fee•<u>loh</u>* v kiss

φλέβα *<u>fleh</u>•vah* vein

φλεγμονή *flegh•moh•<u>nee</u>*
inflammation

φλιτζάνι *flee•<u>jah</u>•nee* n cup

φοβερός *foh•veh•<u>rohs</u>* terrible

φοβισμένος *foh•veez•<u>meh</u>•nohs*
frightened

φοιτητής *fee•tee•<u>tees</u>* student

φόρεμα *<u>foh</u>•reh•mah* n dress

φόρος *<u>foh</u>•rohs* duty (customs),
tax

φορώ *foh•<u>roh</u>* v wear

φούρνος *<u>foor</u>•nohs* oven

φούρνος μικροκυμάτων
*<u>foor</u>•nohs
mee•kroh•kee•<u>mah</u>•tohn*
microwave (oven)

φούστα *<u>foo</u>•stah* skirt

φούτερ *<u>foo</u>•tehr* sweatshirt

ΦΠΑ *fee•pee•<u>ah</u>* sales tax

φράγμα *<u>frahgh</u>•mah* n lock
(river, canal)

φράση *<u>frah</u>•see* n phrase

φράχτης *<u>frahkh</u>•tees* n fence

φρέσκος *<u>frehs</u>•kohs* adj fresh

φτάνω *<u>ftah</u>•noh* arrive

φτηνός *ftee•<u>nohs</u>* cheap,
inexpensive

φτιάχνω τις βαλίτσες
*ftee•<u>ahkh</u>•noh tees
vah•<u>lee</u>•tsehs* v pack (baggage)

φυλακή *fee•lah•<u>kee</u>* n prison

φύση *<u>fee</u>•see* nature

φυτό *fee•<u>toh</u>* n plant

φως *fohs* n light (electric)

φώτα *<u>foh</u>•tah* lights (car)

φωτογραφία
foh•tohgh•rah•<u>fee</u>•ah v photo

φωτογραφική μηχανή
*foh•tohgh•rah•fee•<u>kee</u>
mee•khah•<u>nee</u>* camera

φωτοτυπικό
foh•toh•tee•pee•<u>koh</u>
photocopier

Χ

χαμηλώνω *khah•mee•<u>loh</u>•noh* v
turn down (volume, heat)

χαλί *khah•<u>lee</u>* rug

χαλκός *khahl•<u>kohs</u>* copper

χάπι *<u>khah</u>•pee* tablet

χάρτης *<u>khahr</u>•tees* n map

χαρτί *khar•<u>tee</u>* paper

χαρτί κουζίνας *khah•<u>rtee</u>
koo•<u>zee</u>•nahs* kitchen

χαρτί υγείας *khah•<u>rtee</u>
ee•<u>yee</u>•ahs* toilet paper

χαρτομάντηλο
khahr•toh•<u>mahn</u>•dee•loh tissue

χαρτομάντηλο
khah•rtoh•<u>mahn</u>•dee•loh
handkerchief

χείλη *<u>khee</u>•lee* lips

χειροκίνητος
khee•roh•<u>kee</u>•nee•tohs
manual (car)

χειρότερος *khee•<u>roh</u>•teh•rohs*
worse

χιλιόμετρα *khee•<u>lioh</u>•meh•trah*
mileage

χιονίζει *khioh•<u>nee</u>•zee* v snow

χλιαρός *khlee•ah•<u>rohs</u>*
lukewarm

χόμπυ *<u>khoh</u>•bee* hobby (pastime)

χοντρός *khohn•<u>drohs</u>* thick

χορεύω *khoh•<u>reh</u>•voh* v dance

χορτοφάγος *khohr•toh•
<u>fah</u>•ghohs* vegetarian

χρειάζομαι *khree•<u>ah</u>•zoh•meh*
v need

χρέωση υπηρεσίας
*<u>khreh</u>•oh•see ee•pee•reh•
see•ahs* service charge

χρήματα *<u>khree</u>•mah•tah* money

χρησιμοποιώ
khree•see•moh•pee•<u>oh</u> v use

χρήσιμος *<u>khree</u>•see•mohs*
useful

χρονική περίοδος
*khroh•nee•<u>kee</u> peh•<u>ree</u>•
oh•THohs* period (time)

χρυσός *khree•<u>sohs</u>* n gold

χρώμα *<u>khroh</u>•mah* n color

χρωστώ *khroh•<u>stoh</u>* owe

χτένα *<u>khteh</u>•nah* n comb

χτενίζω *khteh•<u>nee</u>•zoh* v comb

χτες *khtehs* yesterday

χώρα *<u>khoh</u>•rah* country (nation)

χωριό *khohr•<u>yoh</u>* village

χωρίς *khoh•<u>rees</u>* without

χώρος *<u>khoh</u>•rohs* n space (area)

χώρος κάμπινγκ *<u>kah</u>•mpeeng
<u>khoh</u>•rohs* campsite

χώρος στάθμευσης *<u>khoh</u>•rohs
stahth•<u>mehf</u>•sees* car park [BE]

χώρος στάθμευσης *<u>khoh</u>•rohs
stahth•<u>mehf</u>•sees* parking lot

Ψ

ψαλίδι *psah•<u>lee</u>•THee* scissors

ψάρεμα *<u>psah</u>•reh•mah* fishing

ψάχνω *<u>psahkh</u>•noh* look for

ψηλός *psee•<u>lohs</u>* tall

ψύλλος *<u>psee</u>•lohs* flea

Ω

ώμος *<u>oh</u>•mohs* n shoulder
(anatomy)

ώρα αιχμής *<u>oh</u>•rah ehkh•<u>mees</u>*
rush hour

ώρες λειτουργίας *<u>oh</u>•rehs lee•
toor•<u>yee</u>•ahs* opening hours

INDEX

Berlitz pocket guide

RHODES

9th edition 2019

Editor: Carine Tracanelli
Authors: Lindsay Bennett, Marc Dubin
Head of DTP and Pre-Press: Rebeka Davies
Picture Editor: Tom Smyth
Cartography Update: Carte
Photography Credits: Alamy 5M;
Bridgeman Art 20; Britta Jaschinski/Apa
Publications 4TL, 6L, 6R, 7, 7R, 11, 12,
14, 19, 23, 28, 31, 33, 34, 36, 40, 42, 44, 46,
48, 51, 52, 54, 56, 58, 60, 62, 65, 71, 73, 74,
76, 80, 84, 86, 89, 90, 92, 99, 101, 102, 105;
Getty Images 26; iStock 1, 4MC, 4ML, 5TC;
Marcus Wilson Smith/Apa Publications 16;
Pete Bennett/Apa Publications 24, 38, 67;
Pictures Colour Library 94; Shutterstock
4TC, 5T, 5MC, 5MC, 5M, 39, 50, 69, 78, 82
Cover Picture: Shutterstock

Distribution
UK, Ireland and Europe: Apa Publications
(UK) Ltd; sales@insightguides.com
United States and Canada: Ingram
Publisher Services; ips@ingramcontent.com
Australia and New Zealand: Woodslane;
info@woodslane.com.au
Southeast Asia: Apa Publications (SN) Pte;
singaporeoffice@insightguides.com
Worldwide: Apa Publications (UK) Ltd;
sales@insightguides.com

**Special Sales, Content Licensing
and CoPublishing**
Insight Guides can be purchased in bulk
quantities at discounted prices. We can
create special editions, personalised jackets
and corporate imprints tailored to your
needs. sales@insightguides.com;
www.insightguides.biz

Contact us
Every effort has been made to provide
accurate information in this publication,
but changes are inevitable. The publisher
cannot be responsible for any resulting loss,
inconvenience or injury. We would appreciate
it if readers would call our attention to any
errors or outdated information. We also
welcome your suggestions; please contact
us at: berlitz@apaguide.co.uk
www.insightguides.com/berlitz